)

# AIRPORTS: PERFORMANCE, RISKS, AND PROBLEMS

# AIRPORTS: PERFORMANCE, RISKS, AND PROBLEMS

PIERRE B. LARAUGE
AND
MARTIN E. CASTILLE
EDITORS

Nova Science Publishers, Inc.
*New York*

LIBRARY OF CONGRESS CATALOGING-IN-PUBLICATION DATA

Airports : performance, risks, and problems / edited by Pierre B. Larauge and Martin E. Castille.
    p. cm.
 Includes bibliographical references and index.
 ISBN 978-1-60692-393-1 (hardcover)
 1. Airports--Design and construction. 2. Airport capacity. 3. Airports--Planning. I. Larauge, Pierre B. II. Castille, Martin E.
 TL725.A52 2009
 387.7'36--dc22
          2008047202

Published by Nova Science Publishers, Inc. ✦ New York

# CONTENTS

# PREFACE

An airport is a location where aircraft such as airplanes, helicopters, and blimps take off and land. Aircraft may also be stored or maintained at an airport. An airport consists of at least one surface such as a runway, a helipad, or water for takeoffs and landings, and often includes buildings such as hangars and terminal buildings.

Larger airports may have fixed base operator services, seaplane docks and ramps, air traffic control, passenger facilities such as restaurants and lounges, and emergency services. A military airport is known as an airbase or air station. The terms airfield, airstrip, and aerodrome may also be used to refer to airports, and the terms heliport, seaplane base, and STOLport refer to airports dedicated exclusively to helicopters, seaplanes, or short takeoff and landing aircraft. In some jurisdictions, the term airport is used where the facility is licensed as such by the relevant government organization (e.g. Federal Aviation Administration (FAA), Transport Canada)

This new book brings together important research related to airports.

The Advanced - Surface Movement Guidance and Control System (A-SMGCS) has been defined by ICAO and Eurocontrol to ensure the safety and efficiency of surface traffic on the airport movement area (runways, taxiways and apron area). State-of-the-art information and communication technologies enable the implementation of A-SMGCS components for the surveillance, control, guidance and routing of any mobile circulating not only in the movement area, as required by A-SMGCS ICAO Manual, but on all the airside area of an airport (movement area and peripheral roads). A conceptual approach for that implementation is presented and a concrete example of an A-SMGCS experimental platform implementation is presented as it was deployed at the Porto and Lisbon airports in Portugal. In Chapter 1, the importance of the use of EGNOS for vehicle surveillance purpose is pointed out, the implemented A-SMGCS services and Decision Support services are described and the different options for the wireless communication networks are discussed. The operational benefits of the use of this platform are also analyzed.

Chapter 2 looks at the relationship between airlines and airports on a European level, with a special focus on the relationship between low-cost carriers and secondary airports. Recognizing the main steps in the liberalization process of the aviation industry allows us to understand the challenges that arose in supply and demand in the air transportation market and analyze development trends. With the arrival of new competitors, carriers and airports have changed their market strategies and progressively focused on the exploitation of potential demand. A survey of published literature is made on this theme and new airline-airport development trends are discussed. Examples are drawn from the European and the Italian market whilst a case study on airports in Rome illustrates the main competitive issues.

Chapter 3 provides a case study of conservation efforts at the Indianapolis International Airport near Indianapolis, Indiana, USA that illustrates how small programs aimed at meeting regulatory requirements can develop into projects of regional and national importance, how adaptive management works in the real world, and the potential for reconciliation ecology. Of particular legal and conservation concern is the presence of the endangered Indiana bat (*Myotis sodalis*), for which the airport agreed to undertake extensive conservation and mitigation efforts including the preservation of existing forest, planting of new forest, installation of experimental roost structures, and intense monitoring of the bats. After 17 years, the site is surrounded by commercial and residential areas, but the Indiana bat is still present. Monitoring has provided detailed information about how this and other bat species respond to a variety of landscape-level challenges and conservation approaches.

As presented in Chapter 4, the context of the airport operator, especially in market-oriented, environments, is changing rapidly, due to such developments as the deregulation of the airline market, terrorist threats, more stringent environmental regulations, the rise of low cost carriers, and increased opposition to growth from some stakeholders. History shows that airport operators have difficulty in dealing with such changes.

Airport planners and decisionmakers have to anticipate changes to their business environment and provide solutions for mitigating the adverse effects of growth that are satisfactory to their stakeholders (e.g. communities, airlines, governments). Doing this successfully is difficult. Many airport strategic plans fail to deliver their promise and there is growing opposition from an increasing number of stakeholders against airport expansion plans.

Explicit consideration of the uncertainties that the future will bring and meaningful involvement of all airport stakeholders is essential for the long-term economic and social performance of the airport. Use of computer-based decision support for airport strategic planning can provide a way to deal with the uncertain future and meaningfully involve the stakeholders. HARMOS is a Decision Support System that we developed with these requirements as the starting point for its design and implementation.

Occupational exposure in airport personnel is very complex and still poorly characterized and includes either chemical pollutants (influenced by environmental factors associated to different climatic and meteorologic conditions), or physical agents such as microwaves-radiofrequency radiations and noise pollution. Airport ground personnel performs different tasks such as aircraft fuel tank, aircraft routine maintenance procedures, airplane parking/towing, baggage charge/discharge, that can induce exposure to complex chemical mixtures including several polycyclic aromatic hydrocarbons (PAHs) produced by vapours or combustion of commercial Jet A-A1 fuels and by combustion of diesel/gasoline engines of runway shuttles and baggage trolleys operating in the vicinity of the planes. Although the airport workers are exposed to low levels of PAHs there is a possibility of long-term health effects following chronic exposure by inhalation or skin contamination. The most available studies on health effects of airport pollution concern military aviation that employs a different kind of jet propulsion fuel in respect to civil aviation and report some genotoxic and carcinogenic effects. For civil aviation only a few data are available on PAHs levels in airports, biological monitoring of occupational exposure and on health risks for airport personnel. In particular genotoxic and oxidative DNA damage, neurotoxic, respiratory, irritant and reproductive effects have been reported by biomonitoring and epidemiological studies. In addition to scarcity of data on health effects of airport pollution on workers there are not enough studies on health risks for populations living and working in surrounding of the airport. Chapter 5 will present the most important studies actually available on health risks of airport occupational exposure giving prominence to effects of chemical pollution.

An airport is like a complicated factory. Any problem that may happen in any situation can directly be a restrictive factor for the airport capacity. It is necessary to develop a reasonable model in which the time is considered between the plane lands and passengers get out of the airport. One of the most important issues in the capacity analysis of airports is check-in unit capacity analysis. Any airport must have enough number of check-in counters providing necessary and facilitated transportation that takes passengers and their luggage into account. In the literature there is limited work available including the capacity analysis of check-in units in airports to obtain a relation applicable to actual problem. In Chapter 6, two different approaches will be presented for the capacity analysis of check-in units of airports which includes many passengers intensively. One is artificial neural network (ANN) method and the other is fuzzy logic approach.

ANN is an efficient method for the analysis of a broad range of engineering problems. In the current problem, an ANN structure predicts the functional time depending on the number of passengers and luggage affecting the capacity. Proposed ANN model is a dynamic model and is a new approach in capacity analysis of airports. A method of relationship is improved to be used in the check-in department with neural network education. Different ANN models have been used and a number of results have been obtained.

Fuzzy logic approach is also extensively used in the analysis of many engineering problems in different disciplines. In the control mechanisms of events linguistic uncertainties may play a significant role. Fuzzy approach considers this role as in the key elements in human thinking. Besides ANN approach, this study also considers the capacity analysis of a check-in department in an airport with the view of those linguistic variables of number of passengers and their luggage adopted.

Both ANN and Fuzzy Logic methods for the capacity analysis of check-in units in airports are used for the check-in unit analysis of a national airport (Antalya Airport). The results have shown both methods work well and as a result, required number of counters in the airport can be determined to provide passengers suitable and facilitated transportation.

During the last decades the limited capacity of runways has become an important source for delays on major airports. Particular safety regulations require asymmetric separation times for aircraft during their landing operations. If there are two or more runways available, aircraft can be assigned to runways in such a way that large separation times are avoided. This increases the actual throughput of the system and reduces additional delays.

In Chapter 7 we formulate the assignment problem as a mathematical optimization model. Though we cannot find optimal assignment strategies analytically, we can use the model as a framework for the simulation of strategies and as a tool for the heuristic optimization of strategies. We examine two classes of strategies that reduce the waiting times of arriving aircraft in simulations.

In particular, we can show that in realistic simulation scenario of a German airport, one of our strategies performs much better than the manual assignment as it is used by flight operators today. As our strategies are essentially simple look-up tables, they may well be incorporated into future flight assistance systems for airports.

In the first Short Communication, we first build a model that shows that a monopolist supplier's profits depend negatively on the market power in the buyers' industry. The model depicts an input market with Stackelberg competition and a market leader amongst buyers but with only one seller. We then proceed with an empirical study for airport and airline industries, and with the theoretical model we consistently get evidence that airports' financial performance depends negatively on the market power in the airline industry. Thus we conclude that airlines are able to extract rents from airports when they have a large market share.

As explained in the second Short Communication, in times gone by the aviation meteorological forecaster was concerned with the issue weather forecasts for the departure airport, en-route and the destination airport. These days the airport aviation meteorologist is increasingly being required to be more knowledgeable about the airport environment and more intimately involved in, the day to day operational decision making and activities at airports so as to increase safety and productivity, lower costs and minimise environmental effects. The increased diversity of aviation meteorological forecasting for airports is commented on by briefly looking at the role the forecaster plays in the issue of forecasts and warnings to air traffic controllers, airside managers, ground operators and airlines as well as a comment on modern trends in the dissemination of the information and into the future.

In traditional single-airport regions, air traffic forecasting is often a simple case of nearest-centre assignment based on national forecasts and local market shares. However, the emergence of multi-airport regions (MARs) has challenged the "golden rule" that air passengers would naturally choose the nearest airports. Within MARs, air passengers may bypass the nearest airports but travel longer distances for cheaper air fares, more frequent flights, more convenient departure/arrival time or services of particular airlines. In this Chapter, the characteristics of MARs are first discussed. Then, the implications of MARs on the airports' relationships with air passengers, airlines and other airports operating within the same MARs are analyzed. The third Short Communication concludes by highlighting the need for more research on air passengers' travel behaviour, the benefits of fostering closer relationships between airlines and airports, and the opportunities for strengthening coordination among airports.

Air transportation has been becoming a major part of transportation infrastructure worldwide. Hence the study of the Airports Networks, the backbone of air transportation, is becoming increasingly important. In complex systems domain, airport networks are modeled as graphs (networks) comprising of airports (vertices or nodes) that are linked by flight connectivities among the airports. A complex network analysis of such a model offers holistic insight about the performance and risks in such a network. The last Short Communication reviews the performance and risks of networks with the help of studies that have been done on some of the airport networks. We present various network parameters those could be potentially used as a measure of performance and risks on airport networks. We will also see how various risks, such as break down of airports, spread of diseases across the airport network could be assessed based on the network parameters. Further we review how these insights could possibly be used to shape more efficient and safer airport networks.

In: Airports: Performance, Risks, and Problems
Editors: P.B. Larauge et al, pp. 1-31

ISBN: 978-1-60692-393-1
© 2009 Nova Science Publishers, Inc.

*Chapter 1*

# A Platform to Increase the Safety of Ground Movements in the Airside Area of Airports

*Augusto Casaca[a,b], Gabriel Pestana[a,b], Isabel Oliveira[c]*
*and Tiago Silva[b]*
[a] IST
[b] INESC
[c] ANA-Aeroportos

## Abstract

The Advanced - Surface Movement Guidance and Control System (A-SMGCS) has been defined by ICAO and Eurocontrol to ensure the safety and efficiency of surface traffic on the airport movement area (runways, taxiways and apron area). State-of-the-art information and communication technologies enable the implementation of A-SMGCS components for the surveillance, control, guidance and routing of any mobile circulating not only in the movement area, as required by A-SMGCS ICAO Manual, but on all the airside area of an airport (movement area and peripheral roads). A conceptual approach for that implementation is presented and a concrete example of an A-SMGCS experimental platform implementation is presented as it was deployed at the Porto and Lisbon airports in Portugal. The importance of the use of EGNOS for vehicle surveillance purpose is pointed out, the implemented A-SMGCS services and Decision Support services are described and the different options for the wireless communication networks are discussed. The operational benefits of the use of this platform are also analyzed.

**Keywords:** A-SMGCS, Airport airside area, EGNOS, Wireless Communication Networks.

## 1. Introduction

Generally, operations at an airport are dependent on air traffic controllers, pilots and vehicle drivers using visual observations to estimate the respective relative positions of aircraft and vehicles. Pilots and vehicle drivers rely on visual aids (lighting, markings and signaling) to guide them along their assigned routes and to identify intersections and holding positions.

During periods of low visibility, controllers must rely on pilots' reports and surface movement radar to monitor spacing and to identify potential conflicts. Under these conditions, pilots and vehicle drivers find that their ability to operate based on the "see and be seen" principle is severely impaired. There is no prescribed minimum separation, and controllers, pilots and vehicle drivers share the responsibility that operations will not create a collision hazard.

The situation of aircraft and vehicle ground movements in European airports raises a number of issues that have led Eurocontrol to define a strategy for the implementation of an Advanced Surface Movement Guidance and Control System (A-SMGCS) for the surveillance, guidance, routing and control of aircraft and vehicle movements on ground [1].

More recently, SESAR - the Single European Sky Implementation Program from the European Commission – recognized that European airspace is fragmented and will become more and more congested, as traffic is forecast to grow steadily over the next 15 years and air navigation services and the systems that support them are not sufficiently integrated and are based on technologies which are already running at maximum. In order to accommodate future air traffic needs, it will be necessary to rethink the European Air Traffic Management (ATM) system and a "paradigm shift" is required, supported by state-of-the-art and innovative technologies.

The AIRNET platform presented in this chapter, whose main objective is to ensure the safety and efficiency of airport surface traffic with the increasing density of traffic and in all weather conditions can be seen as a component of the A-SMGCS, but not less important are the Decision Support Services also available in that platform, which are in line with the SESAR Program Strategy.

The implementation of the AIRNET platform implies the existence of advanced localization techniques, state-of-the-art wireless communication networks operating in the movement area of the airport, low cost performing embedded systems for installation in vehicles and the use of advanced geographical information systems (GIS) for airport cartography.

Although the A-SMGCS strategy has already been proposed about five years ago, only in the most recent years the right technological systems, which are able of efficiently implementing A-SMGCS, started being available. The existence of the European Geostationary Navigation Overlay Service (EGNOS) was a key factor for obtaining a relatively precise localization of the vehicles. Also the availability of recent high bit rate wireless communication technologies like Wi-Fi (IEEE 802.11) and WiMAX (IEEE 802.16) and the possibility of their deployment in the airport airside facilitated the communications based on IP between the vehicles and a central station used for control of the ground movements. Together with the present availability of low cost embedded systems and performing GIS, all these components are the basis for not only an efficient implementation of A-SMGCS, but also for the implementation of a re-engineered European ATM network more efficient, better integrated, more cost-efficient and safer.

This chapter gives an overview of the main issues and design of a concrete EGNOS based system, which includes A-SMGCS services and Decision Support services. The platform has been implemented and can be the basis for future widespread deployments to increase airport safety and efficiency. The implementation has resulted from research and development work done in several European and national R&D projects. The original project, which was supported by the European Commission, was named AIRNET. This is the reason why the platform presented here is identified by that name.

The chapter is organized in the following way. In section 2 the main objectives of A-SMGCS, namely its vehicle navigation component, are introduced. The architecture of the deployed platform and its main components are described in section 3. Section 4 discusses the strategy for the use of wireless communication networks in this environment and presents the main characteristics of the communication technologies to be considered. Also the integration with the airport local area network is described in this section. Section 5 is concerned with the implementation of the different A-SMGCS services and Decision support services and describes with some detail the design of the software modules that were implemented. Finally, section 6 concludes the chapter.

## 2. A-SMGCS Objectives

The surveillance and control on the movement area of an airport are performed visually by the air traffic ground controller. All the operational procedures depend on the actors involved, i.e. pilots, air traffic controllers and vehicle drivers. There is also an articulation between the airport operations and control tower operators done by voice or through other electronic communication mean. Concerning guidance, pilots and vehicle drivers rely on visual aids or on the air traffic controller's instructions to guide them along the assigned routes on ground. With respect to low visibility conditions there are operational procedures, which vary from airport to airport, that are restrictive and need to be strictly followed for ground movements.

Despite the implementation of Surface Movement Guidance and Control System (SMGCS) procedures along the past years, the continuous growth of air traffic, the complexity of airport layouts and of operations in low visibility and congestion situations are leading to an escalating number of incidents and accidents on ground movements. This originated the need to define an advanced approach, which improves SMGCS services to facilitate more efficient procedures. A-SMGCS looks for the application of state-of-the-art information and communication technologies to improve the safety of the ground movements in the movement area of airports. Namely, it intends to maintain the airport throughput in low visibility conditions, to allow controllers to issue clearances and instructions on the basis of surveillance data and to better coordinate the airport activities. This includes the improvement of the airport ground control services, of conflict detection and alerts, and of routing and guidance procedures on the movement area. The technology cost is a concern and, whenever possible, the deployment of low cost systems with no impact in the efficiency of airport operational services is an objective.

It is foreseen that A-SMGCS will be implemented progressively in a phased approach consisting in a package of services addressing Surveillance, Control, Guidance and Route Planning. Surveillance provides controllers, and eventually pilots and vehicle drivers, with the situational awareness in the movement area. The control functionality allows preventing conflicts and collisions by providing alerts for incursions in runways and restricted areas, and activating protection devices. Guidance gives indications to pilots and vehicle drivers to enable them to follow an assigned route. Through the routing functionality, a more efficient route, either manually or automatically, is designated for each aircraft.

Each package of services is structured according to four different implementation levels [2]. The main concerns of levels I and II rely on the improvements of safety, whereas the ground movement's efficiency is dealt with in levels III and IV. The first criteria for implementing A-SMGCS relates to operational needs. The services that address urgent operational needs should be implemented first. This means that services like surveillance and control have priority over aircraft route planning.

Indeed, as presented in Figure 1, the surveillance service is a pre-requisite for implementing all the other A-SMGCS services.

Figure 1. Dependencies between A-SMGCS services.

The primary aim of a surveillance service is to have a real time situational awareness of the position and identification of all vehicles and aircrafts with the guarantee of a predefined reliability and integrity level. In general, the surveillance service provides identification and accurate positional information on aircrafts, vehicles and obstacles within the required area.

A control service will necessary detect the critical operational situations but should, progressively, monitor for other less severe situations. For instance, such a service may be first developed to detect runway incursions and later on to deal with more complex situations or less critical hazardous situations, e.g., detection of a non-authorized vehicle in a stand area or in a restricted area. Alarms and alerts should be generated when appropriate.

The guidance service assigns continuous, unambiguous and reliable information to pilots and drivers to keep their aircrafts or vehicles on assigned routes intended for their use.

Finally, the routing service addresses the planning and assignment of a route to an individual aircraft to provide safe, expeditious and efficient movement from its current position to its intended position.

Table 1 shows the Eurocontrol proposed levels for A-SMGCS implementation. The AIRNET platform described in this chapter addresses the four A-SMGCS levels for vehicles circulating in the airside area for safety and operational management procedures. The goal is to provide accurate surveillance, control, routing and guidance services.

The AIRNET platform described in this chapter has been experimentally deployed at the airport of Porto in Portugal and another one is being deployed at the airport of Lisbon in Portugal. For illustrative purposes the layouts of both airports are shown in Table 2. The critical aviation operations are generally included in the movement area where security and safety are more tightly regulated. But AIRNET provides services for all the airside area, which corresponds to a clearly visible perimeter fence containing the movement area (runway, taxiways and apron), peripheral roads and other restricted access areas within the airport airside.

**Table 1. A-SGMCS levels overview.**

| Levels | Surveillance | | Control | | Routing | Guidance | |
|---|---|---|---|---|---|---|---|
| | Users | Mobiles and areas covered | Users | Conflicts detected | Users | Users | Type |
| **0** | SMGCS | | | | | | |
| | Strict application of SMGCS (considered as pre-requisite for the A-SMGCS) | | | | | | |
| **I** | A-SMGCS | | | | | | |
| | Surveillance | | | | | | |
| | Air Traffic Controller (ATCO) | All vehicles in the maneuvering area  All aircrafts in the movement area | | | | | |
| **II** | | | | | | | |
| | ATCO | All vehicles in the maneuvering area  All aircrafts in the movement area | Control | | | Guidance | |
| | | | ATCO | Runway incursions | | Drivers | Airport Static Map & mobile position on a screen as an option. |
| **III** | | | | | | | |
| | ATCO  All participating mobiles | All vehicles in the maneuvering area  All aircrafts in the movement area | ATCO  Equipped mobiles | All conflicts | Route Planning  ATCO | Pilots  Drivers | Airport Dynamic Map (e.g., with runway status), mobile position on a screen; Automatic switch of ground signals. |
| **IV** | | | | | | | |
| | ATCO  All participating mobiles | All vehicles in the maneuvering area  All aircrafts in the movement area | ATCO  All participating mobiles | All conflicts + Conflict Resolution | ATCO  Equipped mobiles | Pilots  Drivers | Airport Dynamic Map (e.g., with runway status), mobile position & route (from route planning function) on a screen; Automatic switch of ground signals. |

**Table 2. Characterization of the airports of Lisbon and Porto.**

| Airport characteristics | Airport layout |
|---|---|
| Lisbon Airport<br><br>Aerodrome movements = Declared 36/hour<br><br>N° of runways = 4 (03;21;17;35)<br><br>N° of Taxiways<br><br>TAXIWAY<br>WIDTH<br><br>P<br>35M<br><br>C, G, I, K, L, M, N, R, S, T, U, V, W, HN and RET HS<br>23M<br><br>TAXILANE<br>WIDTH<br><br>A1, A2, F and J<br>23M<br><br>B, D and E<br>WIDTH<br><br>Annual Passenger<br>2007 - 13.418.747 Million | |
| Porto Airport<br><br>Aerodrome movements = Declared 18/hour<br><br>N° of runways = 2 (17;35)<br><br>N° of Taxiways<br><br>TAXIWAY<br>WIDTH<br><br>A1, A2, A3, B, C, H, J<br>23M<br><br>D, F<br>25M<br><br>Annual Passenger<br>2007 - 3.988.881 Million | |

## 3. Airnet Platform Architecture

The present level of technological development in the information and communication technologies allows the definition of a low cost platform for the vehicle navigation component of A-SMGCS. The solution relies on the existence of EGNOS for the localization of mobile vehicles on ground, on the deployment of IP-based wireless communication networks in the airside area of the airport, on low cost embedded equipments with EGNOS receivers in the vehicles, on central servers for communication management and application running, and, finally, on the existence of state-of-the art GIS for cartography purposes in the displays connected to the application server and in the on-board vehicle displays. This solution is appropriate only for cooperative vehicles (vehicles with on-board system). It can be extended to non-cooperative vehicles if the appropriate systems, e.g., radar and multi-lateration, are deployed and the data coming from those systems go through a data fusion process together with the data originated in the cooperative vehicles as foreseen in the A-SMGCS strategy. The solution for non-cooperative vehicles is outside the scope of this paper.

Figure 2 shows the architecture of the platform and identifies its main components [3]:

- On-board System – Equipment installed in the vehicle to communicate with the ground system. The information exchanged is very diverse, but we are mostly interested on data about vehicle position, speed and direction of movement, driver identification and task which is being performed.
- Wireless Communication Network – There are several options for the wireless communication network technology to be used in the airside. This network allows the communication between the on-board systems and the ground system. The main candidate technologies are WiMAX, Wi-Fi, CDMA and TETRA. Usually, only one of these technologies is deployed, but if more than one is deployed, a back-up solution for communication becomes feasible.
- Communication Server – Responsible to accurately provide the data collected from the on-board systems to the ground system. The communication server is equipped with the appropriate transponders to adapt to the wireless network in use and manage the communication between vehicles and the ground system through the airport local area network.
- Ground System – The ground system consists of the application server and a set of monitors for the users of the platform. The application server has two models designated as online and offline manager. The first one focuses on operational management issues and the second one on historical data analysis. The Geo Database Manager deals with the cartography issues of the GIS in use. The Air Traffic Controller (ATCO), Airport Operations Officer (AOO) and other airport stakeholders, like the Ground Handler Manager, interact with the platform via monitors, known as Ground Human-Machine Interface (GHMI), connected to the application server in a client-server model. It is foreseen the possibility of users to connect to the application server via PDAs too.
- External Systems – These are existing airport operational systems, which contain information about flight schedule, airport operational tasks, vehicle allocation, allocation of tasks to personnel, airport equipment and airport status.

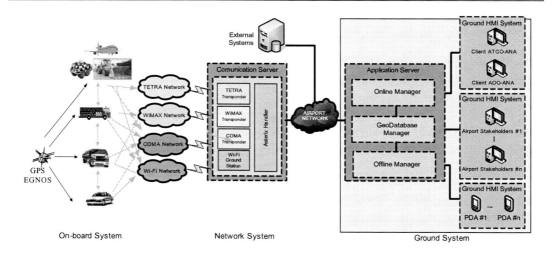

Figure 2. AIRNET platform architecture.

There is one embedded system installed in each vehicle. The system is connected to an on-board display for the vehicle driver, known as the Driver Human-Machine Interface (DHMI). The embedded system includes a GPS/EGNOS receiver, the wireless communication network transponders and a PC board.

The on-board system uses a GPS/EGNOS receiver to obtain its position and communicates the vehicle position to the ground system, which after being geo-processed by the application server, is then displayed at the GHMI. EGNOS augments the two satellite navigation systems presently operating, GPS and GLONASS, and makes them suitable for safety critical applications. It consists of three geostationary satellites and a network of more than 30 ground stations [4]. EGNOS achieves its aim by transmitting a signal containing information on the reliability and accuracy (integrity data) of the positioning signals sent by GPS and GLONASS. It includes accurate information on the position of each GPS and GLONASS satellite, the accuracy of the atomic clocks on board the satellites and information on disturbances within the ionosphere that might affect the accuracy of positioning measurements. The EGNOS receiver decodes the signal to give a more accurate position than is possible with GPS or GLONASS alone, and an accurate estimate of the errors. It allows users to determine their position to within 2 meters. EGNOS is a joint project of the European Space Agency, the European Commission and Eurocontrol. It is in operation since 2006 and it might be considered as a precursor to Galileo, the global satellite navigation system under development in Europe.

The software modules that implement the AIRNET services on-board run in the PC board. There are four distinct software modules, which are identified according to the services that they provision, namely Conflict/Infringement Detection, Traffic Context, Service Monitoring (monitors the equipment status) and Decision Support. These modules have equivalent, although more complex,  modules in the application server and by running symmetrically in both systems they implement the A-SMGCS and Decision Support services supplied by the platform.

As the on-board system software structure is analogous to the one implemented in the ground system, we will focus into the description of the application server software structure and on the corresponding functionalities, outlining whenever applicable specific aspects of the on-board system that contribute to the enhancement of safety procedures. The description of the software structure will be done in section 5.

The wireless communication networks allow the exchange of data between the on-board systems and the ground system. They cover the whole airside area. Four distinct networks are considered for this purpose: Wi-Fi, WiMAX, TETRA and CDMA. The main emphasis should be on the use of the Wi-Fi or WiMAX networks, which are novel and high bit rate technologies for an airport airside environment. However, the platform can also work, although with a lower quality of service, with lower bit-rate communication technologies like CDMA or TETRA. These last two networks are sometimes found in an airport environment and that is the main reason of their choice as an alternative technology. It should also be noted that CDMA and TETRA are networks run by telecommunication operators whereas Wi-Fi and WiMAX might be networks operated by the airport authorities, which is preferable. Finally, an aeronautical network, e.g. VDL-4 or MODE-S, might also be used for communication of the platform with aircrafts, although the communication with the aircraft is not covered in this chapter. The communication server is the entity responsible for managing the heterogeneity of the wireless communication networks, presenting a common network interface to the ground system.

# 4. Communication Networks for the Airnet Platform

The platform shown in Figure 2 has been implemented first as a result of an R&D European project named AIRNET [5] and later on, it was enhanced and made more robust for a new deployment at the airport of Porto in Portugal. In this case, trials have been done with Wi-Fi, CDMA and TETRA communication networks. As a result of those trials it was decided that, because of operational and performance reasons, Wi-Fi is the main communication network at the airside in Porto airport and CDMA will be used as a back-up. A second deployment of the platform is being done at the airport of Lisbon in Portugal. Here, the wireless communication network in the airside uses the WiMAX technology. This is a more recent technology that was not available yet at the time of technology choice for the Porto airport. By using Wi-Fi and WiMAX in different airports, it will be possible to compare the performance of both in full operational conditions and extrapolate the results for future deployments.

## 4.1. Selection of the Wireless Communication Network

Wireless communication networks have a key role in the A-SMGCS platform. They allow the seamless data communication between vehicles and the ground system. The objective is to cover the whole airside with a high bit rate private wireless network, which can be operated by the airport authority. IP based communications will be run over this network. The cost issue concerning deployment is also an important factor to consider. The two strongest candidate technologies are Wi-Fi (IEEE 802.11 standard) and WiMAX (IEEE 802.16 standard). Both are high-bit rate technologies and available at a fair cost.

As referred previously, a Wi-Fi network was deployed at the airport of Porto. At that time, WiMAX was not a realistic option yet. Nowadays, WiMAX products are widely available and the platform, which is being installed at the airport of Lisbon will use WiMAX. It will have the advantage of using a very small number of antennas to cover the airside compared to Wi-Fi and of having a more controlled quality of service. However, WiMAX is more expensive and operates in licensed frequencies, which implies the need for the airport authority to get operation authorization from the country telecommunication regulator.

The optional use of CDMA and TETRA is justified because these two communication technologies are deployed in many airports, not only for telephony but also for data communication. Both technologies have data rates smaller than Wi-Fi and WiMAX, but they might be used as back-up to the main network. The quality of service will be significantly degraded in TETRA because TETRA operates with a few tens of kbps only, which means that TETRA will be always the last option to consider. CDMA might reach 2 Mbps in some deployments and at this speed most A-SMGCS services might operate satisfactorily. We must not forget, however, that CDMA and TETRA networks are under the management of a network operator, which represents a disadvantage for the airport authority, which would like to have the full control of the network for the AIRNET platform.

The most relevant characteristics of the four wireless communication technologies referred above are described next having in view their use in the AIRNET platform.

### 4.1.1. Wi-Fi Network

In the A-SMGCS platform of Porto the Wi-Fi network is based on the IEEE 802.11a standard [6], which operates in the 5 GHz frequency band, supporting physical bit rates between 1 Mbps and 54 Mbps. IEEE 802.11a was selected in detriment of its 2.4 GHz counterpart standard IEEE 802.11b/g due to the fact that the Portuguese communications regulation authority has authorized the use of higher transmission power in the 5.470-5.725 GHz frequency band for vehicular applications (1 W E.I.R.P versus 100 mW E.I.R.P for the 2.4 GHz frequency band), which greatly reduced the number of access points required to cover the airside area. In this deployment about 15 access points have been used for that purpose.

Among the analyzed Wi-Fi architectures, the IP-based Routed-WLAN architecture turned out to be the most advantageous. The Routed-WLAN architecture uses high layer management protocols on top of TCP/IP to configure the network elements: Central Controller and Access Points. The Central Controller concentrates all the Wi-Fi network "intelligence". Its main responsibilities are network management services, Radio Frequency channel management, access point transmission power management that automatically adapts to interference conditions, handover logic and mobility management, enforcement of security and quality of service policies, network monitoring and automatic reconfiguration in response to failure conditions. The access points have their functionality limited to the physical and medium access control layers, except for the management plane.

### 4.1.2. WiMAX Network

WiMAX is one of the most promising broadband wireless access systems. WiMAX is based on the IEEE 802.16 standard, which defines the medium access control and physical layers of a fixed and mobile solution [7]. WiMAX implementations are also based on the WiMAX Forum specifications. The WiMAX carrier frequency is less than 11 GHz. For the moment, the frequency bands considered are 2.5 GHz, 3.5 GHz and 5.7 GHz. WiMAX is built on the

Orthogonal Frequency Division Multiplexing (OFDM) transmission technique known for its high radio resource use frequency. The average data rate is about 10 Mbps, although some reports give more ambitious figures up to 70 Mbps. This high value only applies for a very good state of the radio channel and for a very small cell. The distance can go up to 20 km. This value for distance contrasts with the value of hundreds of meters achieved in Wi-Fi, which justifies the advantage of WiMAX in the airport coverage, although WiMAX is a dearer technology than Wi-Fi.

The main components of a WiMAX network are:

- End-User devices (clients);
- WiMax Base Station, Adaptive Antenna System, scalable OFDMA combined with smart antenna technology;
- Wireless Access Controller responsible for access control, security and authentication, accounting, traffic routing and mobility;
- Operation & Maintenance Center  responsible for advanced radio network optimization and performance management,

The WiMax network supports fixed and mobile clients, end-to-end quality of service and low latency; it can be used to support different types of applications simultaneous, including VoIP.

The airside of the airport of Lisbon is covered with only three Base Stations.

### 4.1.3. CDMA Network

The public CDMA network available in Portugal operates in the 450 MHz range (CDMA450). It basically follows the specifications of CDMA2000 defined by 3GPP2, with the physical layer modifications required for use in another frequency band and with lower bandwidth channels (1.25 MHz).

The CDMA network operates in two modes: 1xRTT (Radio Transmission Technology) [8] and EV-DO (Evolution, Data Optimized) [9]. In the EV-DO network the maximum bandwidth per sector is 2.4 Mbps downstream and 153.6 Kbps upstream. In the 1xRTT mode the maximum bandwidth per sector and connection is 153.6 Kbps for both downstream and upstream directions. Presently the EV-DO is only available in urban and suburban areas, which includes the entire Porto aerodrome, requiring, however, that the ground vehicles are equipped with external antennas.

An important advantage of CDMA450 is that as it operates in a frequency band much lower than Wi-Fi, it has a lower attenuation in open air and better coverage in non-line-of-sight environments, what means that it can cover a wide area with a single base station controller, making it a possible alternative to support the A-SMGCS services.

### 4.1.4. TETRA Network

The TETRA network is centered on a base station and supports packet data services via the Specific Connectionless Network Service (S-CLNS). The S-CLNS allows the transmission of IP packets between a TETRA mobile terminal and terminals located in either a fixed IP-based

LAN or other mobile terminals using the S-CLNS. In the Porto airport, the proprietary DIMETRA S-CLNS implementation is used [10].

Due to the low bit rate supported by the TETRA technology (maximum of 28.8 kbps per carrier per direction of communication) the platform functionality will be substantially reduced when this technology is used. Pre-operational tests have been conducted to evaluate the performance of the deployed wireless network. The results have shown that the performance is low and not satisfactory to run the A-SMGCS services for a large number of vehicles.

## 4.2. Integration with the Airport Local Area Network

The deployed wireless communication networks are managed by the communication server of the ground system. These wireless networks should be integrated with the airport Local Area Network (LAN) via the communication server to allow the communication of the airport operational systems with the vehicles. This will be especially useful when display of operational information, like schedule of flights or allocation of vehicles to certain aircraft stands, is required in the vehicle display as an aid to the vehicle driver. The implementation has considered this approach and the Airport Operational Management System (AOMS) of the Porto airport communicates with the on-board systems of the vehicles through the interconnected networks. AOMS is an example of the External System referred in the A-SMGS architecture in Figure 2. Figure 3 shows the interconnected network architecture deployed in the Porto airport.

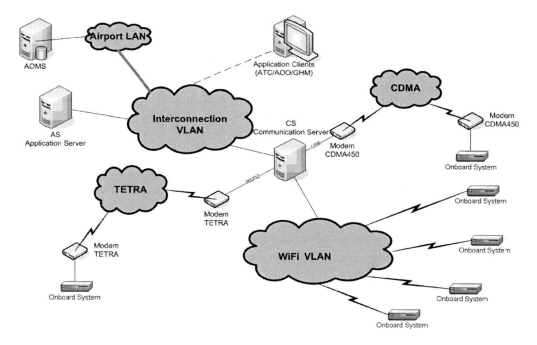

Figure 3. Network interconnection in the Porto airport.

The communications are completely based on the IP protocol. The core of the network consists of an interconnection VLAN that is separate from the airport LAN where the AOMS is located. As the airport authority has complete control of the Wi-Fi network, an independent VLAN was defined for the Wi-Fi network, which connects to the airport interconnection VLAN.

## 5. Airnet Services Implementation

The AIRNET services are implemented in the application server, which works in articulation with the on-board systems at the vehicles. The AIRNET services include the A-SMGCS and the Decision Support services.

The internal software structure of the Application Server is presented in Figure 4. The focus of the Online Manager is into operational efficiency, namely the continuous display of the vehicles position in real-time at the airport stakeholder's monitors. The focus of the Offline Manager is to provide a collaborative decision making environment with GIS functionalities enabling the airport stakeholders to perform historical safety data analysis.

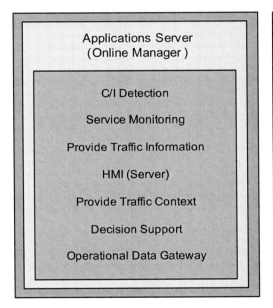
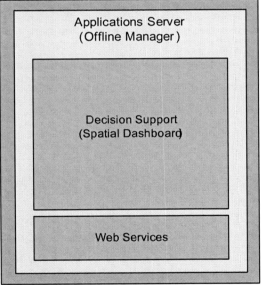

Figure 4. Application Server modules.

Airport operational data are first compiled by the Online Manager modules and stored in a specific database that is accessed by the Offline Manager for historical data analysis. The main functionalities of the Online Manager modules are the following:

- Traffic Information (TI) – receives the vehicle location from the Communication Server and validates the data before passing it to the CID and HMI modules;

- Conflict/Infringement Detection (CID) – provides information about conflicts, incursions, and infringements by permanently monitoring TI data. The module also addresses route planning algorithms to cope with changes in operational data;
- Traffic Context (TC) – provides information about gradual changes to the airport cartographic context, with the metadata managed in a dynamic way by authorized users;
- Operational Data Gateway (ODG) – manages the connection to external systems providing operational business data about flights, fleet, drivers, and tasks;
- Human Machine Interface (HMI) – provides a map-based interface with surveillance, control, guidance, alert messages and decision support information for the airside area;
- Decision Support (DS) – supports stakeholder's daily management activities and data communication between the ground and the on-board systems;
- Service Monitoring (SM) – stores information about the status of the system components; within the scope of this paper the functionalities addressed by the module are not of interest, hence it is not detailed.

In short, the vehicle location-awareness data passed from the on-board systems to the application server are processed by the TI module. After checking the accuracy of location-based parameters and their conformity to the cartographic parameters at the ground system the data are passed into the HMI and CID modules. The platform operates with WGS84 geographic coordinates, therefore location-based data are expressed in latitude and longitude angles. The interoperability between the modules within the Online Manager is described in the following sub-sections.

The Offline Manager module is responsible for managing historical data, namely to seamlessly integrate data provided from external systems, including operational data collected by the ODG module (e.g., flight information, tasks, vehicles), data concerning aircrafts at the ground provided by Air Control and data about driver's provided by the resource management system, with location-based data about cooperative vehicles provided by the TI module.

The data structure of the Offline Manager module is a multidimensional spatial database optimized for multi-criteria decision making and spatial data analysis. This database provides support for airport stakeholders to monitor gradual changes to business performance, enabling them inclusively to check for geometric evolutions derived from changes to the airport layout when analyzing historical hazard situations.

The main goal of the Web Services module is to enable airport stakeholders to monitor their fleet operational activities in useful time without requiring their physical presence in the airport. The web services are performed offline because, in this case, the major requirement does not relate to real-time data access constraints. In a web environment a time delay of just a few seconds is acceptable.

## 5.1. CID and TI Modules

Airports are excellent examples of very large, dynamic and complex systems with many interacting traffic modes and numerous services. The interdependencies between traffic modes and services, and therefore the system complexity, are a result of the number of groups of stakeholders, each group operating within different fields with different goals but all generally aiming into significant improvements of the airport safety and efficiency.

Most of the A-SMGCS control and surveillance issues are depending on the successful execution of the data fusion process performed in real-time. The term data fusion besides addressing the process of combining traffic information also includes operational data related to operational efficiencies of drivers and vehicles on the airside. For instance, when a driver logs into a specific vehicle a set of validations are performed, a successful login requires the transmission of the driver's task to the corresponding on-board system of the vehicle. For each task that is being performed a dynamic route is automatically determined and presented as a recommendation to the driver at the DHMI. This route is determined based on the current location of the vehicle, the target destination and additional parameters such as circulation directions, speed limits and time of day. Route suggestions are provided on-the-fly as changes to the task plan are communicated to the ground system, for instance, by the airport task planning system.

**Table 3. Types of safety hazards**

| Safety hazards | Scenarios |
|---|---|
| Conflict - possibility of collision between aircrafts and/or vehicles | • Vehicle entering or crossing a closed RWY or TWY.<br>• Vehicle not stopping at the road holding position.<br>• Vehicle going beyond road holding position.<br>• Near collision (same intersection or short proximity). |
| Incursion - unauthorized entry by an aircraft, vehicle, into pre-defined, protected, dangerous, or restricted areas | • Restricted area incursions, e.g., TWY incursion without a clearance level.<br>• Incursions into TWY strips closed area, e.g., vehicle circulating on a closed service road.<br>• Incursions to critical and sensitive areas established for radio navigation aids.<br>• Incursions to emergency areas. |
| Infringements - occurrences related to airport traffic rule infractions | • Driver without a valid license.<br>• Vehicle circulation without airport vehicle access permission.<br>• Vehicle exceeding speed limit.<br>• Vehicle circulating out of the areas authorized by the airport authority.<br>• Vehicle parked in an unauthorized area. |

The CID module also relies on the data fusion process to accurately detect safety hazards, e.g., incursions, infringements and collisions. To ensure that airport operations are conducted efficiently and within the required safety level for all visibility conditions and emergency situations, the CID module classifies each vehicle movements according to one of the three types of hazard situations presented in Table 3. The location-awareness algorithm of the CID module can be configured to operate with most of the airport safety rules for multiple domain entities including vehicle category, access permissions or traffic circulation rules.

The surveillance of safety hazards is performed by the CID module in multiple ways, namely by monitoring vehicles location against restricted access boundaries or by correlating data received from the on-board system with data collected from undergoing aircraft assisting tasks or any other airport maintenance task.

As part of the data fusion process data integration is accomplished by linking the data provided by the on-board systems (e.g., vehicle and driver identities) with the data collected from external systems (e.g., task and flight identities). Such level of data integration enables the CID module to ensure the accomplishment of very granular business rules, namely to check for driving license expiration dates, validate if a driver is qualified to drive a specific vehicle, or to trigger an alert when the vehicle inspection date expired.

One important aspect when creating a business rule is the rule expression, that is, if it relates to a business process with a direct impact on operational activities. For instance, some operational tasks may require drivers to provide periodical feedback information about the task completion status (started, aborted, changed, and finished) enabling airport stakeholders at the ground system to monitor work progression. Any business rule violation will trigger an alert informing that the vehicle is in an infringement situation. The efficiency of operations for ground surface movements is therefore improved by preventing safety hazards due to vehicles and by preventing airport congestion in crisis situations.

The CID module makes use of dynamic operational business rules, expressed as configuration parameters to describe business semantics, and on specific data access constraints for checking the compliance of airport operations with the airport safety requirements. The CID module is also responsible for classifying safety hazards according to their severity level and for structuring them hierarchically. In this way, when monitoring vehicles movements the surveillance algorithm addresses the most appropriate alert message whenever a safety hazard situation is detected. The CID module also correlates the current position of the vehicle against pre-defined protection areas where its presence is permanently or temporarily forbidden. The boundaries of pre-defined protection areas are represented as features with a specific boundary for each airport operational level.

Protection radius around mobiles (vehicles and aircrafts) is another type of features supported by the CID module for topological validations, namely to validate safety distances between conflicting vehicles, between a vehicle and an aircraft, or between a vehicle and fixed obstacles. This radius takes the form of a circle when the mobile is stopped and an ellipse when the mobile starts moving.

The TI module has an important role in the data fusion process since it receives from on-board systems information about the mobiles position, their directions, speed, and HPL[1] values, as well as the driver, operator and vehicle identities. Without these data the CID would not be able to implement the surveillance service of the A-SMGCS. The location-based data that the TI module receives must be precise and accurate. Such accuracy is determined by the position integrity algorithm in the on-board system, namely to determine HPL values.

---

1  Horizontal Protection Level (HPL).  The Horizontal Protection Level is the radius of a circle in the horizontal plane (the plane tangent to the WGS-84 ellipsoid), with its center being at the true position, which describes the region that is assured to contain the indicated horizontal position.

After checking the conformity of the location-based parameters with the cartographic parameters, the TI module sends the information to both the HMI and the CID modules.

The on-board system equipped with an EGNOS/GPS receiver, offers a good accuracy in locations where there is good visibility of the geostationary satellites. However, the lack of availability, especially in congested areas near or beneath airport terminals, is a known problem for most of the EGNOS/GPS receivers in the market. Although an EGNOS/GPS receiver offers an improvement in the calculated position, the integrity of this position might not be good enough for location based services. In Figure 5 the usefulness of the position integrity is shown. Here the vehicle goes through the true path (striped stars), but the navigation system indicator estimates that the trajectory is another one (filled stars). The difference between the erroneous and correct paths is the horizontal position error (HPE). The calculation of the integrity parameters is based on the real time processing of the data broadcast by EGNOS, which contains correction information for all red measurements. The integrity algorithm developed for the HPL calculation accuracy presents the following range values:

- Vehicle position accurate → HPL $\in$ [0; 7.5[
- Lack of surveillance services→ HPL $\in$ [7.5; 12[
- Lack of control services  → HPL $\in$ [12; ∞[

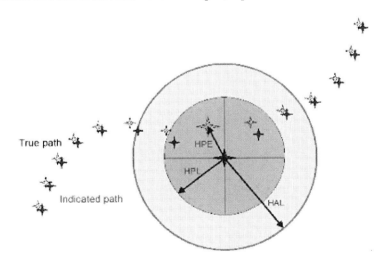

Figure 5. Horizontal Protection Level.

In the airport environment, the HPL parameter is vital in order to enclose the confidence area of the EGNOS/GPS receiver, providing a good estimation of the system reliability based on the fact that the true position is within a circle around the computed position. The horizontal alert limit (HAL) can be defined as a proper upper bound for the HPL value. If HPL>HAL the integrity alarm is triggered and the vehicle point feature at the HMI for both the ground and on-board systems is displayed in gray. Figure 6 shows the block diagram of the on-board system. It is equipped with a wireless antenna, an EGNOS/GPS receiver and an embedded computer component with wireless communication connectivity.

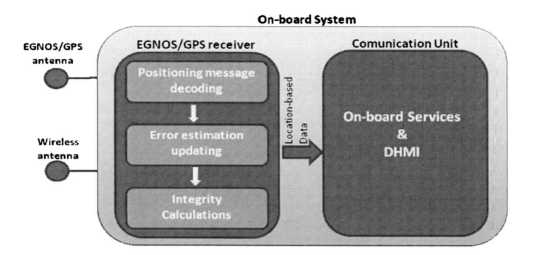

Figure 6. Internal structure of the on-board system.

According to the specified requirements, for each on-board system the lag time between sending its position and receiving feedback information from the ground system is less than one second. The feedback information relates mostly to alert messages, as well as to flight and task data updates to be presented at the on-board DHMI. This means that as soon as the CID receives a new mobile position, the module initiates a validation procedure to check if the mobile is in an infringement, incursion or conflict situation, for instance, if the mobile exceeds speed limits or is in an area where its presence is permanently or temporarily forbidden or if two vehicles are within a collision path. Whenever such hazard situations are detected a specific alert message is sent to the ground HMI module and to the on-board system of the vehicles that caused the hazard situation.

The HMI module has the responsibility to continuously update the location of the mobiles, representing them as point features over the airport map-based display. To accomplish with the lag time requirement expressed before, the screen refreshing cycle time must occur periodically in less than 500 milliseconds.

## 5.2. TC Module

The TC module is responsible for managing the airport map layout, namely to represent gradual changes and assure conformity of the map features to specified standards. The map features are structured into a set of thematic layers for the representation of the airport cartographic context. Some of these layers are mandatory because they provide the essential map features for a good understanding of the airport map-layout.

The airport map layout, or cartographic context, is based on the ED-119 standard [11]. This standard describes requirements for the interchange of geographic data products that represent terrain, obstacles, and airport mapping features. These requirements apply the concepts of the ISO 19100 series of standards to previously published requirements for data content and quality. Specifically, this standard represents an intermediate specification level between abstract conceptual requirements and a compliant interchange implementation. The

ED-119 standard also specifies requirements for the scope, metadata, content, reference system, quality and maintenance of cartographic information.

The ISO 19100 series of geographic information standards establishes a structured set of standards for information concerning objects or phenomena that are directly or indirectly associated with a location based service. As outlined in Figure 7, this family of standards specifies methods, tools and services for management of geographic information, including the definition, acquisition, analysis, access, presentation and transfer of such data in digital/electronic form between different users, systems and locations.

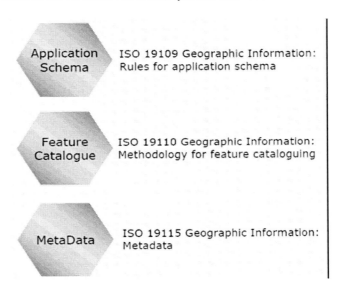

Figure 7. Related ISO19100 Standards.

The three ISO 19100 series of geographic information standards are of particular relevance for the specification of airport mapping database, namely to:

- define the basic semantics and structure for data management and data interchange purposes;
- define airport mapping service components and their behavior for data processing purposes;
- define the formal description of the data structure and content of data sets, in particular for the feature catalogue and metadata.

The ISO 19115 is of particular interest because it corresponds to an abstract metadata model essential to support data management and discovery. As presented in Table 4, the standard provides a common and consistent method to describe map features [12].

The knowledge of information resources and their description in a metadata catalogue based on an international standard are recommended as one of the first actions to be undertaken for the development of Spatial Data Infrastructure (SDI). The term SDI encompasses the policies, standards and institutional arrangements involved in delivering spatially related information from all available sources to all potential users. The TC module provides a graphical interface for authorized users to manage airport features, namely to add new thematic layers to the airport cartographic context, add/remove descriptive attributes from a specific layer or add new attributes to all the existing layers. In addition to basic operations (e.g. management of the attribute values, feature color, transparency level, order of visualization) end-users can change the status of some features. For instance, the status of a TWY or a Stand can be set to deactivate causing the CID module not to trigger an incursion alert whenever a vehicle is within the deactivated TWY or Stand. Changes are stored centrally at the application server and a broadcast message is automatically sent to all HMI-clients to update their current version of the airport layout.

**Table 4. Metadata key aspects.**

| Metadata Aspect | Description |
|---|---|
| Content | Which feature catalogue is used? |
| Distribution | How can I access the data? |
| Identification | What kind of dataset? |
| Data quality | What is the quality of the data? |
| Responsible party | Who is the responsible publisher and what is the contact information? |
| Maintenance | How frequently is the data updated and maintained? |
| Spatial representation | How are the data spatially represented? |

According to the ED-119 an airport map must be represented as a vector data model with its spatial features structured as a stack of overlapped layers. From a spatial point of view, the representation of correlated spatial features as a set of overlapped layers provides a clear picture of the causes and effects between spatially related features. A feature data set is a collection of spatial objects sharing the same spatial reference system within a common geographic area, usually with pre-defined business relationships between features. The features that characterize the airport layout also define most of the airside circulation and operational rules. This is why it is useful to group them into meaningful data sets using features such as points (e.g. fixed obstacles, lights), lines (e.g. TWY lanes, Stand parking lines), or polygons (buildings, stands).

Thematic layers are also grouped into meaningful more generalized geographic areas, for instance, runways, taxiways and apron areas are grouped into a global area represented by the movement area layer, the aircrafts parking places and corresponding support areas are grouped into the stand layer and the different types of roads into a roadway layer. Each layer is time-stamped enabling accurate representations of gradual changes to the spatial context. This procedure enables the representation of changes to spatial features, a parameter critical for historical data analyses requiring data to be monitored within the right spatial-temporal context.

## 5.3. ODG Module

Airport stakeholders working at the airport share the same resources and services. Although services are the responsibility of different stakeholders, they need to co-operate to contribute to the common transportation objective. The ODG module is responsible for collecting data from the existing airport operational systems, namely to provide airport stakeholders with information about:

- Airport operational plan - detailed information about all scheduled flights;
- Tasks - information about scheduled and ongoing tasks relative to aircrafts assistance or airport maintenance;
- Drivers - detailed information about the drivers, namely their role and professional data as well as historical information about their conflict and infringements record;
- Vehicles - detailed information about the vehicles, including historical data about the conflict and infringements caused by the vehicle.

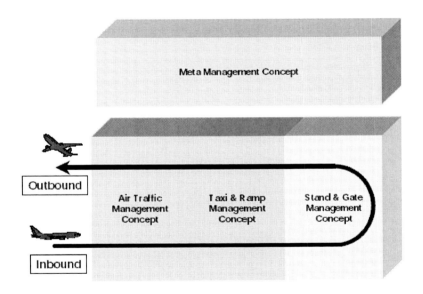

Figure 8. Macroscopic view management layer.

The type of information provided is limited to one single airport and is not structured to the execution of decisions at the ad-hoc level but rather to support airport stakeholder's daily operational decisions such as surveillance of mobile movements at the airside area. As outlined in Figure 8 the emphasis of this data fusion is to characterize the main operational aspects and interdependencies for the basic management areas:

- Air Traffic Management;
- Taxi and Ramp Management;
- Stand and Gate Management.

Figure 8 provides a macroscopic view on the aircraft's turn-around cycle in relation to the stakeholders involved. It depicts (from left to right) the aircraft's inbound phase described in terms of geographical location and operation centers grouped by the basic management areas.

Macroscopic view in this context means the local view of current operations (status tracking) and future operations (plans of operations) transferred beyond the scope of the area of responsibility of a single local operation centre. Transfer is not just a physical transmission of some information to a "downstream operation centre"; transfer also includes the aggregation, transposition, synchronization and harmonization of information. The integration of operational data should result into an optimized traffic flow during "normal" conditions to increase the punctuality or throughput. In this way the macroscopic view should be seen as an enabler for:

- global access to airside maintenance tasks;
- global access to flight plans;
- global aircraft flight/ground status and key-event tracking;
- global aircraft assisting tasks and planning status tracking.

The goal is to guarantee the current maximum available flow, which could mean that, for example, a single aircraft already delayed is delayed even more to fulfill the overall goal of maximum flow. Macroscopic identification and awareness of deficiencies and bottlenecks, and their mutual effects, is furthermore a prerequisite for global airside operational efficiency.

Indeed the lack of data integrity of the overall model might influence the force of expression of later results due to inconsistency of information used by different airport stakeholders especially when information is "crossing" the basic management areas. Hence the overall goals for the design of the macroscopic view management layer were based on the following features:

- Comprehensive and well-directed information flow to all stakeholders despite of their different objectives;
- Automatic coordination between the basic management areas;
- Clear definition of the responsibilities;
- Identification of the systems and procedures for the movement area with a common performance specification.

In this way, it was possible to identify the data sources at the airport systems and to organize the information flow to provide the "logical macroscopic view" to each airport stakeholder. From a safety perspective this is particularly important because airport authorities need to have access to the most updated operational tasks at the movement area.

The ODG module acts therefore as a gateway to keep operational data updated as they change at the central "head office". Furthermore, the ODG module enables the development of automated planning tools to help airport stakeholders in achieving a better level of performance. In this way all airport stakeholders involved are informed about any changes to flight schedule, flight status, ongoing tasks, drivers and vehicle descriptive data.

## 5.4. HMI Module

The Ground Human Machine Interface (GHMI) at the Application Server is the link between the system and the end-users, in particular Air Traffic Controllers, Airport Operation Officer and Ground Handler Managers. The GHMI provides a view of what is contributing or influencing the safety performance, alerting for underperforming situations together with information about the appropriate actions to improve performance. Hence, it is most important that the HMI displays location-based information in a continuous and accurate way.

The design objective of the GHMI was to provide surveillance and control services for all cooperative vehicles in one single screen with a map-based layout at least 2/3 of the screen display, with basic GIS functionalities (e.g. pan, zoom, feature selection, feature identify) as the main way for end-users to interact with the system. The GHMI satisfies the functionalities defined in A-SMGCS. However, since aircraft assisting tasks all have an addressed stand or terminal gate, the route for each task is automatically calculated based on the vehicle current position, destination and operational parameters such as time of day, airside traffic circulation rules, speed limits, and characteristics of the road segments (e.g., category, status, and average circulation time).

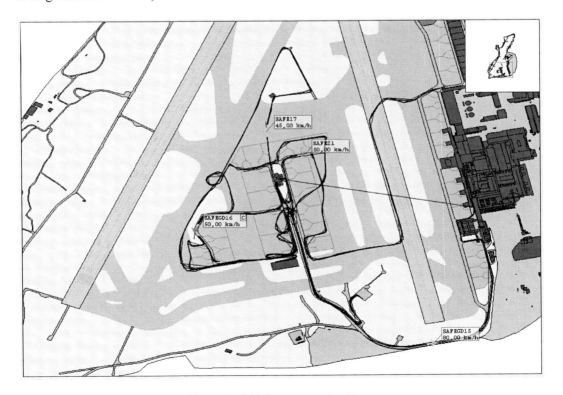

Figure 9. Vehicle movement patterns.

Airport stakeholders, in particular drivers at the on-board system, can activate/deactivate the functionality to visualize the vehicle's movement path as line features. The analysis of movement patterns of vehicles is particularly useful to fine tune the route planning algorithms for better operational efficiency. The vehicle movement patterns can be filtered by date/time, type of task or by airport operator for a better understanding of driving habits, bottlenecks caused by traffic congestion, identification of operational inefficiencies or strange vehicle movements. Figure 9 presents an example of movement's patterns derived from four vehicles during field tests on the airside of the Lisbon airport.

The implementation of pop-up windows, according to ICAO [13] requirements, was avoided as much as possible because they are a distractive element and their overlapping behavior eliminates the surveillance capability of the end-users. An effort was also applied to minimize the number of mouse clicks that the end-users need to perform to reach the required information.

The GHMI surveillance and control services derive from a closed interaction between the TC module and the CID module. Besides the airport mapping background context, the displayed data also includes traffic information about all the vehicles in the airside. Figure 10 exemplifies one of the airport views that can be seen at the GHMI. In this case all thematic layers are considered (see the Map Feature tab at the left side) including the representation of the RWY and TWY protection areas. The user might choose to hide these layers for simplification reasons. By default, vehicles are represented as icons with their identification and current speed assigned as transparent labels. In Figure 10 one of the labels is represented with a red color. A red label means one of two critical situations: vehicle located within a restricted access area or that the driver is in a "Panic Alert" situation requesting immediate help.

The colour code presented in Figure 10 representing the vehicles surveillance status is defined as:

- Green – to represent a vehicle operating normally;
- Blue – vehicle stopped;
- Gray – Lack of HPL accuracy, surveillance and control services are not provided;
- Yellow – vehicle caused a level 1 incursion (e.g. stand incursion) or caused an infringement (e.g., speed limit exceeded);
- Read – vehicle caused a level 2 incursion (e.g. RWY incursion) or Panic Alert was pressed.

All alerts are provided with a visual indication of the failure including a time indication. These alert messages are presented at the Alert Viewer according to their severity level, type, and user profile. An end-of-alert timestamp is automatically added whenever the vehicle stops being in an infringement or incursion situation. At the Alert Viewer, the alert messages are ordered by date; end-users can use graphical scrolls to search the list to see the history of alert messages. A double click in one of the alert messages centers the GHMI display at the current location of the vehicle that caused the selected alert message. End-users have also the possibility to assign a specific sound to each type of alert to call their attention in a more proficient way, namely to alert them for those critical situations requiring their immediate attention or intervention. Sound alert messages are presented at the map-based display as a transparent label with information describing the occurrence and its location for audit purposes.

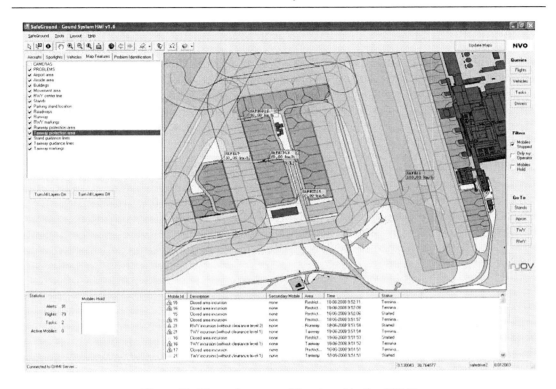

Figure 10. View of an area of the airport in the GHMI.

The screen refreshing time cycle occurs every second. This means that at the GHMI, the information about the vehicle location is updated every second. It is therefore possible to continuously monitor the vehicle position. Airport stakeholders have also the possibility to label only their fleet vehicles. This means that the locations of all vehicles are displayed but only the vehicles from their fleet are labeled.

The GHMI provides a problem reporting tool that enables airport stakeholders at the ground system to manage field reported problems in real-time, namely to assign a task for each reported problem. All reported problems are represented as point features.

The guidance service is dedicated to drivers and includes all the areas of the airport. This service allows drivers to visualize their own positions on a moving map of the airport, which is one of the functionalities provided by the DHMI.

## 5.5. DS Module

In most organizations, decision makers seek to improve their decision process by managing the tradeoffs between precision, consistency, agility, speed and cost of decisions. The DS module addresses these decision making requirements by providing information targeted to the specific needs of airport stakeholders. It provides a collaborative decision making environment that enables decision makers to monitor, evaluate and analyze safety performance on-the-fly, reducing costs, and contributing to improve their perception about business behavior.

The functionalities of the DS module are mostly dedicated to provide efficient interactions between both systems (i.e., ground and onboard) as well as to provide an alternative text message communication channel between drivers and end-users at the ground system. These functionalities are not strictly an implementation of A-SMGCS services, but rather a planning support service for an European ATM network engineered to become more efficient, better integrated, more cost-efficient and safe. The decision support service, in concrete, provides real time information about aircrafts (departing and landing times, departing positions, air companies, etc.), text messages with instructions to the drivers, data about the airport and vehicle status, in addition to problem reporting and video surveillance functionalities.

DS services operate in two ways: support operational daily activities or historical data analysis. The first one aims to help airport stakeholders and vehicle drivers to take efficient and pertinent decisions in order to optimize operational performance through a better management of the resources (human, vehicles and equipment) in particular for the apron area. The second one aims to provide a full spatial context for historical data analysis. The main goal is to provide risk assessment and diagnosis functionalities to help decision-makers to better understand hazard events. Decision-makers have the possibility to monitor gradual changes to spatial object's geometric evolutions or to analyze historical hazards within their spatial-temporal context.

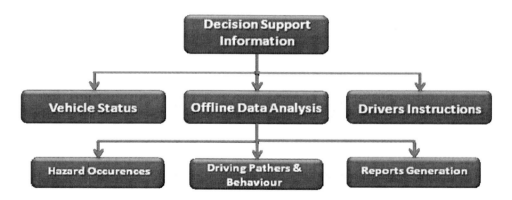

Figure 11. Decision support information chart.

As presented in Figure 11, the real time operational component of the DS provides the airport stakeholders with information about the vehicle status and a function to communicate with the drivers using text messages. The communication request and data synchronization between ground and on-board systems is started by the on-board system based on the switch-on procedure, i.e. when the driver logs at the Login interface of the DHMI. This procedure is responsible to validate the driver login request and for each successful login a well-structured set of data is exchanged between the DS module in the on-board system and the DS module in the ground system.

The on-board DS module is just a simplified version of its ground system counterpart. It should be seen as a gateway to comply with data request concerning information, which is stored only at the ground system. This means that no functionalities for historical data analysis are provided, only information for drivers operational daily activities, namely information about flight drivers' tasks and text messages exchanged between both systems.

The communication between the on-board and the ground DS modules is particularly useful for the acknowledgment of messages related to assigned tasks or panic alert situations. The former enables airport stakeholders at the ground system to monitor the evolution of the assigned tasks complementing the reported task status with location based data and, in some cases, with video images collected from mobile cameras installed within the vehicles.

The offline component of the DS module comprises automatic data fusion tasks in order to bundle data from different sources and to put them into a context appropriate for historical data analysis. The collected data are stored in a Data Warehouse with a multidimensional spatial data structure optimized for decision making purposes and spatial data analysis [14]. This is accomplished without consuming too much time or requiring specific domain-expertise.

Offline data analysis operates only at the ground system, because it intends to support airport stakeholder's historic data analysis and subsequent decisions. When analyzing historical data, airport stakeholders are mainly interested in analyzing the facts within the same spatial and temporal context in which they occur. Therefore, the DS module shall periodically collect all the data generated by the other AIRNET modules and store them in the Data Warehouse database. All Alert messages are stored to be audited.

The offline DS functionalities are particularly helpful for the Safety Manager to have, in a single screen, the history of all safety occurrences detected by the system. DS offline functionalities also include information related to disruptions to airport operations. As presented in Figure 12, an incident report should provide as much information as possible, for instance to help Safety Managers in auditing safety occurrences. The proposed approach conforms to this requirement by providing a set of activities to semantically characterize and describe business artifacts from a spatial-temporal point of view so that they can be represented as features at the GHMI. The red scroll bar at the top of the DS offline application interface represents the hazards that were detected by the system for the selected period.

The offline interface provides a set of graphical tools, such as Time slider to enable airport stakeholders to seamlessly position their search at the instant relevant for their data analysis. The GIS functionalities also provide a visualization paradigm for an accurate visualization of the sequence of events within the exact space-temporal context. Besides the stack of overlapped thematic layers that form the mapping background context, topological operations enable the visualization of correlations between the reported alerts and operational constrains such as temporary or fixed obstacles, vehicle status and vehicles movement density. It is also possible for airport stakeholders to correlate the data in a different way. For instance, when analyzing a safety occurrence it is possible to look for relationships between reported problems (represented as point features), shifts to the operational routes provided by the system to the driver (represented as line features), and strict time schedules to perform an aircraft assisting task derived from a change to the flight schedule.

Spatial-temporal functionalities enable airport stakeholder's to perceive dynamic evolutions to the business domain. The offline interface, besides offering the visualization of a stack of overlapped thematic layers that form the mapping background context, also provides a collection of spatial analysis techniques to help airport stakeholders to analyze business behavior, trends and anomalies at a glance.

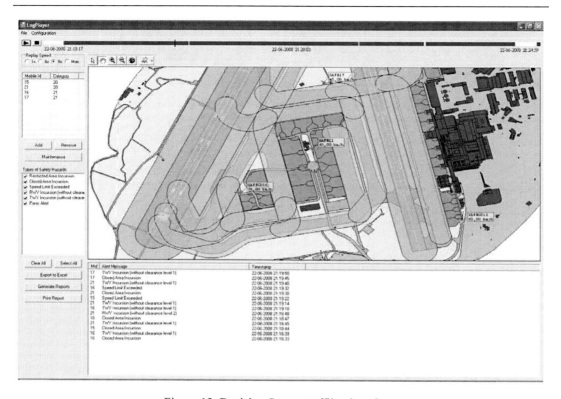

Figure 12. Decision Support offline interface.

The ability to monitor business safety performance in a context of dynamic evolutions is a distinctive functionality. The DS module enables airport stakeholders to review historical operational procedures in order to identify strengths, weaknesses or risk opportunities. Although it is not possible to eliminate accidents or safety risks, it is possible to progressively minimize the likelihood of safety risks. The proposed approach can detect and prevent incidents, accidents or critical situations using countermeasures. Nevertheless, external events such as weather conditions, traffic congestion, fleet age, airport infrastructure and site-suitability can contribute to raise the probability of safety hazards. Therefore, risk events must be carefully monitored and continually evaluated to determine when it is adequate to take action.

## 6. Conclusion

The A-SMGCS vehicle management component defined by Eurocontrol can be already implemented with the available information and communication technologies used in AIRNET platform. By using EGNOS, embedded computer systems with EGNOS/GPS receivers, performing servers for running the A-SMGCS services, advanced GIS software and IP-based communications on wireless communication networks covering the airside area, surveillance, control, guidance and routing A-SMGCS services can be implemented.

In previous sections we have demonstrated however that the AIRNET platform already integrates cohesive decision-making services that will allow to evolve for a a more effective and integrated air traffic management architecture, which could support future developments that will contribute for the optimal use of European airports meeting the users' needs. Indeed, the goal of this platform was to provide accurate surveillance, control, guidance and routing services together with gradual changes to the business context using airport dynamic maps,

The platform architecture was described to emphasize the flexibility and scalability of the proposed approach, including the description of the components that are responsible to provide surveillance, control and guidance services, as well as decision support facilities to the different actors, facilitating the synchronization of the plans and actions of the different users and resources.

In general, we may say that the AIRNET platform contributes to improve airside operations by providing the means to increase the safety and efficiency of airports operations, namely to:

- analyze safety hazards within the right spatial-temporal context;
- implement an airport vehicle surveillance, monitoring, guidance and decision support system fully integrated with any Airport Operational Management System and an Aeronautical Telecommunication network;
- deploy data fusion capabilities to provide information of different stakeholders acting on the aircraft's turn-around-cycle;
- adopt standards for spatial and non-spatial data interoperability collected from existing airport systems;
- detect underperforming situations that are difficult to perceive using traditional spreadsheets and non-spatial data processing alone;
- implement a spatial decision support system for the management of airside-related ground traffic, ground support, and ground supplier services;
- identify the driving elements for each stakeholder to accurately monitor how well its fleet is performing against operational and safety requirements.

Without such a solution, airport stakeholders and, in particular, Safety Managers, will hardly be able to obtain accurate information about safety related problems, because in current safety management systems the identification of safety hazards, especially minor occurrences, depends on the workers willingness to report those occurrences. The platform contributes to solve this problem by increasing context and location-awareness, enabling Safety Managers to proactively and continuously monitor safety hazards and to receive alerts whenever their intervention is required.

Airport stakeholders can track and manage the location of field crews and mobile resources, integrating asset and spatial data with work order tasks and resource status from the field data. The term "tracking" refers to monitoring the movement of vehicles and mobile workforces using a GPS/EGNOS satellite navigation system. The Conflict/Infringement Detection and Decision Support modules cope efficiently with any amendments to regulations or operational procedures without the need to implement updated software releases.

The authors have been involved in several R&D projects, which validated solutions for the implementation of the system. An experimental platform, like the one described in this paper is deployed at the Porto airport and another one is being deployed at the Lisbon airport. One of the main differences between both platforms resides in the wireless data communication technology used for the airport. Whereas in Porto a Wi-Fi network has been used with good results, in Lisbon, WiMax is being deployed for the same purpose. The main aim is to significantly reduce the number of locations to install access points in the airport and also to increase the robustness of the network and to be aligned with SESAR Master Plan, which considers 802.16 a wireless technology candidate to be used for communications between vehicles and central control systems.

The use of EGNOS is an aspect that we should strongly underline. EGNOS is a precursor of Galileo and the positioning accuracy that we have obtained with EGNOS has been well within the 2 meter precision announced in the EGNOS specifications. One of the applications foreseen for EGNOS is for aviation and airports and the A-SMGCS implementations can take a great advantage of its existence.

## Acknowledgment

The authors acknowledge with thanks the collaboration of their colleagues in the projects AIRNET and Safedrive, and also of all those involved in the platform deployments in Porto and Lisbon airports. The opinions expressed in this paper only commit the authors and not their companies.

## References

[1]   Eurocontrol, A-SMGCS Project strategy, September 2003, http://www.eurocontrol.int/airports/public/standard_page/APR1_Projects_ASMGCS.html
[2]   Eurocontrol, Definition of A-SMGCS Implementation Levels, September 2003, http://www.eurocontrol.int/airports/public/standard_page/APR1_Projects_ASMGCS.html
[3]   A.Casaca, T.Silva, A.Grilo,, M.Nunes, F.Presutto, I.Rebelo, The Use of Wireless Networks for the Surveillance and Control of Cooperative Vehicles in an Airport, Telecommunication Systems Journal, Springer, DOI 10.1007/s11235-007-9063-z, Vol. 36 (2007), Nos. 1-3, ISSN 1018-4864, pp. 141-151, November 2007.
[4]   ESA, EGNOS Navigation, http://www.esa.int/esaNA/egnos.html
[5]   AIRNET Validation Report – Plan and Results for Porto Platform Prototype, Deliverable D4, AIRNET/D4/ANA/WP4/VP&RASC/0.1, August 2006.
[6]   "IEEE Standard for Telecommunications and Information Exchange Between Systems - LAN/MAN Specific Requirements - Part 11: Wireless Medium Access Control (MAC) and physical layer (PHY) specifications: High Speed Physical Layer in the 5 GHz band", IEEE 802.11a standard, IEEE.
[7]   L. Nuaymi, WiMAX – Technology for Broadband Wireless Access, Wiley, 2007.
[8]   S. Agrawal, I. Acharya, S. Goel, "Inside 3G Wireless Systems: The 1xEV-DV Technology;" TATA Consulting Services, 2003.
[9]   L. Harte, "Introduction to EVDO, Physical Channels, Logical Channels, Network and Operation", Althos Publishing, 2004.
[10]  Motorola, "DIMETRA Packet Data Service – Programmer's Guide," Release 3.1, 2000.

[11] EUROCAE, "Interchange Standards for terrain, Obstacle, and Aerodrome Mapping Data", http://www.eurocae.org, 2004.

[12] H. Hartmann, "Final Report of Preliminary Study Total Airport Management", Institut für Flugführung (Institute of Flight Guidance), 2001,http://www.dlr.de/fl.

[13] ICAO, "Safety Management Manual, International Civil Aviation Organization", Doc 9859 AN/460, 2005.

[14] G. Pestana, M. Silva and Y. Bédard, "Spatial OLAP Modeling: An Overview Base on Spatial Objects Changing over Time", Proc. of the IEEE 3rd International Conference on Computational Cybernetics, April 2005.

In: Airports: Performance, Risks, and Problems      ISBN: 978-1-60692-393-1
Editors: P.B. Larauge et al, pp. 33-50      © 2009 Nova Science Publishers, Inc.

*Chapter 2*

# NEW FRONTIERS FOR EUROPEAN AIRPORT MANAGEMENT: PERFORMANCE, RISKS AND DEVELOPMENT TRENDS [1,2]

## *A. Nucciarelli[a,*] and P.O. Achard[b]*

[a] Department of Industrial Engineering and Innovation Sciences,
Technische Universiteit Eindhoven – Den Dolech 2, 5600MB Eindhoven,
The Netherlands
[b] Universitá dell'Aquila – Department of Economic Systems and Institutions
Piazza del Santuario, 19 – 67040 Roio Poggio – L'Aquila, Italy

## Abstract

This chapter looks at the relationship between airlines and airports on a European level, with a special focus on the relationship between low-cost carriers and secondary airports. Recognizing the main steps in the liberalization process of the aviation industry allows us to understand the challenges that arose in supply and demand in the air transportation market and analyze development trends. With the arrival of new competitors, carriers and airports have changed their market strategies and progressively focused on the exploitation of potential demand. A survey of published literature is made on this theme and new airline-airport development trends are discussed. Examples are drawn from the European and the Italian market whilst a case study on airports in Rome illustrates the main competitive issues.

---

[1] This chapter is an extension of two studies that have already been published or are in press in International Journals: Nucciarelli, A. and Gastaldi, M., 2008, Information technology and collaboration tools within the e-supply chain management of the aviation industry, *Technology Analysis & Strategic Management*, 20(2), pp.169-184; Nucciarelli, A. and Gastaldi, M., 2007, Collaboration in the airport business through the development of an IT platform, *International Journal of Production Economics*, doi:10.1016/j.ijpe.2007.02.017 (in press).

[2] Data reported and analyzed in the chapter are taken from companies' websites and reports as well as from: ICCSAI – International Center for Competitiveness Studies in the Aviation Industry, 2008, Fact Book, ICCSAI.

[*] Corresponding Author

# Introduction

Over the last two decades, changes in the structures of supply and demand in the European airline industry have led to a re-definition of the relationship between airlines and airports. The reasons for this evolutionary path stem from a number of factors including the modification of the legislative framework, the introduction of Information and Communications Technology (ICT) into stakeholders' operations and, last but not least, a dynamic and somewhat challenging economic (and political) environment.

This chapter aims to investigate the current competitive European passenger air transport scenario taking into consideration: a) the structure of demand as a result of the liberalization of Member State and international markets; b) the evolving needs of the demand for aviation services and the effect on carrier market strategies; c) the nature and importance of partnerships between carriers and airports in the light of new strategic and competitive issues; and d) a specific example of reorganization carried out by Rome's International Airport – Leonardo da Vinci, one of the most important airport systems in the European market. The chapter is divided into three main sections. In the first section the process of liberalization is analyzed, focusing on the main features and its impact on the current structure of supply. Parallels are drawn with the US deregulation process to identify analogies and differences and understand how institutions in the European Union (EU) addressed change. The results of two decades of the liberalization process are then considered and the business models of competing carriers (i.e. flag carriers and low-cost carriers) are briefly compared taking into account the "hub-and-spoke" and "point-to-point" network management system. The analysis of network architecture then leads to the investigation of the role of airports: while international airports are the hubs around which worldwide alliances plan and operate their international and intercontinental connections, secondary airports develop specific strategies in close relation to low-cost carriers (LCCs). Interestingly, the increasing competitiveness in the international market has not led to a sidelining of secondary and regional airports which act as value generators for wide regional areas fostering tourism and enhancing business activities, and examples from the Italian aviation industry are discussed. The third section looks at Aeroporti di Roma (AdR) – the Italian company responsible for managing the Leonardo da Vinci (Fiumicino-FCO) and the Pastine (Ciampino-CIA) airports in Rome. The study of the management of a major airport contributes to the understanding of new market strategies and orientation in the European market.

## 1. The Deregulation of the European Aviation Industry

The decision of the European Community (2007/339/CE) on April 25th 2007 opened a new chapter for the development of a liberalized international aviation system. Published in the Official Journal of the European Union on May 25th 2007, the Air Transport Agreement between the United States of America (USA) and the Member States of the European Union (EU) is more widely known as the "Open Skies" agreement. As the most recent step towards the opening of market of transatlantic flights, it is rapidly changing the already relatively, unstable competitive equilibrium in the European aviation industry. Indeed the deregulation of the European aviation industry has long been considered overdue (Sochor, 1991; Good et al., 1993; Lawton, 1999)[3]. There are many explanations for the length of time it took Member States and European Institutions to completely open the market to competition. Though the time it took could be interpreted as a delay, especially when compared to the US, explanations can be found by looking at two aspects of EU institutional dynamics: the "permanent negotiation" and the "technical-functionalist paradigm" (Verola, 2006).

Scharpf (2001) argues that the European Union is mainly based on a "negative integration" process even with respect to the creation of a Single Market. The "negative integration" process arises from the observation that every economic and political decision taken by Member States as well as national and supranational Institutions is the result of a complex confrontational view, which is the legacy of the EU since its foundation after the Second World War (see Haas, 1958; Mazey, 1996). The permanent negotiation attitude is what single Member States have always insisted upon for each decision process to maintain a certain degree of independence while addressing economic and political policies. In the wake of this "machine à négocier" (De Silguy, 1996 cited in Verola, 2006), Member States have gradually accepted a slight reduction in their sovereignty to European Institutions to allow joint management of some policy aspects. A second basic issue permeates decisional process in the EU. Considering the historical bases of European Integration (i.e. the *Treaty of the European Coal and Steel Community*, the *Treaty of the European Atomic Energy Community* and the *Treaty of the European Economic Community*), the proof of the existence of a technical added value in the integration process lies in the fact that specific common policies are based on the existence of a *de facto* joint liability among Member States. Accordingly, supranational decisions have been interpreted as the best *technical* answer to political and economic issues. The adoption of this dichotomy between the "permanent negotiation" and the "technical-functionalist paradigm" has often led to time-spending processes of which the liberalization of the aviation industry is a clear example.

The first timid attempts to proceed towards the creation of a European policy for civil aviation date back to the late 1940s. According to Lawton (1999), citing Sochor (1991), even in 1949 - after the establishment of the Council of Europe - the possibility of setting up a regional form of co-operation in air transport was considered. However, in the 1950s the creation of the European Civil Aviation Conference (ECAC) and the almost simultaneous failure of the first air traffic control system (Eurocontrol) made it clear that economic interests (namely, financial participation) in the capital of flag carriers by national governments, and differences in airlines' competitive strategies were crucial obstacles towards the adoption of a European decision system. It was only in the 1980s, when a means was found to apply the principles of the Rome Treaty (articles 81-86) that the first steps could be made in the deregulation process. This was also a result of events in the US between 1975 and 1978. At that time the Civil Aeronautic Board authorized competition between national carriers and charter flights (1975) leading to the first significant fare reductions applied by traditional network carriers. Then the Airline Deregulation Act (1978) was approved by the American Congress which led to great price reductions within the internal market. There followed an intense process of transformation of the entire market characterized by economic effects for both the airline industry and travelers (Morrison and Winston, 1986). In 1985, in the wake of this new deal, liberalization landed in Europe. Negotiations took place between British and

---

[3] Barrett (1990) analyzes the liberalization of the European aviation industry discussing market contestability, price levels and degree of competition.

Dutch authorities leading to a bilateral agreement and "a first significant break with the past and one of the major steps towards European-wide airline deregulation" (Lawton, 1999). However, in spite of pressure by consumer groups, air carrier associations and the European Commission, the reluctance of national governments delayed the implementation of the dictates of the Single Market Programme with respect to the deregulation of the industry and the enhancement of a greater degree of competition. In 1986, the *Nouvelles Frontières*[4] case opened a new chapter limiting the authority of Member States; as a result of the innovative contents of the decision of the European Court of Justice, a three-package deregulation program was gradually implemented. Articles 85-90 of the Rome Treaty were applied as a result of stricter control by the European Commission on applied fares, the extension of the laissez-faire regime to the whole European Union, the cancellation of restrictions on low fares, the introduction of the consecutive cabotage (1993) and full cabotage (1997) (Dogson, 1994)[5]. More specifically, licenses to operate flights within the EU were made accessible to all carriers meeting specific safety, ownership and operating requirements, thus opening the market to newcomers (e.g. the low-costs carriers). One of the most critical issues addressed during the liberalization was slot allocation; as Nucciarelli and Gastaldi reported in 2008 and Sentance in 2003, airport access is controlled by "grandfather rights", namely the historic usage of rights/slot holdings by flag carriers. Though liberalization opened the market, it did not result in significant change to access to congested airports by newcomers. However in the wake of the implementation of the EC Treaty on competition, the "new entrant rule" was introduced. So now the slot regime, in addition to "grandfather rights", is established through schedule co-ordination conferences, the "new entrant rule" and independent slot co-ordination[6]. Agreements are made during conferences attended by ICAO (International Civil Aviation Organization) airlines to plan activities and flights scheduling according to their strategies. However, to make access to airports equal, the "new entrant rule" has meant that not all slots can be assigned during conferences. As stated by Sentence (2003), after historical slots have been allocated at conferences, 50% of the available remaining slots are allocated to new entrants. A scheduling committee coordinator assigns these slots, which are not controlled through the historic usage rights and the remaining slots are allocated according to IATA (International Air Transport Association) regulations. This system has allowed low-costs carriers to operate their flights on traffic-intensive routes in order to generate a high volume of profits.

This changing and challenging scenario is now opening new business opportunities across the EU. The already cited Open Skies agreement is on the way to dramatically modifying competition in the European as well as in the transatlantic market. As BA Chief Executive Willie Walsh recognized in a press release published on www.ba.com on January 9th 2008 - announcing the US-EU subsidy airline 'OpenSkies' operating daily flights from New York to Brussels and Paris – declaring that the name 'OpenSkies' was to celebrate "the

---

[4] In this dispute between a French travel agency and the French regulatory authority, the European Court of Justice decided that the dictates of the Rome Treaty on competition rules had to be applied to air transport.

[5] The consecutive cabotage refers to the permission granted to a carrier to fly between two airports of another Member State but originating or terminating in the airline's home country. Specific restrictions also applied to the percentage of capacity sold. The full cabotage deals with the possibility for carriers to operate between airports of another Member State without any connection with the airline's home country.

[6] The description of the slot allocation system is taken from Nucciarelli and Gastaldi (2008). Further suggested reading on the strategic implications of slot allocation is: Madas and Zografos (2006).

first major step in 60 years towards a liberalized US/EU aviation market". In fact, according to the Open Skies agreement, any European carrier is allowed to operate flights between the EU and the US without any restriction in terms of routes, number of flights and airplanes. Hence overseas cooperation agreements can now be signed among carriers who are also able to fix prices in function of market features. Finally, it has been established that, from June 1st 2008 onwards, European investors can own more that 50% of US carriers' equity. Further expansion of this rule is still under negotiation between EU and US parties.

# 2. Airport-Airline Interaction in the Liberalized EU Market

## 2.1. Changes in the Passenger air Transportation Market

The liberalization of the air transportation market has been studied in depth by numerous authors. Some (Lawton, 2002; Delfmann et al. 2005; Dennis, 2007; Iatrou and Oretti, 2007) have analyzed changes in the structure of supply and strategic management, whilst others (Mason, 2005; O'Connell and Williams, 2005) have focused on the dynamics of demand or looked at the relationship between airlines' strategic decisions and travellers' behaviour (Mason and Alamdari, 2007). What emerges from differing studies is the competition between two main business models: 1) the low-cost carrier model – LCC (e.g. Ryanair, Easyjet and Wizzair) and; 2) the network carrier model (e.g. Alitalia, British Airways, KLM). The adoption of a no-frills business model has allowed LCCs to achieve competitive advantages especially in terms of cost leadership. It has led to high levels of penetration in specific markets such as the leisure market where the price elasticity of demand can sensibly affect the competition.

The low-cost business model was first developed by Southwest airlines in the US market in the early 1990s (O'Reilly and Pfeffer, 1995) and since then many other models have been developed. On the European scene, Ryanair and Easyjet (Kuman and Rogers, 2000; Bain, 2008) are two of the most successful examples of European no-frills carriers. Though differences exist between these and the "original" Southwest model, there are many common features in their strategies[7]. Operating international point-to-point flights from secondary and regional airports[8], the LCCs' business model relies on a "passenger and baggage" service gaining the highest advantage from an intensive use of price levers (Kangis and O'Reilly, 2003)[9]. A dedicated yield management system and a dynamic pricing system[10] help LCCs to achieve high load factors (up to 85%) on their flights. Because of intertemporal price discrimination, ticket prices are the same for all clients but vary significantly as the departure date draws closer (ICCSAI, 2008; Nucciarelli and Gastaldi, 2008). Again according to ICCSAI (2008), in the week before the flight the dynamic pricing system leads to offering left

---

[7] Divergences exist between US and EU markets. Flexibility of the labour market is one of the most relevant variations.

[8] European LCCs operate international flights within the EU. In the wake of the Open Skies deal, further expansions of the low-fares flights have already been planned by Ryanair, which is planning to launch budget transatlantic airline by mid-2009.

[9] Forsyth (2007) discusses whether lower charges are a durable competitive advantage for LCCs.

[10] No market segmentation is made by LCC with respect to ticket pricing. Economy class is the only available class on low-cost flights since no tariff proliferation is adopted.

seats at 1.5-2 times higher prices than the ones of two months before[11]. In addition to the previously mentioned characteristics of the low-cost business model adopted by LCCs, an extensive cutback of costs also stems from: 1) the adoption of a standardized fleet to achieve significant reduction of costs (economies of scope) in maintenance and repair overhaul as well as in crew management; 2) the outsourcing of non-core activities (e.g. passenger handling and maintenance of aircrafts); 3) the absence of any free on-board service and frequent-flyer programs (FFPs)[12]; and, 4) the streamlining of booking and pre-flight operations through Information Technology (IT) tools that allow not only on-line booking but also boarding pass printing and self check-in.

Traditional European airlines have adopted specific responses to LCCs. Despite differences in the way they have been affected by the increased competition, most of the flag carriers have changed their approach to the market in recent years or even set up low-cost subsidiaries to serve specific market niches[13]. As Dennis reported in 2007, European flag carriers have reacted differently to the initial loss of market shares. Though Alitalia, Iberia and Olympic airlines still lack behind Air France, British Airways, Lufthansa and KLM in concentrating on their major hubs and off-loading peripheral routes as well as implementing cost reduction policies, several common strategies emerge[14]. In fact, both on the European and international scenario, major trends in competitive behaviour emerge. Many airlines opted for the rationalization of their hub-and-spoke system limiting connections with peripheral airports and intensifying hub activity. Air France is a typical example: about 55.2% of traffic in terms of ASK at the Paris' Charles De Gaulle is managed by Air France, underlining the strategic importance of carriers' international hubs as one of the incumbent's core assets and international partnerships (for example the relationship between Air France and the Dutch KLM, which has become the biggest operator in terms of ASK and revenues in the European market). As ICCSAI sustains, catching up with the operational dimensions of for example, the Air France-KLM group, is crucial in both intercontinental market and inter-European ones where LCCs present high though stable growth rates[15]. However, the importance of carriers' dimensions is currently under debate. As Iatrou and Oretti (2007) noted, the three main international alliances (i.e. Oneworld, SkyTeam and Star Alliance) were initially created to significantly reduce costs, streamline operations, increase customer satisfaction, generate synergies (to achieve economies of scale and scope) and most importantly, to avoid destructive head-on competition. Though many of these multiple targets have been somehow achieved, it is still difficult to quantify the real impact of alliances on revenue generation. Moreover, financial crises as well as unexpected capacity cuts have led to a re-thinking of the role of these worldwide alliances principally with respect to the way risks are shared among business partners. Finally, worth mentioning is the changes flag carriers have made in the provisioning of on-board services leading to more accentuated differences

---

[11] Many differences characterize levels of price for low-cost flights. Variations also depend on routes and carriers and seasonal availability of seats.

[12] For an analysis of possible evolutions in terms of FFPs see Klophaus (2005).

[13] The Australian carrier Quantas is also to start operating long haul connections with a low-cost subsidiary (Forsyth, 2007).

[14] Other carriers (e.g. Swiss) have successfully recovered from a financial unraveling situation (Suen, 2002) selling non-strategic assets, cutting jobs and better addressing medium-long term investments.

[15] The Air France-KLM group is also planning to invest in Czech Airlines as well as in the combined Delta Air Lines and Northwest Airlines carrier in exchange for a board seat (www.usatoday.com; www.reuters.com).

between the revenue-intensive business class and economy class. In addition, a cutback of distribution costs, optimization (and increase) of fleet utilization and reduction of operations costs have resulted in significant increases in terms of passengers, ASK and Revenues per Kilometer (RPK)[16] for flag carriers.

## 2.2. The Challenge of the Airports

The airport industry is in transformation as a result of liberalization and privatization (Costas-Centivany, 1999; Thompson, 2002; Zhang and Zhang, 2003; Oum et al., 2006)[17], globalization and new competitive positioning (Graham and Guyer, 2000; Jarach, 2001) and the introduction of Information Technology (Buhalis, 2004; Nucciarelli and Gastaldi, 2007). Only a decade ago, airports were simply considered capacity providers by airlines; they were charged with providing carriers basic services that met the technical and operational needs of traditional network, regional and charter carriers. The new competitive scenario – as described above – has altered this role and brought about a radical change in the relationship between airports and airlines, with airports acting as 'a system within the system' (Nucciarelli and Gastaldi, 2007). As de Neufville (2006) noted, this new scenario requires a compatible evolution of airport access. LCCs have spread air traffic over a larger number of airports within the same metropolitan area opening up a debate concerning airport connectivity and accessibility. Private medium and long-term investments as well as public involvement are deeply impacted by these issues and can, rather simply, determine market exploitation or competition distortion[18].

Before analyzing the role of international as well as secondary airports, it is important to note the rapid escalation of interest in the airport business over recent years. As Sinatra's (2001) studies show, banking, insurance and transportation companies (namely, investors operating in other capital-intensive sectors) are heavily investing in airport management. This often leads to complex market strategies where airports become the means to differentiate investments within a multiple-oriented market strategy. In the following subsections, our analyses will focus on: a) airports being part of international networks (that is, airports considered the main hubs of alliances like Rome Fiumicino, Paris Charles De Gaulle and London Heathrow); and, b) airports of secondary importance including national hubs as well as regional airports. The analysis of networked international hubs (NIBs) is intended to provide information about the strategic choice of major hubs in the new competitive scenario. Investigating the main trends in NIBs facilitates the comparison with the strategic choices of secondary and regional airports. International hubs which are not only part of a network but are considered the 'pivot' of  hub-and-spoke strategies of international alliances and secondary airports (national and regional), which are the originating (or terminating) airports

---

[16]  Between 2006 and 2007: Air France-KLM passengers +2.7%, ASK +3.7% and RPK +4.1%; Lufthansa passengers +5.8%, ASK +4.7%, RPK +6.5%.

[17]  Studies have quantitatively measured the impact of liberalization and privatization on airport management. For a detailed analysis of airport performance after the privatization process see also Martin and Roman (2001) and Barros and Dieke (2007).

[18]  More specifically, public involvement in the accessibility issue led to State Aid (EC Treaty 87(1)). For a detailed analysis see Barbot (2006) and Gröteke and Kerber (2004). Further correlated readings: Commission of the European Communities (2007) and various reports on www.europa.eu.

of both hub-and-spoke as well as point-to-point strategies are compared. Secondary airports are characterized by lower levels of traffic and are not the main hub of international alliances. The distinction between these two categories is made in order to understand possible future developments in airport management across the EU. A special section is dedicated to secondary airports in this chapter and to understand and evaluate secondary airport development trends, a brief analysis is made of international hubs.

## 2.3. International Hubs and Secondary Airports: From Capacity Providers to Value Generators

Many are the trends which are currently re-shaping the role of international hubs in the European passenger transportation scenario. An analysis of data and reports[19], reveals some of the major trends:

1) after a diffused stagnation of passenger traffic from 2000 to 2002, an increase of 84.4% and 80.3% was recorded for 2006 and 2007;
2) from year 2005 onwards, international hubs have been reducing the gap with secondary airports in term of yearly percentage of growth in managed passengers;
3) comparing data for the years 2006-2007, it is evident how concentration is increasing in many international hubs (e.g. Paris Charles De Gaulle, Zurich)[20];
4) almost each international hub is now affiliated to an alliance (i.e. Oneworld, SkyTeam, Star Alliance) and this acts as a junction for all the intercontinental connections.

These four main trends highlight the close relationship between airlines and airports. Indeed they can no longer be considered separately owing to their growing interdependence. The policy of restructuring of many European incumbents has resulted in the development of international hubs. An example of this is London Heathrow and the management decision to proceed with the building of Terminal 5. The expansion of the intercontinental flights market - also sustained by the role of international alliances - is leading to a general expansion of major hubs. Considered multi-business companies rather than simply capacity providers, international hubs are also experiencing a significant increase in concentration. Paris Charles De Gaulle, Frankfurt Hahn, Amsterdam Schiphol, Vienna's and Zurich's airports are currently dominated, with respect to the past, by national flag carriers mainly as a result of their performance in terms of passengers and scheduled flights[21]. The domination of a specific carrier in an airport is not only related to the interaction between international hubs and traditional carriers: a close airline-airport relationship also exists between LCCs and regional airports albeit of a different nature.

Many studies (O'Reilly and Pfeffer, 1995; Doganis, 2001; Kangis and O'Reilly, 2003; Franke, 2004) have focused on the strategic decisions taken by LCCs. Scarce attention has

---

[19] Various airports' reports and ICCSAI (2008).

[20] Concentration is analyzed using the Herfindahl-Hirschman Index (HHI) and the Entropy Index in ICCSAI (2007; 2008).

[21] Among the most important hubs, Rome Fiumicino has the lowest concentration rate. This is mainly due to the weakness of Alitalia's international strategy as well as its financial losses.

been given to the importance of airline-airport interaction, which appears to be crucial in generating added value for both carriers and airports as well as for passengers (Gillen and Lall, 2004). Indeed, this relationship can be considered a durable competitive advantage for both partners. Airports can expand their capacity and generate revenues from aeronautic and non-aeronautic activities while carriers can provide high potential demand areas with low fare transportation services. However, the success or failure of an airline-airport relationship is heavily dependent on the way market risks are allocated and the bargaining power of each player. In this section, airline-airport interaction is analyzed with respect to: 1) the key factors influencing a carrier's choice of secondary airport; 2) the implications (threats and opportunities) for secondary airports used by low-cost carriers; and, 3) future development trends.

The airline-airport relationship and in particular the LCC-secondary airport one, is a self-standing business deal based on economic criteria as well as on a mutual agreement on expanding potential travel demand. Warnock-Smith and Potter (2005) illustrate, with a questionnaire-based methodology, the key factors guiding LCCs in their choice of airport. This research integrates differing opinions on the role of LCCs and does not assume that all LCCs are 'market making' airlines, pointing out that "this does not apply to all LCCs and therefore it is important that an airport has either a high demand for LCC traffic or a positive economic forecast to increase demand for point-to point traffic" (Scheers, 2001 cited in Warnoch-Smith and Potter, 2005). Among the most critical choice factors for LCCs, is the high demand for LCC services within the airports' catchment area, meeting both airline and airport expectations in order to reach the critical mass of passengers to cover costs and generate profits. This also ensures increasing competition between carriers and airports. In addition, aeronautical and non-aeronautical charges (or revenues) are seen as crucial factors, which are able to determine the success of an airline-airport partnership and heavily impact on the long-range investment planning for both players. In the ranking of airport choice factors, Warnock-Smith and Potter (2005) also listed quick and efficient turnaround facilities as well as convenient slot times among the highest positions. This reflects what has been largely argued by several authors (Doganis, 2002; Barrett, 2004) with respect to the centrality of maximization of fleet organization and streamlining of flight procedures in the LCC's business model. As for airlines, airports managers carefully analyze the potential of close relationships. According to Francis et al. (2004: p.508) "airports depend on airlines making the decision to operate services from their airport. Without the airlines, airports have no market". Moreover, "the airlines have a strong bargaining position because they can threaten to fly elsewhere unless reductions in charges or commercial incentives are granted by the airport" (p.510). This illustrates the sense of the evaluations that airport management make. In fact, investigating potential low-fare demand for air transportation in the catchment area aside, airport management must forecast costs and revenues flows in order to plan investment and negotiate the best aeronautical charges with carriers. The case studies reported by Francis et al (2003; 2004) clarify the need for accurate and innovative models for airline-airport interaction. Moreover, the specific market segmentation created by LCCs and secondary airports has led to a reclassification of travelers who are no longer just passengers but customers whose time spent at the airport dramatically impacts on non-aeronautical airport revenue. In the wake of this scenario several trends can be forecast:

1) growing competition between airport-airlines systems. In particular, competition among LCCs operating in airports within the same catchment areas resulting in a significant increase in uncertainty and risk factors for the evaluation of potential demand;

2) competition among systems due to expansion into the intercontinental market as LCCs start operating long distance flights;

whilst risks and opportunities in airline-airport agreements will have to be assessed and distributed carefully to avoid disparities in bargaining strength.

Three strategic choices emerge for secondary airports: a) being part of a national/global network; b) focusing on regional development or; c) adopting an intermediate strategy (Nucciarelli and Gastaldi, 2007).

The first implementable strategy (being part of a national/global network) would entail joining a hub-and-spoke system, especially in the case of expansion of the strategic influence by one of the leading network carriers (or an international alliance). These airports are not properly "regional" since they are often close to important cities with relevant business activities. However, they cannot be considered as international hubs such as Rome Fiumicino or London Heathrow because of their lower strategic importance, number of passengers and number of scheduled flights. The catchment area of these regional airports is considered particularly attractive in terms of potential customers and compatibility with a strategy of expansion into new geographical markets. Thereafter, the expansion of the operations into a new niche market can easily become a competitive advantage when trying to limit the growth of competitors. When joining a hub-and-spoke network, regional airports are pushed towards the rapid adoption of the standards established by major airlines for handling services, passengers' management and slot allocation. There are many examples of airports being part of international networks. One of the most significant examples in the Italian market is the Florence Peretola airport[22]. Situated in a high tourism area, the Florence airport is fast becoming a (regional) hub for network carriers like Alitalia, Air France[23], Austrian Airlines, Lufthansa and Swiss. It also has daily and/or weekly connections to Eastern European countries (Albania and Rumania) following agreements with Belle Air (Albania) and Carpatair (Romania). Florence has exploited the potential of new business partners while strengthening its own weight in the international network. Some interesting data emerge from the analysis of traffic in the Florence airport in 2007. More than 1.9 million passengers were carried by 10 carriers, bringing Florence airport 16th in ranking within Italy and 113th in the Europe. The first carrier operating out of this airport, in terms of Available Seats per Kilometer (ASK), was responsible for 50.2% of passenger traffic while the first three airlines transported more than 68% of the total passengers. The strategic choices made by Florence airport are supported by the fact that the ASK share of low-cost carriers is 0.6% or in a nutshell, Florence airport is characterized by a high degree of concentration, which has not been significantly influenced by the presence of low-cost airlines or the strong competition from other airports in the same catchment area, leading to a 95.9% of ASK in competition.

---

[22] The Lyon-Saint Exupéry airport in France has developed a similar strategy. Till only a few years ago, the strategy of both these airports was more intermediate orientated (see Nucciarelli and Gastaldi, 2007).

[23] Air France offers the most important connection to Paris Charles De Gaulle in terms of ASK.

The second viable strategy (focusing on regional development) requires close collaboration with local stakeholders in order to exploit any possible synergy among business partners. Interdependences among differing sectors (tourism, real estate, transportation and generally industrial and business activities) have to be carefully evaluated within a medium to long-term strategy. Accordingly, the airport system can act as a flywheel for an entire local economic environment facilitating process streamlining in tourism management and information access as well as rationalization of transport services through passenger (customer)-orientated policies. Examples on the Italian and European scenario can be found, for example the Alghero Fertilia airport[24]; its 1.3 million passengers in 2007 were mainly transported by low-cost carriers (72.9% share of low-cost connections in terms of ASK) with several scheduled flights operated by Ryanair. Being the 20th airport in the Italian ranking system for managed passengers – and 136th in the Europe – its business is mainly focused on regional development. Initially a military airport, after the demilitarization of flight assistance services, it focused on tourism development and close collaboration with local stakeholders. After a period of decline at the beginning of the 1990's, the Alghero airport benefited from the Sardinia North-Western "strong operative pushing action from local economic actors, from institutions to public administration, clearly supported by the willing to determine the following social-economic new era and to value local resources and skills" (www.aeroportodialghero.it). Its highly attractive catchment area and the lack of airports in very close competition are the ingredients for its astonishing success and the main reasons of the interest of low-cost carriers as well as other traditional vectors (i.e. AirOne). This is especially true because of the development of several tourism channels and niche markets in Sardinia. Hence, the increasing tendency to use flight connections across EU has been one of the leading factors in the success of Alghero Fertilia's business model. Comparing data from 2006 and 2007, the 21.5% increase in passenger numbers brings it into line with the general expansion of the industry in Italy as well as in the EU[25].

The third possible strategy (adopting an intermediate strategy) has been one of the most commonly implemented, especially over recent years. Airports situated in strategic areas where network carriers are interested in gaining passengers have adopted this strategy. However, these airports' business models remain focused on the development of the local economic area and resources for tourism. Figure 1 summarizes the complexity of such a local/global system.

Differing stakeholders concur with the development of complex strategies. As public institutions are the natural counterpart in implementing territorial marketing policies, regional airports are asked to deal with private investors and business partners interested in providing new passengers with value added services (e.g. tourist packages associated with travel solutions). The visibility of the airport also depends on investment-intensive policies aimed at stimulating business initiatives and economic development within the catchment area. Competing airports can also be crucial. The easy connection among different airports (e.g. Rome Fiumicino International Airport and Rome Ciampino) can contribute to developing important synergies especially between international hubs and regional structures. Examples

---

[24] Other Italian examples are: Bergamo Orio al Serio, the International Abruzzo Airport of Pescara, Perugia Sant'Egidio, Parma and Pisa Galileo Galilei. In the EU panorama: Brussels South Charleroi (Belgium), Eindhoven (The Netherlands) and Girona (Spain) airports.

[25] For a detailed analysis of European airport connectivity see Malighetti et al. (2008).

of Italian airports are: 'Bologna Marconi', 'Catania Fontanarossa' and 'Torino Caselle' airports. All of them show significant (though different) low-cost shares in terms of ASK (i.e. 13%, 41.7% and 9.6%) associated with high passenger traffic (i.e. 3.5 million, 6 million and 4.4 million) and number of carriers (i.e. 29, 23 and 24) flying to/from the airport.

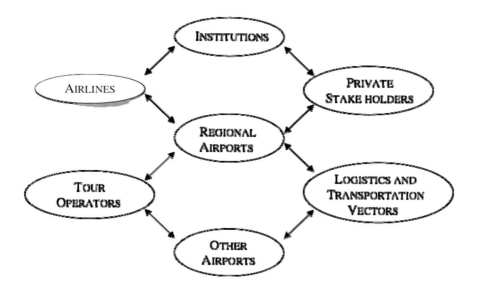

Figure 1. The star scheme (Nucciarelli and Gastaldi, 2007).

# 3. Special Focus: AdR S.p.A. Managing Roman Airports

S.p.A. AdR is an interesting example of how synergies among stakeholders can generate value for a wide business and social environment. Indeed, the model followed by AdR relies on the Airport-city concept, which ICAO (Airport Economics Manual – Doc 9562 ch. 6 – 6.14)) defines as The Airport City concept which *acknowledges the notion that large airports take the characteristics of a real city. They develop non-aeronautical services far beyond the core business of providing a location for passengers. Airports have not only become catalysts for employment and economic growth, but they have attracted a full range of business to the airport vicinity, which are reminiscent of the way seaports and river deltas became centres of economic activity in past centuries.* The Airport of Rome "Leonardo da Vinci", located in Fiumicino, opened in 1961. In 1974, a public society, the S.p.A AdR, was created and granted management of Rome's two airports by the Italian Government. The first important event affecting airport management took place in 1983, when the Italian flag carrier, Alitalia, acquired the society. As a consequence of this acquisition, AdR became the main capacity provider for Alitalia. The direct control of the most important Italian airport was an important asset for Alitalia, allowing important synergies among its own businesses, and in particular those concerning the supply chain, although the carrier did not give much weight to possible synergies among support activities, particularly customer-orientated ones. In 1995, the carrier and the S.p.A. AdR separated when the Italian flag carrier started experiencing financial difficulties. Two years later, in 1997, a new era started, at the beginning of a long and difficult privatization process, which was only completed in 2001. The society was quoted on the Stock exchange, while, all over the world, liberalization process of the air transportation market was flourishing, accompanied by diversification into non-aeronautical activities. These were also the years of the change from traditional aviation activities to customer-orientated activities: the S.p.A. AdR started looking at its customers and at business communities and it began to work not only in terms of operations but also in terms of effectiveness and financial performances. AdR is now owned by Gemina S.p.A. (95.8%), Local Organizations (3%) and by other minor shareholders (1.2%). AdR is also shareholder of the society charged for managing the airports of Genoa and Lamezia Terme. In 2008, AdR served 40 million passengers and 210 different destinations can now be reached from the two airports of Rome, thanks to the 140 carriers flying from these two airports. The traffic in the Roman airport system is still growing[26]. Total revenues in the first three months of 2008 were € 119.9 million, i.e. 0.7% more than in the same period for 2007. Total revenues in the field of non-aeronautical activities were € 60.7 million (+4.5%). EBITDA (Earnings Before Interest, Taxes, Depreciation and Amortization) was € 46 million, slightly less (-11%) with respect 2007. The increase in investment made by AdR in this period (€ 45.2 million) is important as it more than tripled, the main investments being in flight management infrastructures to increase the quality and the efficiency of services offered to customers. Therefore, great efforts are currently being made to reduce the gap with international hubs' average investments per passenger (€2.4 vs. €7). AdR is now responsible for managing, in Fiumicino alone, an area of about 400,000 square meters, 25,000 car parking places, more than 20,000 square meters of offices and the same surface of technical spaces and stores. Moreover, AdR furnishes all services related to the location of its spaces. Revenues from "property" represent about 30% of total "non-aeronautical" revenues.

AdR is also currently active in three different but closely related core businesses: "Aviation", which is the traditional core business; "Retail", which is the most recent field of activity; and "Real Estate", which is most closely tied to the territory. In addition, AdR is involved in ITC services, advertising, development, and engineering, with AdR Tel, AdR Advertising, AdR Sviluppo, and AdR Engineering. Due to its activities in differing fields, AdR represents a perfect partner for the development of new business opportunities; an airport, in fact, is an articulated reality, offering many possibilities to new enterprises. The competitive advantage of its strategic placement makes the Roman airport system an important figure in territorial development, not only as an operative structure, but also as a center of economical activity. AdR has studied airport accessibility for passengers, employers and suppliers of commercial and logistic services very carefully and is planning a €1.8 billion investment over the next 10 years for the new "Airport-city". The development plan has to take into account passenger forecasts of 50 million in 2020 rising to 90 million in 2044. One of the main objectives of the plan is the complete integration of airport and public and private transportation systems, on a local, regional and national scale. Another priority is the efficiency of the transport system inside the Airport-city and the safeguarding of the internal and external environment as well as the archeological heritage of the area.

---

[26] Over the next couple of years, traffic currently managed at Ciampino airport will be routed to Viterbo airport (about 100 kilometers north of Rome) while traffic at Fiumicino airport should benefit from a strategic willingness to make it the "main door" into Mediterranean, Middle and Far East countries.

An example of AdR's new strategic management style is the Department of Aviation Marketing, which is part of the Strategic Planning & Marketing Development Division. This department is responsible for increasing the number of flights to and from Rome, encouraging the extension of the destination network, short and long distance, and increasing the offered capacity for destinations popular with customers. In fact, in 2007 more than 2.6 million passengers had to use other European hubs because of a lack of direct flights from Rome to their final destination. Aviation Marketing has among its customers several carriers that already operate in Rome, or alternatively that are interested in having Rome as their final destination. It sells consultant services for the launch of new flights and for the follow up of new activities. In 2007, seven new carriers decided to fly from Rome's airports, contributing to the opening up of new destinations such as Washington in the USA and Sao Paolo in Brazil. The challenge for AdR will be to act as a central node, with strong leadership based on competency in retail business and real estate, and a power of governance deeply rooted in the territory. This will stem from the strategic approach of AdR, which is currently based on innovative financial assets, ICT and infrastructural investments. Of course, the final aim can only be reached through a new effort in human resources management. The development of competency is one of the most important strategic issues facing AdR. Competency management in AdR is characterized by:

- specialist nature of services;
- the need to introduce a diffused managerial perspective, not limited to apical roles, but extended to all operative units;
- acceleration of competitivity.

Market liberalization has highlighted the importance of distinctive competences as a factor of competitiveness. Nowadays, airports are required to develop organizational structures able to support the creation of individual competences. As a consequence, the distinctive element of the new mission of AdR is the strong integration between consolidated business models and new distinctive competences based on human resources. The latter, in fact, are the main sources for the creation of competitive advantage for the customers.

## Conclusions

On July 29th 2008, during a conference in Madrid (Spain), British Airways Chief Executive Willie Walsh and Iberia Chairman Fernando Conte announced that the two carriers were on their way to creating the world's third-biggest airline (Bowker and Harding, 2008). The immediate response of financial markets, Iberia +21% and BA +6%, underlines how relevant the expectations of the aviation industry are. Commenting on the news Willie Walsh stated: "*I don't see this as a matter of survival, but as two strong companies coming together. We do not see this as the end game but as the start of a new era* […]"; "*the combined balance sheet, anticipated synergies and network fit between the airlines make a merger an attractive proposition*"."[This is a] *consequence of liberalization of the aviation industry. Hand in hand with liberalization is the need for consolidation*" (www.reuters.com). In this sense, the €16.5 billion revenue of the new group makes it the second strategic merger in Europe after the 2004 AirFrance-KLM merger (turnover of €24 billion in 2007). However, the details of the financial agreement aside, it is certain that the new carrier will operate with two separate brands (Iberia and BA) exploiting all of the market opportunities that the Open Skies agreement provides for in the EU and the US. In fact, as Bowker and Harding (2008) reported, *"BA and Iberia would control nearly 45 percent of take-off and landing slots at Heathrow, the core hub for flights between Europe and the United States"*. In addition, a strong impact on South American airports is expected. In fact, BA will have access to all the current destinations of Iberia with unknown repercussions on increase in traffic, new hub development and higher number of connections.

The news of the merger Iberia-BA seems to confirm what John Kohlsaat, the EasyJet regional manager for central and northern Europe (including Baltic states), recently declared: according to him, after the current sector re-organization the European aviation industry will only allow room for British Airways, Air France-KLM, Lufthansa, Ryanair and, obviously, Easyjet to compete. This expected concentration on the supply side may lead to differing repercussions on the demand side. In fact, passengers could assist to a progressive rise in fares and to a reduction in the number of connections particularly between secondary airports especially if oil prices continue to affect carriers' costs structure as it did for Ryanair in the first quarter (Q1) of 2008. Between Q1 2007 and Q1 2008 a passenger increase of 19% and a rise of 12% in revenues scarcely mitigated the drop of adjusted profits after taxes from €139 million to €21 million (-85%) which will probably result in a reduction of the point-to-point route extension plan for the first months of 2009[27].

# References

Bain, J. (2008). Ryanair — How a small Irish airline conquered Europe. *Journal of Revenue and Pricing Management*, **79** (1), 117-118.

Barbot, C. (2006). Low-cost airlines, secondary airports, and the state aid: An economic assessment of the Ryanair-Charleroi Airport agreement. *Journal of Air Transport Management*, **12**, 197-203.

Barrett, S.D. (1990). Deregulating European aviation – A case study. *Transportation*, **16**, 311-327.

Barrett, S.D. (2004). The sustainability of the Ryanair model, *International Journal of Transport Management*, **2** (2), 89-98.

Barros, C.P., & Dieke, P.U.C. (2007), Performance evaluation of Italian airports: A data envelopment analysis. *Journal of Air Transport Management*, **13**, 184-191.

Bowker, J., & Harding B. (2008), British Airways and Iberia in merger talks, July 29th 2008, www.reuters.com.

Buhalis, D. (2004). eAirlines: strategic and tactical use of ICTs in the aviation industry. *Information & Management*, **41**, 805-825.

Commission of the European Communities. (2007). Evaluation of the Performance of Network Industries Providing Services of General Economic Interest. 2006 Report – SEC(2007) 1024, www.eu.org

---

[27]Although the Ryanair founder O'Leary has already announced an aggressive price policy to maintain the low-cost market leadership around Europe.

Costas-Centivany, C.M. (1999). Spain's airport infrastructure: adaptations to liberalization and privatization. *Journal of Transport Geography*, **7** (3), 215-223.

De Neufville, R. (2006). Planning Airport Access in an Era of Low-Cost Airlines. *Journal of the American Planning Association*, **72** (3), 347-356.

De Silguy, Y.T. (1996). *Le Sindrome du Diplodocus*. France, Paris, Albin Michel.

Delfmann, W., Baum, H., Auerbach, S., & Albers, S. (2005). *Strategic Management in the Aviation Industry*. Germany, Köln, Kolner Wissenschaftsverlag.

Dennis, N. (2007). End of the free lunch? The responses of traditional European airlines to the low-cost carrier threat. *Journal of Air Transport Management*, **13**, 311-321.

Doganis, R. (2001). *The airline business in the 21$^{st}$ century*. UK, London, Routledge.

Doganis, R. (2002). *Advice on aviation issues for the Department of Taoiseach*. Ireland, Dublin, Department of Public Enterprise.

Dodgson, J.S. (1994). Competition policy and the liberalization of European aviation. *Transportation*, **21**, 355-370.

Forsyth, P. (2007). The impacts of emerging aviation trends on airport infrastructure. *Journal of Air Transport Management*, **13**, 45-52.

Francis, G., Fidato, A., & Humphreys, I. (2003). Airport-airline interaction: the impact of low-cost carriers on two European airports. *Journal of Air Transport Management*, **9**, 267-273.

Francis, G., Humphreys, I., & Ison, S. (2004). Airports' perspectives on the growth of low-cost airlines and the remodeling of the airport-airline relationship. *Tourism Management*, **25**, 507-514.

Franke, M. (2004). Competition between network carriers and low-cost carriers – Retreat battle or breakthrough to a new level of efficiency?, *Journal of Air Transport Management*, **10** (1), 15-21.

Gillen, D., & Lall, A. (2004). Competitive advantage of low-cost carriers: some implications for airports, *Journal of Air Transport Management*, **10**, 41-50.

Good, D.H., Roeller, L.H., & Sickles, R.C. (1993). US airline deregulation: implications for European transport, *The Economic Journal*, **103** (July), 1028-1041.

Graham, B., & Guyer, C. (2000). The role of regional airports and air services in the United Kingdom. *Journal of Transport Geography*, **8**, 249-262.

Gröteke, F., & Kerber, W. (2004). The Case of Ryanair – EU State Aid Policy on the Wrong Runway: In ORDO, *Jahrbuch für die Ordnung von Wirtshaft und Gesellschaft*. Germany, Stuttgart, Lucius & Lucius Eds.

Haas, E.B. (1958). The uniting of Europe: political, social, and economic forces, 1950-1957. UK, London, Stevens & Sons.

Iatrou, K., & Oretti, M. (2007). *Airline Choices for the Future*. UK, Aldershot, Ashgate.

ICCSAI – International Center for Competitiveness Studies in the Aviation Industry. (2007). *Fact Book: La Competitivita' del Trasporto Aereo in Europa*. Italy, Orio al Serio - Bergamo, ICCSAI.

ICCSAI – International Center for Competitiveness Studies in the Aviation Industry. (2008). *Fact Book: La Competitivita' del Trasporto Aereo in Europa*. Italy, Orio al Serio - Bergamo, ICCSAI.

Jarach, D. (2001). The evolution of air airport management practices: towards a multi-point, multi-service, marketing-driven firm. *Journal of Air Transport Management*, **7** (2), 119-125.

Kangis, P., & O'Reilly, M.D. (2003). Strategies in a dynamic marketplace: A case study in the airline industry. *Journal of Business Research*, **56**, 105-111.

Klophaus, R. (2005). Frequent flyer programs for European low-cost airlines: Prospects, risks and implementation guidelines. *Journal of Air Transport Management,* **11**, (5), 348-353.

Kuman, R., & Rogers, B. (2000). EasyJet: The Web's Favorite Airline. *Case Study, Harvard Business School Cases.*

Lawton, T.C. (1999). Governing the Skies: Conditions for the Europeanisation of Airline Policy. *Journal of Public Policy*, **19** (1), 91-112.

Lawton, T.C. (2002). Cleared for Take-Off: Structure and Strategy in the Low-fare Airline Business. UK, Aldershot, Ashgate.

Madas, M.A., & Zografos, K.G. (2006). Airport slot allocation: From instruments to strategies. *Journal of Air Transport Management*, **12**, 53-62.

Malighetti, P., Paleari, S., & Redondi, R. (2008). Connectivity of the European airport network: "Self-help hubbing" and business implications. *Journal of Air Transport Management*, **14**, 53-65.

Martin, J.C., Roman, C. (2001). An application of DEA to measure the efficiency of Spanish airports prior to privatization. *Journal of Air Transport Management*, **7** (3), 149-157.

Mason, K.J. (2005). Observations of fundamental changes in the demand for aviation services. *Journal of Air Transportation Management*, **11** (1), 19-25.

Mason, K.J., & Alamdari, F. (2007). EU network carriers, low cost carriers and consumer behaviour: A Delphi study of future trends. *Journal of Air Transport Management*, **13**, 299-310.

Mazey, S. (1996). The development of the European idea. In J. Richardson, *European Union: power and policy making*. UK, London, Routledge.

Morrison, S., & Winston, C. (1986). *The Economic Effects of Airline Deregulation*. USA, Washington, D.C., The Brookings Institution.

Nucciarelli, A., & Gastaldi, M. (2008). Information technology and collaboration tools within the e-supply chain management of the aviation industry. *Technology Analysis and Strategic Management*, **20** (2), 169-184.

Nucciarelli, A., & Gastaldi, M. (2007). Collaboration in the airport business through the development of an IT platform. in press on *International Journal of Production Economics*.

O'Connell, J.F., & Williams, G. (2005). Passengers' perceptions of low cost airlines and full service carriers: A case study involving Ryanair, Aer Lingus, Air Asia and Malaysia Airlines. *Journal of Air Transport Management*, **11** (4), 259-272.

O'Reilly, C.A., & Pfeffer, J. (1995). Southwest Airlines (A). *Case Study*, Harvard Business School Cases.

Oum, T.H., Adler, N., & Yu, C. (2006). Privatization, corporatization, ownership forms and their effects on the performance of the world's major airports. *Journal of Air Transport Management*, **12** (3), 109-121.

Piga, C.A., & Filippi, N. (2002). Booking and flying with low-cost airlines. *International Journal of Tourism Research*, **4** (3), 237-249.

Scharpf, F. (2001). *European Governance: Common Concerns vs. the Challenge of Diversity*. In Jean Monnet Working Paper No. 6/01, USA, Boston, Harvard University.

Scheers, J. (2001). Attracting investors to European regional airports: what are the prerequisites? *International Airport Review*, **5** (4), 55-63.

Sentence, A. (2003). Airport slot auctions: Desiderable or feasible?. *Utilities Policy*, **11** (1), 53- 57.

Sinatra, A. (2001). *Aeroporti e Sviluppo Regionale: Rassegna di Studi*. Italy, Milan, Guerini e Associati.

Sochor, E. (1991). *The politics of international aviation*. UK, London Macmillan.

Suen, W.W. (2002). Alliance strategy and the fall of Swissair. *Journal of Air Transportation Management*, **8** (5), 355-363.

Thompson, I.B. (2002). Air transport liberalization and the development of third level airports in France. *Journal of Transport Geography*, **10**, 273-285.

Verola, N. (2006). L'Europa legittima: Principi e processi di legittimazione nella costituzione europea, Italy, Florence, Passigli Editori.

Warnock-Smith, D., & Potter, A. (2005). An exploratory study into airport choice factors for European low-cost airlines. *Journal of Air Transport Management*, **11** (6), 388-392.

Zhang, A., & Zhang, Y. (2003). Airport charges and capacity expansion: Effects of concessions and privatization. *Journal of Urban Economics*, **53**, 54-75.

# Websites

www.ba.com
www.europa.eu
www.icao.int
www.reuters.com
www.usatoday.com

In: Airports: Performance, Risks, and Problems
Editors: P.B. Larauge et al, pp. 51-65

ISBN: 978-1-60692-393-1
© 2009 Nova Science Publishers, Inc.

*Chapter 3*

# RECONCILIATION ECOLOGY AND THE INDIANA BAT AT INDIANAPOLIS INTERNATIONAL AIRPORT

*Dale W. Sparks[1], Virgil Brack, Jr.[1], John O. Whitaker, Jr.[1] and Richard Lotspeich[2]*

[1]Center for North American Bat Research and Conservation, Department of Biology, Indiana State University, Terre Haute, IN 47809 USA
[2]Department of Economics, Indiana State University, Terre Haute, IN 47809 USA

## Abstract

We provide a case study of conservation efforts at the Indianapolis International Airport near Indianapolis, Indiana, USA that illustrates how small programs aimed at meeting regulatory requirements can develop into projects of regional and national importance, how adaptive management works in the real world, and the potential for reconciliation ecology. Of particular legal and conservation concern is the presence of the endangered Indiana bat (*Myotis sodalis*), for which the airport agreed to undertake extensive conservation and mitigation efforts including the preservation of existing forest, planting of new forest, installation of experimental roost structures, and intense monitoring of the bats. After 17 years, the site is surrounded by commercial and residential areas, but the Indiana bat is still present. Monitoring has provided detailed information about how this and other bat species respond to a variety of landscape-level challenges and conservation approaches.

## Introduction

Traditionally, conservation and economic development have been viewed as competing alternatives for the same piece of land (Rosenzweig 2003). While numerous scientific societies including The Wildlife Society, the American Society of Mammalogists, and the North American Section of the Society for Conservation Biology have each recently passed resolutions in favor of steady-state economic paradigms (Gates et al. 2006, American Society of Mammalogists 2007, Society for Conservation Biology, North American Section 2005), such approaches will take years to implement. During that time, habitat will be lost and biodiversity will continue to decline. In the United States, three federal laws are often used by conservationists to slow or stop development: National Environmental Policy Act (NEPA), Clean Water Act (CWA), and Endangered Species Act (ESA), but most conservationists view all three as being broadly unsuccessful in reducing loss of biodiversity. Of particular concern has been the inability of ESA to either recover species from near extinction or to prevent species from becoming critically endangered. Similarly, Section 404 of the CWA is aimed at protecting wetlands, but permits issued under section 404 allow replacement of existing wetlands with newly created wetlands. These new wetlands rarely function as well, at least initially, as those lost to development. Finally, NEPA was intended to ensure that a broad array of environmental impacts by activities funded or permitted by the federal government are considered, employing an analysis of alternatives, so that impacts are avoided and minimized to the degree practicable, and that compensatory mitigation is employed for losses that cannot be avoided, including measures undertaken for ESA and the CWA. Unfortunately, such conservation and mitigation efforts are often undertaken in isolation rather than coordinated with one another. The first purpose of this paper is to provide a case study of how a large, long-term, and broadly successful conservation effort grew out of efforts to comply with regulatory requirements.

In addition to efforts aimed at regulatory compliance, this study also describes a substantial number of efforts made with an eye toward providing conservation benefits beyond those normally attained by similar regulatory compliance activities. Particularly unusual at this site was the incorporation of a research and monitoring component in regulatory documents such as incidental take permit under ESA. Unfortunately, success of a mitigation/conservation project too often is legally achieved when the approved work is completed. For example, habitat preserved for an endangered species as part of a construction project is considered a "success" even if the mitigation habitat is not used by the target species. In the present study, a substantial monitoring component was required partly because some conservation measures were experimental. As it has turned out, because of additional academic research undertaken at the site, monitoring at the airport substantially exceeds typical regulatory requirements. This research has demonstrated that efforts undertaken to benefit Indiana bats have benefited the entire community of bats and a variety of other taxa as well. Because this paper demonstrates a system where conservation has succeeded in the presence of development it also demonstrates how reconciliation ecology (Rosenzweig 2003) can be coordinated with regulatory requirements to provide synergistic benefits.

Our experience is that large–scale, real-world conservation efforts rarely proceed on a direct course. Rather, like this project, they boom when funding is available, and essentially shut down when it is not. Thus, we have chosen to provide a review of conservation efforts by describing the study site, providing a review of conservation and regulatory decisions made during this project, and finally examining proposed future activities on the site.

## Study Site

This paper details conservation efforts that centered on a large series of properties owned and managed by the Indianapolis International Airport (IND), although many privately owned parcels are interspersed in the landscape. These properties extend south and west along US Highway 40 (US-40) from the Airfield to Indiana Highway 267 (IN-267) in the west and Indiana Highway 67 (IN-67) in the south with Interstate Highway 70 (I-70) bisecting the study area from east to west. The East Fork of White Lick Creek, a medium-sized permanent stream, bisects the study area north to south. In 1991 the study area included many small, fragmented forest remnants within a matrix of corn/soybean agriculture. Since 1991, most agricultural areas north of I-70 have been developed into residential and commercial properties. Properties south of I-70 remain primarily agricultural although 54.5 ha of wetlands have been created and 323 ha have been reforested as part of the conservation effort.

## Airport Expansion

In 1991, the Indianapolis International Airport (IND) began to expand from a regional airfield with 1 runway into a major freight airport with 2 operational runways, and another being planned. As part of this effort, the Indianapolis Airport Authority (a public governing board) began efforts to comply with a variety of regulatory agencies including the Federal Aviation Administration (FAA), Federal Highways Administration (FHWA), US Fish and Wildlife Service (USFWS), US Army Corps of Engineers (USACE), US Environmental Protection Agency (USEPA), Indiana Department of Natural Resources (IDNR), Indiana Department of Environmental Management (IDEM), Indiana Department of Transportation (INDOT), and the Cities of Indianapolis, Mooresville, and Plainfield, Indiana, USA. Early in this effort 3 major compliance issues were identified.

First, expansion of the airport would take air-traffic over a rural area that included some suburban developments. Thus, part of the cost of expansion would include purchasing or noise-proofing these homes to comply with FAA noise pollution regulations. Second, the new runway and its associated developments would remove several jurisdictional wetlands, mostly fragments of seasonally or temporarily flooded deciduous forests. In order to comply with section 404 of the CWA, wetlands destroyed by construction would be replaced at a 4:1 ratio. Third, scattered forest remnants (woodlots hereafter) were considered by USFWS as potential habitat for the US endangered Indiana bat (*Myotis sodalis*). Construction of the additional runway would thus need to minimize impacts to this endangered species. These concerns were intensified when IND was approached by United Airlines which sought to develop a regional service hub at IND.

## Impacts of Airport Expansion

Within this document, we most often use mitigation to refer to efforts to replace habitats removed or damaged during development, and conservation indicates efforts to preserve and improve pre-existing habitats. However, the terms that are applied to dealing with adverse impacts vary under NEPA, ESA, and CWA, making the language used when referring to all of them collectively confusing or inaccurate.

Under NEPA, the Council on Environmental Quality (1978) defines mitigation as: *"(a) Avoiding the impact altogether by not taking a certain action or parts of an action, (b) Minimizing impacts by limiting the degree or magnitude of the action and its implementation, (c) Rectifying the impact by repairing, rehabilitating, or restoring the affected environment, (d) Reducing or eliminating the impact over time by preservation and maintenance operations during the life of the action, and (e) Compensating for the impact by replacing or providing substitute resources or environments."*

The definition of mitigation for wetlands impacts is taken from that used for NEPA, and follows a path from avoidance and minimization of impacts, to compensatory activities that replace losses that cannot be avoided (USACE 1985). Such mitigation typically revolves around creation of new wetlands or the restoration and enhancement, and preservation of existing wetlands.

In contrast, under ESA (United States Code, 2002.), the term mitigation is essentially replaced with the term conservation and are defined as: *"to use and the use of all methods and procedures which are necessary to bring any endangered species or threatened species to the point at which the measures provided pursuant to [the] Act are no longer necessary."* Conservation Measures *"are actions to benefit or promote the recovery of listed species that are included by the Federal agency as an integral part of the proposed action. These actions will be taken by the Federal agency or applicant, and serve to minimize or compensate for, project effects on the species under review."* As with NEPA and wetlands, the preferred option is to avoid impacting endangered species.

Initially, habitat loss at IND consisted of about 240 ha of woodlands and 40 ha of wetlands. Approximately 90% of the existing wetlands were deciduous forests that were seasonally or temporarily flooded. Mitigation for wetlands was set at a 4:1 ratio and for woodlands (i.e., bat habitat) at 1:1. Wooded wetlands were considered to provide mitigation for both wetlands and bat habitat. At this site, some activities achieved both mitigation of wetlands and conservation of endangered species.

## Early Mitigation and Conservation Efforts: 1992-1999

The Airport Authority agreed to mitigation and hired a private consulting firm (3D/Environmental Services, Inc. (3D/ESI), Cincinnati, Ohio) to conduct the work in 1992. Initial conservation and mitigation efforts were composed of three major efforts, all aimed at providing potential bat roosts: (1) preserve existing woodlands, (2) enhance short-term suitability of these woods for bats with artificial roosts, and (3) provide long-term contributions to bat roosting and foraging habitat through creation of both forested wetlands and upland wooded areas.

First, IND purchased a series of existing woodlots (72 ha) that would potentially provide bats with roosting areas. Second, to supplement natural roosts, a series of 9 types of artificial roosts were placed in these woodlots (see Whitaker et al 2006). Several of these artificial roosts were specifically designed to mimic natural roosts of the Indiana bat. There were 2 goals to be attained from these artificial roosts: 1) to experimentally determine if any of the types of artificial roosts could be used as a management tool for the Indiana bat; and 2) provide temporary habitat for the bats until planted forests could mature and begin producing natural roosts (approximately 75 years).

In most managed forests of a suitable size, providing long-term roosting habitat would require managing for standing timber of varying ages, including large and over-mature trees (Kurta and Kennedy 2002). Near the airport, however, little standing timber existed in 1992. Thus a third conservation activity was to plant agricultural land with seedlings of hardwood trees. Land for these plantings was obtained within a noise reduction zone in which the FAA provided funds to purchase or retrofit existing residential properties to reduce noise impacts of aircraft. Traditionally, these properties are redeveloped as support structures for the airport or industrial facilities. At IND, this area included a substantial amount of agricultural lands that could be modified into conservation areas at low cost. These planted woodlands were placed in and beside areas used to construct new wetlands under the CWA.

Wetland mitigation was designed to meet requirements of the USFWS, USEPA, USACE, IDNR, and IDEM, and also provided the third mitigation effort. Most of these agricultural areas were farmed or prior-converted wetlands that had a high probability of successful wetland mitigation with minimal construction and maintenance requirements. Thus, mitigation was a combination of habitat creation, enhancement, and restoration. Mitigation for wooded wetlands was completed with a minimum of earth-moving, instead relying upon reestablishment of preexisting hydrology by plugging drainage ditches and breaking or plugging drainage tiles (clay pipes that were used to drain surface water from potential farm ground). Mitigation for emergent wetlands was completed using shallow berms and dikes. Mitigation was concurrent with development so that new habitats were built in the same year that existing areas were lost. Wooded wetlands were typically planted with commercial nursery stock (bare root seedlings) and vegetation maintenance activities were aimed at encouraging natural recolonization, by allowing volunteer plants to grow between planted trees. Species composition of planted stock was based upon detailed studies of species native to the area and typical of the desired future habitats resulting from mitigation. Many species of trees were used and planting ratios were stratified by water tolerance (wet, mesic, and dry zones) of each species according to placement in the mitigation area. Thus, plantings in wet zones included dry zone species, and dry zone areas included wet zone species, but at reduced ratios. Monitoring of bat and wetland habitats, and use of bat roost structures was conducted annually for 5 years.

In 1994, conservation efforts were supplemented by the inclusion of regular mist netting of 10 sites along the East Fork of White Lick Creek (Whitaker et al. 2004). Indiana bats captured at these sites were radio-tagged and followed to roosts. In 1994, these efforts led to discovery of a maternity colony of Indiana bats roosting in a tree on private property. This tree proved to be the primary roost for this colony through the 2001 field season (Sparks 2003, Whitaker et al. 2004). This roost was just south of the rapidly-developing commercial area at the junction of I-70 and IN-267, suggesting that these bats would lose much of their foraging habitat to development. Thus, starting in 1996, bats were radio-tracked to not only their diurnal roosts, but also to nocturnal foraging areas and roosts.

Following the 1996 field season, management of the Indianapolis International Airport was privatized and day-to-day operations came under control of BAA International. At that time, implementation of mitigation and conservation efforts was contracted to American Consulting Engineers, Inc. of Indianapolis, who in turn subcontracted bat conservation efforts to Indiana State University (ISU) for the 1997 - 1999 field seasons (Whitaker et al. 2004). ISU instituted regular emergence counts (i.e., numbers of bats exiting diurnal roosts at dusk) on primary and secondary roost trees as they were discovered. The first roost tree, discovered in 1996, was the center of Indiana bat activity until it fell following the 2001 field season (Sparks 2003, Whitaker 2004). Because artificial roosts were rarely used by Indiana bats at that time (Whitaker et al. 2004, 2006), structure monitoring was scaled back following the 1997 field season to check types of structures within woodlots that bats had previously used. Reduced monitoring allowed a focus on telemetry studies of foraging bats. However, 4 of 9 types of structures were used by the northern myotis (*Myotis septentrionalis*), and that became the subject of studies that began in 1998 (Sparks 2003, Farrell Sparks et al 2004).

Formal mitigation and conservation associated with airport expansion ended following summer 1999. A greatly reduced monitoring effort was implemented in 2000 and 2001 by ISU students conducting research on northern myotis (Sparks 2003, Farrell Sparks et al 2004), and the foraging biology of the big brown (*Eptesicus fuscus*) and evening bat (*Nycticeius humeralis*) (Duchamp et al. 2004). Study of the Indiana bat was restricted to occasional emergence counts of Primary roosts, telemetry studies on 1 animal each year, and examination of roost structures for northern myotis. These data have proven critical, however, to conservation efforts undertaken under the Habitat Conservation Plan.

## Habitat Conservation Plan: 2002 - Present

In 2002, conservation and research targeting the Indiana myotis was reinstated. The reason for this was the addition of a new interchange (Six Points Road) to I-70 and its secondary impacts (Raymond 2006). The interchange is in the center of the study area, and it connects I-70 with private developments near the southern end of the project area. This construction effectively added another multilane highway that bisects the study area from north to south. In many respects, the HCP mitigation plan mirrored that of 1992 - 1999. Mitigation was centered on purchasing land and planting of 147 ha of woodland, and further monitoring and studies of bats. This effort in combination with property protected under other conservation efforts resulted in permanent protection of 860 ha of woodland. Because woodlands near the airport are in an agricultural matrix, many additional hectares of undeveloped land have also been protected, which provide foraging habitat for several species of bats (Duchamp et al. 2004, Sparks et al. 2005 *a, b, c*, Walters et al 2007). Monitoring of the Indiana bat continued to include use of telemetry, emergence counts, and regular mist-net surveys.

## Specific Achievements and Results

### Artificial Roosts

Artificial roosts are a management tool that could (theoretically) provide an important step in protecting Indiana bats, and artificial roosts may provide research opportunities that are not possible in the loosely-hanging bark of dead trees. However, they also have the potential to be abused. Development of a successful artificial roost could be an important conservation tool that could be used in areas where few suitable roost trees are present such as in stands of pole timber. Because primary roosts (large, dead trees with sloughing bark) cannot be developed on a short-term basis; a successful artificial roost could be combined with planted forests to provide a tool for enhancing habitat, both for general conservation of the species and potentially for mitigating loss of habitat.

The experiment conducted at the airport has offered valuable insight into use of structures (including the widely available bird-house style box) for bats. Artificial roosts at this site were regularly used by northern myotis, but until 2003 received minimal use by Indiana bats (Salyers et al 1996, Ritzi et al. 2005, Whitaker et al 2006). We suspect these structures were not heavily used by Indiana bats for 3 reasons. First, despite the large number of trees removed during development many suitable roost trees were still present in the woodlots preserved as part of the conservation strategy. Second, structures did not adequately resemble sloughing bark. Third, many structures were placed in shaded areas, because the value of solar exposure was unknown at the time. In 2003, however, Indiana myotis began to make regular use of 2 artificial roosts (Ritzi et al 2005) and both the rate of use and the number of structures used increased in both 2004 and 2005 (Whitaker et al. 2006), with routine use continuing to present. Success of the artificial roost program is dependent on perspective. Structures were not extensively used until they were in place nearly a decade, and at that time many had fallen. However, a decade is substantially shorter than roughly 75 years required to grow potential roost trees (Whitaker et al. 2006). In addition, this effort was intended as an experiment, and this experiment has provided a wealth of data that has influenced management decisions across the range of the bat. Effective artificial roosts should not be approached or perceived as a panacea, but the potential to aid recovery of Indiana bats and research should not be discounted. Ultimately, long-term management for the species must emphasize trees of sufficient size and number to support a healthy population of bats.

We believe researchers should continue efforts to develop a successful artificial roost for this species. Specifically, we should strive to develop roosts that provide suitable microclimates (Boyles 2007) and that resemble sloughing bark enough to attract bats (Whitaker et al. 2006). Recent use of a variety of man-made roosts by maternity colonies of Indiana myotis include a vacant church and nearby metal batbox in Pennsylvania (Butchkoski and Hassinger 2002), a barn in Iowa (Kurta 2005), and 2 houses in New York (A. C. Hicks personal communication; Brack unpub. data); roost boxes in Illinois (Carter et al. 2001); 3 utility poles in central Indiana (Brack unpub. Data, Hendricks et al. 2005.); and under bridges (Kiser et al 2002). Given the sudden emergence of these observations across the range of the species, it seems likely that we are seeing a behavioral shift by Indiana bats wherein they are becoming acclimated to anthropogenic structures. As such, this might provide an important model to study this process that must also have occurred as other species such as big brown and little brown bats adapted to buildings following settlement.

The most viable conservation strategies incorporate a combination of preservation, creation, restoration, and enhancement of natural habitats with active management. Use of artificial structures is one management tool appropriate to some, but not all situations. Unfortunately, at times, use of bat boxes at the airport overshadowed other mitigation efforts that have been broadly successful. At the airport, the goal is to provide a mosaic of habitats that include foraging and roosting areas for the Indiana bat. Preservation and planting of woodlots have been successful as these areas are now the most extensively used roosting and foraging habitats on the study area. Use of bat boxes in planted areas (habitat creation) and in young stands (enhancement) or stands that otherwise do not provide a suitable number of sufficient roost sites (restoration) may help support the species until forests mature and natural roosts become available. In addition, artificial roosts may benefit other bats, particularly the northern myotis.

## Habitat Conservation and Creation

Since loss of the main roost following the 2001 field season most primary roosts have been in areas purchased for conservation by the airport. Only 1 new primary roost is in the private woodlot that contained the initial primary roost. Together, protected and replanted forests provide the most important foraging habitat for Indiana bats (Sparks et al. 2005 *a, b*). When purchased, many of these woodlands were surrounded by agricultural lands, which the airport has continued to farm. These open habitats financially benefit the airport, and provide important foraging habitat for at least 5 species of bats (Duchamp et al. 2004, Sparks et al. 2005 a, b, c, Walters et al. 2007), all of which are listed as species of special concern or as endangered in Indiana, including the Indiana bat. This is an important "bonus" because these other bats were not targets of initial conservation efforts. Without this effort, most of the area would have been developed. Instead the conservation area controlled by the airport provides an island of habitat in a sea of suburbia.

## Netting Survey

At its inception, netting targeted obtaining Indiana bats for telemetry studies. A second goal was added in 1998—to provide baseline data on composition of the bat community (Sparks et al. 1998, Whitaker et al. 2004) and how that community changes with seasons (Walters et al. 2006) and land-use patterns (Sparks 2003). The netting effort has been successful in meeting these goals. In addition, comparing capture rates of bats in this heavily disturbed landscape to those at more natural sites was enlightening about the response of bats to landscape changes (Sparks et al. 1998, Ulrey et al. 2005). Continuing to monitor changes in this bat community will require long-term data, obtained from continued netting along the East Fork of White Lick Creek.

## Telemetry Studies

Radio-tagged bats are being used to develop the first comprehensive overview of nocturnal behavior by an entire community of bats. Important contributions of telemetry studies to conservation efforts at IND have been to: 1) target for acquisition, areas of intensively used habit; and 2) demonstrate the intensity of use by bats on lands following purchase. Unlike many conservation efforts, those at the airport are long-term and are guided by direct and current information about which parcels are used by target species (i.e. adaptive management). Part of this effort has been a study of foraging habitat at a landscape scale (Duchamp et al. 2004, Sparks et al. 2005 *a, b, c*, Tuttle et al. 2006, Walters 2007), which aids decision-making for habitat management practices. An unexpected benefit was the opportunity to gain baseline data on movement patterns by migrating bats (Walters et al. 2006). Given the extensive baseline dataset and a rapidly-changing landscape, this site has immense potential to provide insight into how bats respond to development.

## Emergence Counts

To obtain information about the population size of Indiana bats at the airport and their movement patterns, we instituted a series of regular emergence counts at known roosts. Most similar information has been obtained from relatively short-term data sets and from a few trees per site (Sparks et al 2005a). Our data are the most comprehensive to date for the Indiana bat, and thus should supply the best information about long-term population trends at a single site (Whitaker and Sparks In Review).

Combining regular emergence counts with telemetry data over many years has have provided a unique opportunity to understand how bats respond to environmental change, both natural and anthropomorphic. Following loss of the primary roost in winter 2001/2002, our data provided remarkable insight into the response of bats to such an event (Sparks 2003, Kurta 2005). In addition, we noted a pattern whereby many roosts that earlier studies (e.g., Callahan et al. 1997) would have classified as primary roosts are abandoned at IND, often within a week of discovery, while a few are consistently reused for many years. Studies of emergence counts provided data that put in perspective occasional use of artificial roost structures by Indiana bats (Salyers et al. 1996, Kurta 2005, Ritzi et al. 2005, Whitaker et al. 2006).

## Impacts on Nontarget Species

Conservation efforts targeting the Indiana bat and wetlands are providing habitat for many nontarget species. We suspect the state-endangered evening bat would have been extirpated without ever having been detected from this site without conservation activities aimed at Indiana bats. Evening bats were first detected in the netting surveys of 1996, and the first roost was documents in 1997 (Whitaker et al. 2005). The woodlot containing that roost was cleared in winter 1997/1998 and evening bats moved into the woodlot containing the primary Indiana bat roost (Sparks et al. 1998). Evening bats now forage and roost almost exclusively in areas conserved for the Indiana bat (Duchamp et al. 2004).

Local populations of amphibians and reptiles are greatly reduced in developed areas north of I-70 as compared to the IND conservation areas (Foster et al. 2004). Species richness is greatest in the IND mitigation wetlands (Foster et al. 2003, 2004). One species apparently benefiting is Kirtland's snake (*Clonophis kirtlandii*), a state-endangered species first detected in summer 2004 (B. J. Foster unpublished), although populations are known from nearby areas of Indianapolis (Minton 2001). Similarly, local fish diversity and aquatic habitat quality increases from the northern end of the study site and is greatest in the habitat conservation area (Ritzi et al. 2004). No formal survey of birds has been conducted, but three state-listed species (Henslow's sparrow, *Annodramos henslowii*; Red-shouldered hawk, *Buteo lineatus*, and least bittern, *Ixobrychus exilis*) have been detected in mitigation wetlands during the summer breeding season with a fourth (upland sandpiper, *Bartrania longicauda*) occasionally observed near the runways. In short, numerous species, some locally rare, are benefiting from the airport conservation effort.

## Academic Involvement

Having a university conduct monitoring has provided 3 major benefits. First, it documented project impacts on non-target wildlife that typically would not have been obtained by a private consulting company, because these data were primarily collected as a result of student research projects. Second, results have been published rather than be restricted to technical reports. Third, it has improved public perception of the project. These benefits led the airport to contract Purdue University to conduct monitoring of the tree plantations.

## Public Perception and Reception

Initially, airport developments were viewed as positive by the general public, in large part because of anticipated economic benefits. As with most developments, the views of adjacent landowners were typically less favorable. Coincident with a positive view of the development was a similarly positive view of the concern for natural resources, including bats and wetlands. Conservation for bats at the airport was reported on ABC network news as a win-win situation for the airport and for the bats. However, with time, there was a growing perception by the public that mitigation was not as effective as anticipated (i.e. bats were not using the bat boxes), that the financial cost of mitigation was too high, and that concerns for bats were given preference over concerns for humans. These negative views, like the positive ones before, reached the public via television through a segment on a local station. In recent years, involvement of 2 public universities has helped improve perception of the project, including several positive stories in the local media. In retrospect, at least some negative perceptions could have been avoided had not the initial positive perception set unattainable goals. Education of the public is now a major goal of conservation efforts.

## Economic Aspects

A detailed analysis of economic features of habitat conservation and scientific research associated with the project is beyond the scope of this paper. However, it is instructive to provide a cursory description of the economic context of this project. This is particularly true given the tendency by some members of the local community to treat the airport expansion and subsequent economic developments as separate from the cost of conservation efforts. In reality, the conservation efforts were an essential component of obtaining federal funding and permits that allowed the project to move forward. These conservation efforts would not have happened without the airport expansion and resulting building boom, which itself would have proceeded very differently without the conservation efforts.

Expansion of the Indianapolis airport and related transportation infrastructure was a large construction project that will continue to provide substantial benefits to the local economy in future decades. Construction of the new terminal alone required a budget of $974 million (Nunn 2004), while the new highway interchange that will serve as access for both passengers and airfreight cost around $170 million (INDOT 2004). From 1990 to 2001 airfreight grew by 661%, averaging 25.6 million tons annually (Nunn 2004). By 1999 the Indianapolis airport was ranked as the eleventh largest in the U.S. for cargo shipments (Schoettle 1999). From

1990-2001 3.3 million people annually embarked from the Indianapolis Airport while airmail loadings (not included in airfreight) averaged 26.8 million tons annually (Nunn 2004). Expansion of freight capacity directly led to a boom in local construction, which has now resulted in an area of large warehouses that now occupies 800 ha and provides jobs for thousands of people. The airport and associated structures are clearly an important capital asset for the local economy, which is based on services and agriculture as well as manufacturing.

Although airports impose a large spatial footprint, significant parts of the required land also can be used for other activities, including habitat conservation. In this case, presence of the Indiana bat resulted in these lands being used for conservation. Typically one of the largest costs of species protection is the withdrawal of required habitat from economic uses that are incompatible with conservation. In the present case, the airport and the bats can and do co-exist. The collective decision to protect the Indiana bat affirms its social value as a public good, and in this particular case the benefit is attained at low cost.

In addition to providing habitat for Indiana bats, conservation lands can be used for a variety of purposes. Outdoor recreation activities might provide a social benefit from a multiple-use management policy. The conservation area is a large portion of the undeveloped habitat within metropolitan Indianapolis, and thus is particularly valuable for outdoor recreation. Negotiations are underway to designate 132 ha of it as a nature park. It may be necessary to restrict activities to meet the primary goal of protecting the Indiana bat, but even limited recreation would offset some costs of withdrawing the land from commercial development. The presence of natural areas, and even individual trees, is an important, economically demonstrable, contribution to urban and suburban settings. In addition to protecting Indiana bats, the properties provide conservation benefits for numerous species. Finally, this property provides general ecosystem services for the local and regional economies such as carbon sequestration and water filtration.

While limiting uses of land is a key cost of conservation efforts, there is also a financial cost for the research. Again, the work is required by environmental permits and is thus directly tied to airport and highway expansion. This research requires a highly skilled labor pool and minor capital resources. Assessing economic benefits of this research is more difficult than calculating the cost. Monitoring provides essential information about the success or failure of conservation efforts, allows use of adaptive management when unforeseen conservation challenges or opportunities arise. Second, because ISU and Purdue students seek research experience, the airport and regulatory agencies have benefited from a substantial body of research beyond the original mitigation requirements at a relatively low cost. Third, research findings are widely disseminated among the scientific, management, and conservation communities in part by the eventual employment of the students within these professions.

A final benefit of research involves an interaction with the basic cost of habitat conservation. As noted, withdrawal of land from commercial uses is the central cost, and arguably the largest one. A detailed knowledge of bat behavior and the local ecosystem obtained from the research allows a more measured and specific response to competing uses. For example, a local developer sought to acquire parcels of the conservation area for projects incompatible with maintaining habitat for the Indiana bat. However, the developer was willing to exchange other parcels he owned for those he was seeking to acquire. The alternate parcels could improve overall conservation efforts, and so an agreement was reached that benefited both the developer and the bats. Without detailed knowledge of bat use of the project area, this mutually beneficial determination would not have been possible.

## The Big Picture

The size, shape, and composition of ecological preserves is a common theme for theoretical discussions of conservation (Andleman and Willig 2002, Groom et al. 2006). These efforts have and will continue to play an important role in helping conservationist efforts maximize the potential of reservation areas—particularly new reservations in the developing world. Within the past 5 years several scientific organizations dedicated to natural resource management have produced publications or resolutions that support development of steady-state economies (Gates et al. 2006, American Society of Mammalogists 2007, Society for Conservation Biology, North American Section 2005). While these goals are important, conservation biologists must work within the existing economic structure on properties that often were not designed with the aid of modern conservation science.

Most conservation opportunities within developed nations must fit within confines of pre-existing constraints, such as urbanization (this study), reclamation of coal mines (DeVault et al. 2002), or abandoned military bases (Jones and Preston 2000, Everette et al. 2001) which each have their own management problems and constraints. As such, some scientists advocate an alliance between environmental conservation and economic development (Rosenzweig 2003).

At IND we dealt with a situation rarely discussed in conservation texts, but which is far from unique. We had to develop a plan to protect a single endangered species on a rapidly developing landscape. Scientists are often asked to provide habitat to protect poorly known species or replace poorly documented wetlands, including functions and values. In many cases, this combination is a recipe for disaster (Minkin and Ladd 2003; NRC 2001) . We faced a similar mission at IND, but at this site an emphasis was placed on studying the impact of conservation efforts on the target species. The greatest success of the airport project has been the incorporation of traditional approaches like habitat preservation with approaches, such as foraging and artificial roost studies, that clearly document the use or value of measures implemented.

Management of Indiana bats at this site continues to be an interaction among regulatory agencies, private enterprise and academic researchers who rely on site-specific field data. Many challenges remain. That the Indiana bat continues to survive on these conservation lands is a testament to both the success of this effort and the hardiness of the species.

## Acknowledgments

An enormous number of individuals from many organizations contributed to the work at the airport, initially and over the years. These include resource regulators (at all governmental scales), developers, public servants, educators, and private individuals, as both consultants to any of the above or as concerned citizens. There are far too many individuals to mention, and even the task of correctly identifying all of the organizations and their roles would be an onerous one. Nevertheless, we thank each individual and each organization, and readily admit that this work could not have been completed without them. In particular, we thank our students the fruits of whose labor we routinely claim, and the Indianapolis Airport Authority for its willingness to allow us to think "outside the box" for more than a decade. Earlier drafts of this manuscript were improved by comments provided by Marvin Brethauer, Justin Boyles, Lori Pruitt, and Ted Cable.

# References

American Society of Mammalogists. (2007). Economic growth and mammalian species. *J Mammal,* **88**:1571-1573.

Andelman, S. J., & Willig, M. R. (2002). Alternative configurations of conservation reserves for Paraguayan bats: considerations of spatial scale. *Con Biol,* **16**:1352–1363.

Boyles, J. G. (2007). Describing roosts used by forest bats: the importance of microclimate. *Acta Chiroptolog,* **9**:297-303.

Butchkowski, C. M., & Hassinger, J. M. (2002). Ecology of a maternity colony roosting in a building. In A. Kurta & J. Kennedy (Eds.), *The Indiana bat: biology and management of an endangered species.* Bat Conservation International, Austin Texas, pp. 130-142.

Callahan, E. V., Drobney, R. D., & Clawson, R. L. (1997). Selection of summer roosting sites by Indiana bat (*Myotis sodalis*) in Missouri. *J Mammal,* **78**:818-825.

Carter, T. C., Feldhamer, G., & Kath, J. (2001). Notes on summer roosting of Indiana bats. *Bat Res News,* **42**:197-198.

Council on Environmental Quality Executive Office of the President. 1978. 40 CFR. Environmental Protection. National Environmental Policy Act (NEPA), Part 1500: Purpose, Policy and Mandate; 1508.20: Terminology and Index – Mitigation

DeVault, T. L., Scott, P. E., Bajema, R. A., & Lima, S.L. (2002). Breeding bird communities of reclaimed coal mine grasslands in the American Midwest. *J Field Ornithol,* **73**:268-275.

Duchamp, J. E., Sparks, D. W., & Whitaker, J. O., Jr. (2004). Foraging-habitat selection by bats at an urban-rural interface: comparison between a successful and a less successful species. *Can J Zool,* **82**:1157-1164.

Everette, A. L., O'Shea, T. J., Ellison, L. E., Stone, L. A., McCance, J. L. (2001). Bat use of a high-plains urban wildlife refuge. *Wildlife Soc Bull,* **29**: 967-973.

Farrell Sparks, J. K., Foster, B. J., & Sparks, D. W. (2004). Utility pole used as a roost by a northern myotis, *Myotis septentrionalis. Bat Res News,* **45**:94.

Foster, B. J., Sparks, D. W., & Duchamp, J. E. (2003). Urban Herpetology I: new distribution records of amphibians and reptiles from Hendricks County, Indiana. *Herpetol Rev,* **34**:395.

Foster, B. J., Sparks, D. W., & Duchamp, J. E. (2004). Urban Herpetology II: Amphibians and Reptiles of the Indianapolis International Airport Conservation Properties. *Proc Indiana Acad Sci,* **113**:53-59.

Gates, J. E., Dawe, N. K., Erickson, J. D., Farley, J. C., Geist, V., Hands, N., Magee, P., & Trauger, D. L. (2006). Perspectives on The Wildlife Society's economic growth policy statement and the development process. *Wildlife Soc Bull,* **34**:507-511.

Groom, M. J., Meffe, G. K., & Carroll, C. R. (2006). *Principles of Conservation Biology.* Sunderland, MA: Sinauer and Associates.

Hendricks, W. D. (2005). Notable roosts for the Indiana bat (*Myotis sodalis*). In K. C. Vories & A. Harrington (Eds.), *Indiana Bats and Coal Mining, A Technical Interactive Forum.* Office of Surface Mining, U.S. Department of the Interior, Alton, Illinois, pp. 133-138.

IBJ (Indianapolis Business Journal Staff Report). 2003. Power brokers: 16. Lacy M. Johnson, Partner, Ice Miller; President, Board of Directors, Indianapolis Airport Authority. *Indiana Business J.* **23**(53):10-16 March

INDOT (Indiana Department of Transportation). 2004. Wider, safer I-70 unveiled. INDOT News Release 29 December 2004 accessed at http:/www.newindianpolisairport.com/news/122904_i70.htm on 7 April 2005

Jones, C. A., & Preston, C. R. (2000). The role of the bald eagle as flagship species for the Rocky Mountain Arsenal: from superfund site to wildlife refuge. In J. R. Choate (Eds.), Reflections of a naturalist: papers honoring professor Eugene D. Fleharty, Fort Hays State University, Hays, Kansas, pp. 165-171.

Kiser, J. A., MacGreggor, J. R., Bryan, H. D., & Howard, A. (2002). In A. Kurta and J. Kennedy (Eds.) *The Indiana bat: biology and management of an endangered species.* Bat Conservation International, Austin Texas, pp. 208-215.

Kurta, A. (2005). Roosting ecology and behavior of Indiana bats in summer. In K. C. Vories and A. Harrington (Eds.) Indiana Bats and Coal Mining, A Technical Interactive Forum. Office of Surface Mining, U.S. Department of the Interior, Alton, Illinois, pp. 29-42.

Kurta, A., & Kennedy, J. (2002). The Indiana bat: biology and management of an endangered species. Bat Conservation International, Austin TX.

Maurer, K. (2002). Terminal project good news for local contractors. *Indiana Business J,* **25**(35):11-17 November.

Minkin, P., & Ladd, R. (2003). *Success of Corps-required wetland mitigation in New England.* U.S. Army Corps of Engineers, New England District.

Minton, S. A., Jr. (2001). Amphibians and Reptiles of Indiana. Indiana Academy of Science, Indianapolis.

NRC (National Research Council). (2001). *Compensating for Wetland Losses Under the Clean Water Act.* National Academy Sciences Press, Washington, DC.

Nunn, S. (2004). *Airport Development Takes Flight: A Comparison of Aviation Investments in Indianapolis and Eight Regions.* Center for Urban Policy and the Environment. Indiana University-Purdue University at Indianapolis. http://www.urbancenter.iupui.edu/PubResources/pdf/86_04-C09_Aviation.pdf (Accessed 9 November 2007)

Raymond, L. (2006). Cooperation without trust: Overcoming collective action barriers to endangered species protection. *Policy J,* **34**:37-57.

Ritzi, C.M., Everson, B.L. & Whitaker, J.O., Jr. (2005). Use of bat boxes by a maternity colony of Indiana myots (*Myotis sodalis*). *Northeast. Nat,* **12**:217–220.

Ritzi, C. M., Everson, B. L., Foster, B. J., Sheets, J. J., & Sparks, D. W. (2004). Urban ichthyology: changes in the fish community along an urban-rural creek in Indiana. *Proceedings of the Indiana Acad Sci,* **113**:42-52.

Rosenzweig, M. L. (2003). Win Win Ecology: How the Earth's Species Can Survive in the Midst of Human Enterprise. Oxford University Press.

Salyers, J., Tyrell, K., & Brack, V., Jr. (1996). Artificial roost structure use by Indiana bats in wooded areas in central Indiana. *Bat Res News,* **37**:148.

Schoettle, A. (1999). Indianapolis airport: hubless and happy? *Indiana Business Journal* **20**(19):26 July-1 August.

Society for Conservation Biology, North American Chapter (2005). *The Steady State Economy As A Sustainable Alternative To Economic Growth: Position Of The Society For Conservation Biology*, North America Section. accessed at www.conservationbiology.org/Publications/Newsletter/Archives/2005-2-February/ v12n1009.cfm on 11 February 2008.

Sparks, D. W. (2003). *How does urbanization impact bats?* Ph. D. Dissertation, Indiana State University, Terre Haute.

Sparks, D. W., Laborda, J. A., & Whitaker, J. O., Jr. (1998). Bats of the Indianapolis International Airport as compared to a more rural community of bats at Prairie Creek. *Proc Indiana Acad Sci,* **107**:171-179.

Sparks, D. W., Simmons, M. T., Gummer, C. L., & Duchamp J. E. (2003). Disturbance of roosting bats by woodpeckers and raccoons. *Northeast Nat,* **10**:105-108.

Sparks, D. W., Whitaker, J. O., Jr, & Ritzi, C. M. (2005a). Foraging ecology of the endangered Indiana bat. In K. C. Vories and A. Harrington (Eds.) *Indiana Bats and Coal Mining, A Technical Interactive Forum.* Office of Surface Mining, U.S. Department of the Interior, Alton, Illinois, pp. 15-27.

Sparks, D. W., Ritzi, C. M., Duchamp, J. E., & Whitaker, J. O., Jr. (2005b). Foraging habitat of the Indiana bat (*Myotis sodalis*) at an urban-rural interface. *J Mammal,* **86**:713-718.

Sparks, D. W., Ritzi, C. M., & Everson, B. L. (2005c). Nocturnal behavior and roosting ecology of a juvenile *Lasiurus cinereus* near Indianapolis, Indiana. *Proc Indiana Acad Sci,* **114**:70-72.

Tuttle, N. M., Benson, D. P., & Sparks, D. W. (2006). Diet of *Myotis sodalis* (Indiana bat) at an Urban/Rural Interface. *Northeast Nat,* **13**:435-442.

Ulrey, W. A., Sparks, D. W., & Ritzi, C. M. (2005). Bat communities in highly impacted areas: comparing Camp Atterbury to the Indianapolis Airport. *Proc Indiana Acad Sci,* **114**:73-76.

United States Code. 2002. *Endangered Species Act of 1973 as Amended Through Public Law* 107-136. 16 USC 1531.

USACE. 1985. Implementation of fish & wildlife mitigation in the Corps Of Engineers regulatory program. *Regulatory Guidance Letter* 85-08.

Walters, B. L., Ritzi, C. M., Sparks, D. W., & Whitaker, J. O., Jr. (2006). Timing of migration by eastern red bats (*Lasiurus borealis*) through central Indiana. *Acta Chiroptolog,* **8**:259-263.

Walters, B. L., Ritzi, C. M., Sparks, D. W., & Whitaker, J. O., Jr. (2007). Foraging behavior of the eastern red bat (*Lasiurus borealis*) at an urban-rural interface. *Am Midl Nat,* **157**:365-373.

Whitaker, J. O., Jr., Sparks, D. W., & Brack, V., Jr. (2006). Use of artificial roost structures by bats at the Indianapolis International Airport. *Env Manag,* **38**:28-36.

Yurk, M. Airport investments yield uncertain returns. Indiana University-Purdue University Indianapolis News Center, Center for Urban Policy and the Environment, School for Public and Environmental Affairs accessed at http:/www.newcenter.iupui.edu/ newsrelease/airport_04.htm on 6 April 2005.

In: Airports: Performance, Risks, and Problems
Editors: P.B. Larauge et al, pp. 67-103

ISBN 978-1-60692-393-1
© 2009 Nova Science Publishers, Inc.

*Chapter 4*

# SUPPORT FOR AIRPORT STRATEGIC PLANNING: BALANCING AN AIRPORT'S ECONOMIC AND SOCIAL PERFORMANCE

**R.A.A. (Roland) Wijnen[1], H.G. (Dries) Visser[2] and W.E. (Warren) Walker[1]**
[1]Faculty of Technology, Policy and Management, Delft Univ. of Technology, Netherland
[2]Faculty of Aerospace Engineering, Delft University of Technology, Netherlands

**Abstract**

The context of the airport operator, especially in market-oriented, environments, is changing rapidly, due to such developments as the deregulation of the airline market, terrorist threats, more stringent environmental regulations, the rise of low cost carriers, and increased opposition to growth from some stakeholders. History shows that airport operators have difficulty in dealing with such changes.

Airport planners and decisionmakers have to anticipate changes to their business environment and provide solutions for mitigating the adverse effects of growth that are satisfactory to their stakeholders (e.g. communities, airlines, governments). Doing this successfully is difficult. Many airport strategic plans fail to deliver their promise and there is growing opposition from an increasing number of stakeholders against airport expansion plans.

Explicit consideration of the uncertainties that the future will bring and meaningful involvement of all airport stakeholders is essential for the long-term economic and social performance of the airport. Use of computer-based decision support for airport strategic planning can provide a way to deal with the uncertain future and meaningfully involve the stakeholders. HARMOS is a Decision Support System that we developed with these requirements as the starting point for its design and implementation.

**Key Words**: Strategic planning, Master Planning, stakeholders, uncertainty, decision support system

## 1. Introduction

In the private and public sector, strategic planning is often a principal element of strategic management. Bryson,

> A disciplined effort to produce fundamental decisions and actions that shape and guide what an organization (or other entity) is, what it does, and why it does it [6, p.5].

**(author?)** [7] stresses that strategic planning should be viewed as a set of concepts, procedures, and tools that must be carefully tailored to a specific context if desirable outcomes are to be achieved.

Designing an organization's approach to strategic planning needs to consider the way strategies (fundamental decisions) are developed and implemented (actions). The *identity* (what it is), the *purpose* (what it does) and the *values* (why it does it) of an organization also need to be considered[1].

This definition implies that there is not a single approach; many approaches to strategic planning can be defined, such as strategic issue management approaches, logical incrementalism, portfolio models, competitive analysis, among others [7]. In practice, strategic planning is usually a hybrid of a number of these and even other approaches.

Mainly the formalized approaches to strategic planning have been heavily criticized, because of their focus on elaborate methods for analysis, which impeded decision making and left no room for true strategic insights [50]. Strategic planning did therefore not contribute to *strategic thinking*, sometimes resulting in dramatic negative effects on company performance [31, 35].

From an airport management perspective, Wells and Young provide the following definition:

> Strategic planning is the activity that encompasses all other planning activities [facility, economic, financial, organizational, and environmental planning] into a coordinated effort to maximize the future potential of the airport to the community [47, p.368].

This definition does not imply a specific approach to strategic planning either. There are many different approaches to coordinate an all encompassing planning effort with the intention to maximize the future potential of an airport. Besides that, by whom and how should the future potential of an airport be defined? The airport operator and each of its stakeholders probably define the potential of the airport differently, because they have different value systems.

Inherently, airport strategic planning is therefore about balancing different aspects of the airport's performance (rather than optimization of a single objective). Before we discuss the need to find a balance between an airport's economic and social performance in Section 1.2., the next section first describes the problem situation that an airport operator needs to address in their strategic planning effort.

## 1.1.  The Problem Situation

An airport operator has to find an appropriate match between capacity and demand, given a number of constraints (environmental and/or financial). An airport has to be managed such that demand for services matches the capacity of the infrastructure, not only in the short

---

[1]The identity—what an organization is or should become—is usually expressed in a vision statement. The purpose of an organization is expressed in a mission statement. It is also more and more common for organizations to publish the core values of an organization explicitly (separately or as part of their vision).

term but also in the long term. At the same time, the airport operator has to manage the economic, environmental, and land-use effects of the current and future airport operation.

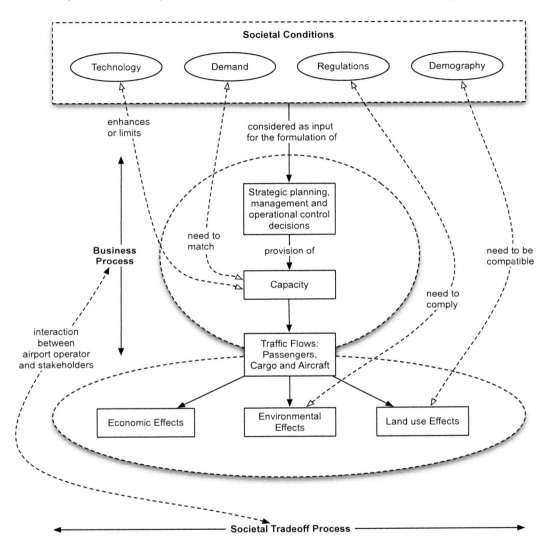

Figure 1. The airport conceptualized as a socio-technical system. **Source**: adapted from (**author?**) [27].

Figure 1 illustrates this problem situation, conceptualizing the airport as a socio-technical system. An airport has a finite capacity, which should be matched with demand. If capacity is below demand, the users of an airport incur high costs because of delays. If capacity is much higher than demand, the airport operator faces substantial costs of maintaining facilities that are underutilised.

In both cases, passenger, cargo, and aircraft flows are created. Processing these flows generates revenues for the airport operator, and provides connections for passengers and freight. Also other effects, such as economic (e.g. employment), and environmental (e.g. degradation of air quality, increase in noise levels), are produced. Additionally, the presence of an airport affects land-use planning in a wide area surrounding an airport (e.g. because of safety zones, noise zones and buffers). We call these impacts*social* impacts because they affect society at large and many specific actors in particular, and usually result in strong public and policy debate.

There are also societal conditions that develop (shown at the top of Figure 1). Regulations are implemented to mitigate environmental impacts. Technology improves or lags behind, which either enhances or limits airport capacity. Demographic developments in the airport region should be compatible with land-use patterns. These social conditions are to a more or lesser extent considered by an airport operator when formulating strategies.

The airport operator deals with the problem situation by controlling the airport's short-term operations (through operational control decisions), allocating and managing resources on the mid-term (through management control decisions), and formulating and implementing strategies for the long-term (through strategic planning decisions). Each of these activities are part of the *business process*, which is a process internal to the airport.

The potential strategies of an airport operator (e.g. building a new runway, or not accomodating specific demand such as low cost airlines) affect the stakeholders quite differently, which is why, in addition to business considerations, a *societal tradeoff process* is needed (or emerges) to determine the strategy (or strategies) that is (are) satisfactory to most, but preferably all stakeholders.

The business process must take into account the societal trade-off process, which goes on simultaneously. This process is external to the airport. The interaction between the business process and the societal trade-off process is stronger for decisions that affect long-term performance, i.e. the strategic planning decisions. The strong interaction clearly manifests itself whenever airport operators present their long-term development plans. Most of the time, these plans are publicly discussed and debated over an extended period among the airport operator and its stakeholders. For example, public discussion about the future of Amsterdam Airport Schiphol seems to reignite every now and then, unfortunately without the emergence of a shared vision for its future.

## 1.2.  Finding the Balance between Economic and Social Performance

Figure 2 illustrates the relationship between economic and social performance of a company [1]. The trends presented obviously apply to airport operators as well.

Airports are intended to perform both a social, as well as an economic function. Throughout aviation history, most airports have fulfilled both functions in mutual accord as shown by the solid line in Figure 2. As long as airport operators manage the airport such that their overall performance remains below point A, both economic and social performance can be increased.

The lower, dashed curve shows what happens if an airport operator would single-mindedly pursue profit maximization. Initially, it is possible to increase profitability, but beyond point B its societal performance will significantly be degraded (e.g. because of in-adequate respect for health and environmental regulations). Pushing for even greater profitability eventually results in active and violent reaction by society against the violation of societal norms, which ultimately jeopardizes economic efficiency (point D). We hypothesize that some airport operators have already arrived at or at least have been in point B or

C, given the strong opposition against airport expansion.

The upper, dotted curve shows the situation in which an airport operator is mainly fo-cused on providing its public service, no matter what the cost. Initially, societal perfor-mance can be improved at the expense of economic performance (point E). Beyond point F, economic performance is degraded to such an extent that it will no longer be possible to maintain adequate social performance (point G).

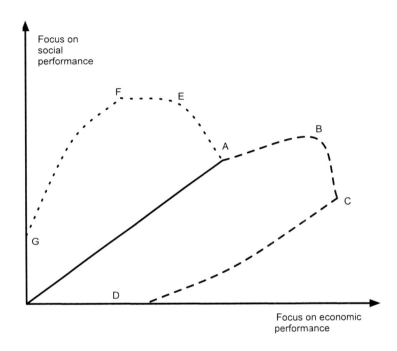

Figure 2. The trade-off between economic and societal performance. **Source: (author?)** [1]

Finding the balance between economic and social performance is difficult for airport operators. Increasing privatization causes airport operators to move toward a more business-oriented management approach. Airport operators are indeed more entrepreneurial in the development of their business, which is not limited anymore to facilitating aircraft opera-tions at their airfield [25]. The Airport City concept, developed by Schiphol Group, is a good example of the result of *entrepreneurial* strategic planning [36].

This approach to developing the business focuses on the products and services offered to the clients of the airport operator [21, 22]. There appears to be no explicit attention in the strategy development process to the externalities (e.g. environmental impacts) of the airport operator's activities.

Of course, the externalities are addressed by airport operators, but many times as an afterthought to comply with local, national, or international regulations. For example, Schiphol's Group long-term vision, which was recently published, merely identifies what needs to happen to secure its profit-making assets [37]. It only vaguely identifies what needs to be done to mitigate environmental impacts. It does not identify any strategies that truly address them.

It is not advisable to just 'copy' an approach to strategic planning that works in other sectors. Managing and planning an airport is fundamentally different from developing, for example, new consumer products. Obviously, there are similarities when the passenger perspective is considered. Passengers are the direct customers of an airport and hence the primary source of income. Developing new services that meet passenger needs (e.g. sport facilities, entertainment) makes perfect sense, as they are essential for creating a competitive advantage.

An approach to airport strategic planning should be more holistic. It should not only focus on the firm's products for their primary customers like passengers and airlines. Proper attention should be given to its 'by-products' as well. Since an airport is a very large system, occupying a vast amount of land and producing significant environmental impacts, there are many stakeholders (see also Figure 1). The airport operator needs to make sure that it offers a product mix, including externalities, that satisfies all stakeholders.

We state that maintaining the balance between economic and societal performance is essential for the sustainability of the airport. Obviously, airport operators should be economically sound and especially privatized airports need to be able to make a profit, but increasing profitability should not be stressed to the limit.

This balance can only be found and maintained if the airport operator and their stakeholders are provided decision support that quantifies the effect of wide range of strategies on the airport's performance, for multiple scenarios representing the many plausible futures that might unfold.

### 1.3.   Outline of Remainder of Chapter

The remainder of this chapter discusses the problems of, approaches to, and resources used for airport strategic planning in Section 2. Section 3. identifies what is needed in terms of decision support, based on the high-level goals of airport decisionmakers. It also describes the HARMOS decision support system and the principles that drove its design and implementation. The functional design of the DSS is described in detail in Section 4., illustrating how the HARMOS DSS has been designed to address the problems with current airport strategic planning. Section 5. concludes the chapter by discussing how the HARMOS DSS meets the generic needs of decisionmakers and showing how its use is compatible with current planning practice.

## 2.   Airport Strategic Planning

This section explores airport strategic planning (ASP) in more detail. The problem areas with current airport strategic planning are discussed in detail in Section 2.1. Section 2.2. describes various approaches to airport strategic planning. The extent to which the different approaches address the problem areas is discussed in Section 2.3. Section 2.4. takes a detailed look at the resources involved in an airport strategic planning effort. Computer-based systems intended to increase the efficiency of using tools for airport performance analysis are discussed in Section 2.5.

## 2.1. Problems with Current Airport Strategic Planning

The way the strategic planning activity is currently undertaken leads to a number of different problems. Many scholars have discussed the practice of airport planning and its associated problems.

(author?) [10] provide a broad overview of the practice of airport planning around the world. (author?) [15] presents a global survey of airport developments, describing failure and success related to airport planning. Based on a case study of Denver International Aiport (DIA), (author?) [23] conclude that decision making and planning theory should be revisited to better account for uncertainty and stakeholder interests. Examples of airport design mistakes and planning failures are frequently used as illustration by(author?) [14].

Each of these authors draw similar conclusions with respect to the underlying causes of airport planning failures. We identified similar and additional problems. For the sake of discussing and addressing them, a division in three problem areas is used:

1. Efficiency of problem-solving;

2. Modeling the future;

3. Stakeholder involvement.

Each of these problem areas is discussed in more detail in the following sections.

### 2.1.1. Problem Area I: Efficiency of Problem Solving

For organizational purposes, the planning problem facing an airport operator is usually divided into smaller subproblems (related to e.g airport capacity and delay, noise, emissions, or finance). The results from the subproblems are later integrated to become part of the solution to the overall planning problem, which leads to the following problems:

**Resources are used inefficiently.** Often, people (or organizations) focusing on different aspects of the system work on different parts of the analysis, each using different models/tools, assumptions, and data.

It is therefore difficult to produce a consistent, integrated set of results that can be used to assess the effect of changes to the airport system [33, 39, 46, 52].

**Inconsistencies.** The specific questions related to a particular planning problem are usually not on the table at the same time, and they may be on different tables within the organization, leading to inconsistent information, and contradictory assumptions.

The risk of introducing inconsistencies is higher within large airport organizations, because different business units, departments, or external consultants are involved, who do not continuously keep each other informed of their progress, preliminary results, and findings.

**Lack of an integral view.** There is not much synergy during problem-solving, because the subproblems are solved by different people (or even different organizations).

An integral view of the airport's performance can be produced only by manually collecting, combining, and post-processing the individual results, which is very time consuming, and often leads to inconsistent results.

So, the airport strategic planning activity is inefficient in terms of time and resources. For example, the Master Plan for Los Angeles International Airport (LAX), which was agreed upon in 2006, took ten years to develop.

### 2.1.2.   Problem Area II: Modeling the Future

The future of aviation is uncertain. Airport planning practice does not recognize this very well, which leads to the following problems:

**Single view of the future.** Planners consider only a limited number of plausible futures (usually only one).

> Many airport development plans are based on only a single view of the future. A single prediction of the future is used as the basis for determining which airport facilities are required.

> Such a *predict-and-act* approach to airport planning is likely to produce a poorly performing strategy or plan, because it is very unlikely that the predicted future will also become the actual future. In reality, 'the forecast is always wrong' as stated by **(author?)** [3] and repeated by many others [14].

**Lack of consideration of external factors.** The future that is considered is usually based on only a single trend extrapolation of demand.

> Other external factors, such as technology, regulations, and demographics, are not considered in detail, if at all. Besides the economic factors that drive traffic demand, other external factors should also be considered. Technology (e.g. the introduction of the new A380 aircraft), regulations (e.g. more stringent noise standards), and demographics (e.g. regional housing and industry development), should be explicitly considered when modeling the future, because they have an impact on the demand itself, the airport operations, and airport performance.

**Too few alternatives are analyzed.** Because of the single view of the future, only a short list of alternative strategies is considered, based on what is known to have more or less worked in the past.

> **(author?)** [10] as well as **(author?)** [4] report that the focus in planning studies is almost exclusively on provision of capacity to meet forecast demand.

Current practice inadequately addresses the uncertain future, leading to either severe congestion or excess capacity at airports, both of which are very costly [14, 26].

### 2.1.3.   Problem Area III: Stakeholder Involvement

Stakeholders are not meaningfully involved in the airport operator's planning process, which leads to the following problems:

**Inadequate collaboration among stakeholders.** The current approach does not facilitate easy and comprehensive collaboration among all the stakeholders, resulting in excluding some of them altogether, or involving them too late.

History shows that this causes serious problems when an airport operator tries to implement its Master Plan. Numerous examples, some of them very successful, exist of legal actions from the excluded stakeholders to prevent a plan from becoming reality [10, 15, 23].

**Exclusion of stakeholders or their concerns.** Stakeholder concerns are not taken into account or the stakeholders themselves are completely excluded from the planning process.

This causes serious problems when an airport operator tries to implement its strategic plan. If some stakeholders feel that the plan for an airport's development does not satisfy their objectives, they will hamper the implementation of the strategy, through legal actions and lobbying, among others.

**Conflicts.** There are often conflicts among the various stakeholders [28, 30, 38].

**(author?)** [10] explicitly mention that within airport planning studies there is a general failure to achieve a transparent balance in areas of competition, air transport, regional development, and local citizen's rights.

Stakeholders are likely to argue about results, assumptions, and the methodologies that were used, either because they were not involved or they do not understand each other (or both).

Two examples of plans that faced major opposition and implementation delay are the plans for the new runways at Boston Logan Airport (proposed in the early 70s and opened in 2006) and the so-called 'Polderbaan' at Amsterdam Airport Schiphol (proposed in the 1970s and opened in 2003).

So, current practice does not facilitate easy and comprehensive collaboration among the people involved in a planning study themselves nor with the airport stakeholders.

## 2.2. Approaches to Airport Strategic Planning

The definition of airport strategic planning by by Wells and Young, presented earlier in Section 2., does not imply a *specific approach* to airport strategic planning. There are many different approaches to coordinate an all encompassing planning effort with the intention to maximize the future potential of an airport. In the following sections, a number of approaches to airport strategic planning are described.

### 2.2.1. Master Planning

Currently, the airport Master Plan is the core artifact of airport planning. Master Planning [18] was born out of the need to interact with existing land use planning processes and to justify investments. The Master Plan is intended to be the strategy for the development of the airport.

The basic purpose of a Master Plan is to set out a plan for future development designed to meet projected needs taking environmental and socioeconomic impacts into consideration [19, 24]. Airport Master Plans are prepared to support the modernization or expansion of existing airports or the creation of a new airport.

In the United States, a Master Plan is required to receive funds from the federal government. Although most other countries do not have such a formal requirement, many airport operators periodically create a Master Plan.

The Master Plan is primarily an engineering and architectural study. The main focus is on the development of the physical infrastructure (i.e. runways, buildings); operational concepts or management issues are not explicitly considered [14, p.62].

The main elements of a Master Plan are (as described in the FAA guidelines):

**Pre-planning.** The pre-planning process is about determining the initial need for a Master Plan, selecting consultants, developing a study design, and apply for funding of the study.

**Public Involvement.** Once a consultant team is under contract, a public involvement program should be established and the key issues of the various stakeholders have to be identified.

**Environmental Considerations.** The environmental requirements need to be clearly understood to be able to move forward with each project in the recommended development program.

**Existing Conditions.** Inventory of pertinent data for use in subsequent plan elements.

**Aviation Forecasts.** Forecasts of aeronautical demand for short-, medium-, and long-term time frames based on a single view of the future.

**Facility Requirements.** Assessment of the ability of the existing airport, both airside and landside, to support the forecast demand. The demand levels that trigger the need for additions or improvements to facilities need to be established. The need for new facilities also needs to be determined.

**Alternatives Development and Evaluation.** Identification of options to meet projected facility requirements and alternative configurations for each major component. The expected performance of each alternative is to be assessed for a wide range of evaluation criteria, including its operational, environmental, and financial impacts. A recommended development alternative will emerge from this process and will be further refined in subsequent tasks. This element should identify the purpose and need for subsequent environmental documents.

**Airport Layout Plans.** A set of drawings that provides a graphic representation of the long-term development for an airport. The primary drawing is the Airport Layout Plan (ALP).

**Facilities Implementation Plan.** Provides a summary description of the recommended improvements and associated costs. The schedule of improvements depends on the levels of demand that trigger the need for expansion of existing facilities.

**Financial Feasibility Analysis.** Identification of the financial plan for the airport, describing the funding of the recommended projects in the Master Plan, and financial feasibility of the program.

Quantifying environmental and socio-economic impacts is not addressed in detail within Master Planning. The FAA only encourages planners to consider possible environmental and socio-economic costs associated with alternative development concepts, and identify possible means of avoiding, minimizing, or mitigating those impacts. Only after the Master Plan is completed, is a more detailed quantitative assessment of environmental impacts carried out, but this hardly affects the decision making process [38].

Most Master Planning studies take a very long time to complete and run the risk of becoming obsolete by the time they are completed, because of new conditions that had not been taken into account in the planning. This is typical because Master Planning assumes a reasonable idea about the future can be determined by forecasting (problem area II). Looking at the events in the aviation industry throughout history shows that there have been many surprises and discontinuities. Most of the time, Master Plans are inflexible and do not provide any means to respond to such events.

## 2.2.2.  Dynamic Strategic Planning

Dynamic Strategic Planning (DSP) is an approach to airport planning that has been proposed by **(author?)** [14, p.81]:

> *Dynamic Strategic Planning emphasizes flexibility.* Its fundamental premise is that airport operators must dynamically adjust their plans and designs over time to accommodate the variety of futures that may occur. This emphasis distinguishes dynamic strategic planning from the traditional master or strategic planning, both of which build upon relatively fixed visions of the future.

One of the key principles of Dynamic Strategic Planning is the examination of several forecasts instead of only one as is typically the case in Master Planning. Another key principle is to encourage planners to be proactive and shape the loads on the system, rather that reacting passively to the load.

DSP extends Master Planning such that planning becomes proactive and flexible. The steps for preparing dynamic strategic plans as presented by**(author?)** [14, p.84] are:

1. Inventory of existing conditions;
2. Forecast range of future traffic, *along with possible scenarios for its major components (international, domestic, and transfer traffic, airline routes, etc.)*
3. Determine facility requirements *suitable for the several possible levels and types of traffic*;
4. Develop several alternatives for comparative analysis;
5. Select the most acceptable *first-phase development, the one that enables subsequent and appropriate responses to the possible future conditions.*

The elements in italics are additions to the Master Planning process. So, DSP still provides the orderly process of Master Planning, but encourages to think strategically about an airport's future by examining the effects of the alternatives on airport performance for several forecasts rather than one. Actual implementation of the alternatices is done through a phased development, adapted to the events as they unfold in the real world. So far, DSP has only been applied on a few occasions (see for example**(author?)** [12]).

## 2.2.3.  Other Approaches

Other approaches for airport strategic planning have been discussed in the literature as well [9, 10, 29]. **(author?)** [10] state that airport planners should *adapt creatively for the future.* **(author?)** [29] discusses how airport planning might potentially benefit from adopting the adaptive approach to policymaking. Their work provides examples of policies that could be implemented to better deal with the uncertain future. **(author?)** [9] propose a flexible planning approach, but this early work only describes characteristics of this planning approach and some basic advice on how to be prepared for the future (e.g. implementing backup systems, buying insurance). **(author?)** [8] describes the flexible planning approach in some more detail, outlining various methods and techniques (e.g. real options) that can be used by planners.

## 2.3. How are the Approaches to Airport Strategic Planning Addressing the Problem Areas?

The question is to what extent the approaches to airport strategic planning (previous section) address the problem areas identified in Section 2.1.. Table 1 provides an overview, which is now discussed in more detail.

### Table 1. Approaches versus problem areas

| Problem area | Approach | | |
|---|---|---|---|
| | Master Planning | Dynamic Strategic Planning | Other approaches |
| Efficiency of problem solving (I) | Sequence of analytical steps | Advice to appropriately use computer-based tools | Not addressed |
| Modeling the future (II) | Single demand forecast | Scenarios | Scenarios, among others |
| Stakeholder Involvement (III) | Advice for early involvement | Fair negotiation process after design of a plan | Not addressed |

The FAA Advisory Circular (AC) on Master Planning provides some support for problem solving (Problem Area I) by defining a series of elements that should be subsequently addressed within the Master Plan. The recent update of the AC on Master Planning also pays some more attention to involving the stakeholders (Problem Area III), by strongly advising to indentify and involve stakeholders as soon as possible. The updated AC still does not provide a way to deal with the uncertain future (Problem Area II).

DSP is more complicated than Master Planning and therefore **(author?)** [14, p.82] advise management of the additional effort related to problem solving (Problem Area I) by the *appropriate use of computer-based tools*. Since DSP is a dynamic approach, uncertainty about the future is recognized very well and multiple scenarios and options analysis are used to deal with this uncertainty (Problem Area II). DSP does not provide any means to involve the stakeholders (Problem Area III). It is only assumed that a fair negotiation process will emerge [13, p.7]. In order to facilitate this negotiation process, DSP includes procedures for dealing with the perspectives and powers of the participants in the planning process.

The other dynamic approaches do not address any aspect of the problem solving process (Problem Area I). Obviously, they do provide an adequate way to address the uncertain future (Problem Area II), very similar to DSP. Stakeholder involvement (Problem Area III) is not addressed by these approaches.

DSP and other approaches to strategic planning that promote flexibility have been around for a while, but have hardly been adopted by airport operators. The lack of adoption of new planning approaches could be due to a resistance to organizational change. Airport operators could also have a blind spot for the urgency to revise their planning approaches to the changing business environment.

In addition to such factors, we think that the lack of adoption could be caused by the fact that these new approaches leave the other two problem areas—efficiency of problem solving (Problem Area I) and the involvement of stakeholders (Problem Area III)—untouched. In our opinion, a new way of supporting airport strategic planning should therefore deal with all three problem areas concurrently.

We have already discussed that the involvement of the stakeholders is crucial for implementation of the proposed strategies. The strategic planning process cannot stay an internal business process that is, often asynchronously, accompanied by a societal trade-off process (see Figure 1). Both processes should merge into an open and single strategic planning process that empowers all stakeholders and allows the airport operator and their stakeholders to commit to action (i.e. implementing the strategies collectively agreed upon).

To improve our understanding of the resources required and used for a strategic planning effort, a generalized description of the tools and other resources is provided in the next section.

## 2.4.   The Resources Involved in a Strategic Planning Effort

Figure 3 provides a conceptual map of airport strategic planning and is not meant to represent any specific airport operator's setting. The map has been determined empirically and shows that many resources are involved, both inside and outside the organization.

A significant number of people (experts, planners, and advisors), some possibly using tools, participate in the effort to turn data into information that is relevant for decision making by the airport's management.

The following description assumes that the airport operator is ultimately responsible for airport strategic planning and coordinates the planning effort. In reality, airport planning consultants might be heavily involved and even responsible for creating definitive plans. The relationship between the airport operator and the consultants depends on the local setting, size of the airport operator's organization, and the regulatory framework. Each of these resources is now discussed in more detail.

### 2.4.1.   The People

As can be seen in Figure 3, there are two types of people involved in planning—those outside and inside the airport operator's organization.

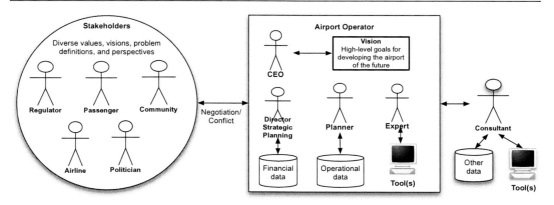

Figure 3. Current planning: a huge coordination effort (Problem Area I) and potential conflicts (Problem Area III).

People inside the airport operator's organization are the ones that are directly involved in the strategic planning process; they carry out different types of activities in order to identify those strategies that have potential for realizing the airport's management vision.

People outside the airport operator's organization are typically associated with organizations or groups that have a stake in the airport's development, which we collectively call the airport stakeholders. These stakeholders (e.g. airlines, air navigation service providers (ANSP), aviation authorities, community groups) have conflicting goals and objectives with respect to the airport's development.

The way the stakeholders are involved depends on the local setting and their role may vary from merely making their views known to being official partners in making agreements about the actual airport development and operations. Stakeholders have significant power (e.g. public campaigns, lobbying, appealing to court) to influence an airport operator's planning process and will do so whenever they think their objectives and goals are not sufficiently taken into account.

### 2.4.2.   The Data and Information

Creating an effective strategic plan requires consistent data and information about a wide range of aspects. The types of data and information are: (i) the business objectives, usually implicitly contained in an organization's vision and further specified (qualitatively or quantitatively) by the airport's management team; (ii) the future context for the airport's operation in terms of economic, technological, regulatory, and demographic developments; (iii) the airport system and its environment, modeled at the appropriate level of detail; (iv) system changes—structural, operational, and/or managerial—due to strategies; and (v) quantitative airport performance information for the given future context and strategies.

With respect to airport performance, information at different levels of detail is required concerning capacity and delay, and environmental impacts (noise, emissions, and third party risk). Nowadays, the financial implications of a plan from the business perspective (as opposed to a socio-economic perspective) are also important. Often, outside consultants are contracted to provide information about some or all of these airport performance aspects.

### 2.4.3.   The Tools

Much of the data and information are generated using analytical tools, typically related to capacity and delay, environmental impacts (noise, emissions, and third party risk), and financial performance. In most cases, this data and information is not generated in a consistent, integrated way. Typically, only a single aspect of the airport's operation (e.g. its capacity and delay or noise or emissions) is evaluated at a single time. Only if there is a problem to be expected with another aspect additional analyses are conducted.

The reason for this is that different aspects are usually assessed by different experts, who are not all from the same organization. First, an expert needs to get appropriate data and information. Next, the data and information have to be processed in order to be used as input to the tools being used. Then the experts execute the appropriate runs with their tools, post-process the outcomes, and return the results to an advisor, who either documents the (aggregate) results in a report or directly communicates the results to the decisionmaker. If either the decision advisor or the decisionmaker is not satisfied with the results, or needs an assessment of another situation, the whole process is repeated.

### 2.4.4.   Underlying Cause of the Problems with Current Airport Strategic Planning

In Section 2.2.2., we mentioned that **(author?)** [14, p.82] state that the additional effort for creating a dynamic strategic plan can be managed by the appropriate use of computer-based tools. They also mention that there are plenty of models and tools available to enable good analysis of alternative developments under different conditions, but that computer models are not a substitute for *strategic thinking*. Tools are necessary for the calculation of the facilities under different loads, but they are not sufficient to develop a good strategic plan.

We believe that it is difficult for airport operators to make sure computer-based tools are used appropriately. Actually, also **(author?)** [33, p.149] aknowledges this fact. Even if airport operators are capable of appropriately using computer-based tools, the actual use of those tools and generating the relevant information for decision making and planning from the tool outputs will probably be a huge effort. This effort might get in the way of strategic thinking, because there is not enough time left or too much attention is needed for tool-related issues.

Our opinion is that the major fundamental cause of the problems discussed in Section 2.1. is the dispersion of people (knowledge), data and information, and tools within the organization of the airport operator and its stakeholders (Figure 3). Resources cannot be easily integrated, consolidated, and focused on producing effective strategies for developing the airport of the future.

People, data and information, and tools cannot quickly be deployed for analysis and subsequent synthesis so that the relevant information for decision making becomes quickly available. Inherently, this leads to an inefficient problem solving process that is not able to support the creation of strategies for an airport's development that are acceptable to all stakeholders.

## 2.5.  Computer-Based Systems for Airport Performance Analysis

From the previous section, it is clear that an airport operator's approach to strategic planning heavily relies on computer tools for providing information about the quantitative effects of the proposed strategies on the airport's performance. Because an airport is a system that produces many effects, including environmental, it is important (and often legally required) to estimate all these effects as a result of changes to the airport's infrastructure, operation, and/or management.

Within a strategic planning study, one of the major tasks is to quickly and easily evaluate the effect on various airport performance aspects due to changes to the airport system and/or operation. Doing this manually requires many tasks to be performed related to preparing data for the various tools, running and coordinating the use of these tools, and processing all of their outputs. The appropriate and efficient use of tools for airport performance analysis is therefore important.

Since the (repetitive) tasks just mentioned are much better performed by a computer-based system, there have been many projects that focus on designing and building systems for airport performance analysis [see e.g. 39, 43, 52]. The goal of those projects is twofold: (i) to remove the burden of users having to select the appropriate tools, and (ii) to provide an end-user with an integrated view of an airport's performance for different situations. As such, the projects focus on integrating tools in a single computer-based system for airport performance analysis (partly addressing Problem Area I).

Since all of these projects strongly focus on tools and models, they result in computer-based systems that support only the *analysis* phase of the problem solving process. The systems provide hardly any functionality to support the *formulation* and *interpretation* phases of problem-solving. Support for the problem formulation phase is important, because during this phase potential problems or opportunities that an airport operator will be facing or can take advantage of are identified. The formulation phase thus includes thinking about scenarios that capture the uncertainties about the future (among other activities).

The interpretation phase needs to be supported as well, because during that phase all the different potential strategies for developing and managing the airport are to be discussed with and explained to all the airport stakeholders. Involvement of all stakeholders has been identified as another essential element of any approach to airport strategic planning.

Strategic planning itself is an iterative process of formulation, analysis, and interpretation. Computer-based systems that support only the analysis phase have, therefore, failed to be used in practice for airport strategic planning. In the next section, we identify what is needed to tackle the problems discussed in Section 2.1. at their root.

## 3.   What Is Needed?

Unfortunately, Master Planning does not provide an adequate way to deal with the uncertain future (Problem Area II). Involvement of the stakeholders is addressed somewhat better by the recent update of the FAA AC on Master Planning [19], which now strongly advises the identification and involvement of all stakeholders as early as possible within a Master Planning study (Problem Area III).

DSP is a new approach to airport strategic planning that is well equipped to deal with the uncertain future (Problem Area II). It does however not provide a way to meaningfully involve the stakeholders (Problem Area III).

With respect to the efficiency of the problem solving process (Problem Area I), both Master Planning and DSP leave the use of various tools—to generate the relevant information for decision making—up to the people involved in a particular strategic planning effort. We believe that this negatively affects the speed and content of the strategic planning study. Too much time is spent on preparing data for tools, running them, and processing their outputs. Additionally, inconsistencies in the generated information are introduced, because the tools are not integrated.

DSP, other approaches, and the computer-based systems for airport performance analysis developed so far do not seem to directly satisfy the needs of planners and decisionmakers, since neither of them have really been adopted by airport operators.

We believe that the lack of adoption is because each of them addresses only one problem area that exists with airport strategic planning today. Our research will therefore address all three problem areas concurrently, thereby closing the gap between the needs of decisionmakers and planners and the design of the decision support.

The increasingly complex and dynamic set of circumstances in airport planning motivates the need for a decision support system (DSS) that offers systematic problem analysis and that supports multiple stakeholders addressing a range of planning problems that cannot be specified in advance.

Our research has found a way to better support airport strategic planning practice through a DSS. We use the definition of DSS by Turban:

> An interactive, flexible, and adaptable computer-based information system, developed for supporting the solution of a non-structured management problem for improved decision making (author?) [40].

(author?) [51] identifies six generic needs that a DSS needs to fulfill: (1) projecting into the future despite uncertainty; (2) making trade-offs among competing goals, which implies that different alternatives can be evaluated and compared; (3) managing large amounts of information simultaneously; (4) analyzing complex situations within constraints on time and resources; (5) visualizing and manipulating those visualizations; and (6) making heuristic judgments, even if they are only qualitative. Our design effort makes sure that these needs are fulfilled.

A vision about decision support is required to identify what is needed to improve the practice of airport strategic planning. The vision identifies the high-level goals of airport operators (Section 3.1.), states the problem to be solved (Section 3.2.), and presents a potential solution to that problem (Section 3.3.). The key principles that drive the design and implementation of our solution to decision support are briefly presented in Section 3.4.

## 3.1.  High-Level Goals

(author?) [2] identified three types of management decisions: (1) strategic planning decisions; (2) management control decisions; and (3) operational control decisions.

Figure 4 shows these decisions, related to potential to add value to an airport, as a function of the planning interval. The most potential to add value, strongly related to strategic planning decisions, is at the left end of the planning spectrum.

*Strategic planning* decisions are decisions related to choosing high-level policies and objectives, and associated resource allocations. By strategic thinking, airport decisionmakers and planners should identify the role of the airport and services to be delivered such that the most value, *preferably for all stakeholders* is added. By doing so, airport operators would be able to balance their economic and social performance (Section 1.2.).

In order to think strategically, a divergent, *intuitive* and creative mode of thinking is required leading to a business *vision* for the airport of the future. A next step is to identify all the potential *strategies* that might help realizing this vision. After these strategies have been evaluated, all the strategies are assessed through comparison among each other and against the objectives of the airport operator, and its stakeholders. The comparison either results in a strategy to be selected for *implementation* or in a request for more analysis, evaluating variations of a strategy, or completely new strategies.

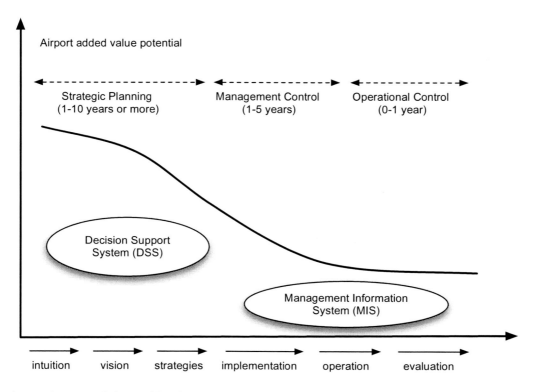

Figure 4. Potential to add value as a function of the planning interval. Source: personal communication with former strategic planner at Amsterdam Airport Schiphol.

The implementation of a strategy is related to *Management Control* decisions, which are decisions made for the purpose of assuring effectivess in the acquisition and use of resources. The implemented strategies result in a different *operation* of the airport.

The effect of the changes to the airport operation should be monitored, i.e. an *evaluation* of the real-world airport performance should be carried out to assess whether the objectives of the intended strategies are truly met. If not, corrective actions should be taken at the operational level; these actions are *Operational Control* decisions, which are decisions made for the purpose of assuring effectiveness in the performance of operations.

Another possibility is to formulate completely new strategies, or even start over with a complete new vision, making the process, shown in Figure 4, an iterative and cyclic process.

Managing the day-to-day operation does not provide many opportunities to substantially change the rules that govern the airport operation, let alone change the airport's infrastructure. Therefore, its potential to add value is low.

However, managers and other staff not directly involved in organizing the daily airport operation can and should take the time to think through how the airport could be developed on the longer term [41, p.2]. Because these people are not completely occupied with the realization of short-term, operational goals, they have the time to *study* plausible futures for the airport and the strategies to face those futures. Since many plausible futures and strategies are conceivable, especially if a planning study spans a period of 10 years or more, it is clear that conducting such a study is very challenging.

The potential of strategic planning decisions to add value can only be realized if airport operators and their stakeholders are appropriately supported for conducting studies that lead to informed decisions.

Our survey and analysis of computer-based systems for airport performance analysis [49] makes clear that Decision Support Systems to support the activities of formulating a vision, and identifying, evaluating, and comparing strategies, do not exist as yet (Section 2.5.).

This is not necessarily true of decision support for management and operational control decisions: For these type of decisions, airport operators usually have some sort of Management Information System (MIS) in place[2] (shown as well in Figure 4).

## 3.2. Problem Statement Driving the Design of the DSS

Airport operators are not very well supported in making strategic planning decisions, which results in a number of problems. Summarizing these problems, leads to the following problem statement, which drove the design of the DSS:

> Airport decisionmakers cannot realize the full potential of an airport to add value because they, and the planners and experts that support them, have difficulties to fully understand the system, its problems, and the potential strategies for addressing these problems.
>
> Although the people that support the decisionmakers try to come up with the relevant information, they are hardly able to do so in a timely manner. Planners and experts do not have the means to execute a systematic problem solving process that efficiently handles (collecting, generating, processing and interpreting) the large amounts of data and information from the various sources within and outside the airport organization (Section 2.1.1.)
>
> Decisionmakers, planners, and experts are not fully aware of how uncertainty about the future would affect the airport's performance. They lack a method to adequately and quantitatively take into account the inherently uncertain developments in demand, technology, regulations, and demography (Section 2.1.2.).

---

[2]Personal communication with Manager Environmental Capacity at Amsterdam Airport Schiphol.

Airport decisionmakers find it difficult to understand how proposed strategies affect their own goals and those of their stakeholders. As a result they are not able to design strategies that are effective in satisfying both. Essentially, the decisionmakers are suffering from a lack of information that is relevant to their decision making in the multi-stakeholder context (Section 2.1.3.).

This problem statement revisits and summarizes each of the problem areas discussed in detail in Section 2.1., and is the starting point for defining a solution (in the next section).

## 3.3.   HARMOS: A DSS for Airport Strategic Planning

The underlying cause of the problems, presented in the problem statement, is the dispersion of people (knowledge), data and information, and tools within the organization of the airport operator and those of its stakeholders (as shown before in Figure 3).

Current airport strategic planning includes many common, repetitive activities, executed by many people, which is very time-consuming and error-prone. It would make a lot of sense to incorporate these resources—the data and information, and tools—into a Decision Support System (DSS) that supports the people in their activities.

By doing so, decisionmakers, planners and experts can work more efficiently and effectively in analyzing problems, thereby unlocking their creative powers, rather than spending large amounts of time on activities that a DSS can do faster and better.

The DSS integrates the problem solving process, data and information, and tools within the organization so that solving a new strategic problem does not require starting from scratch every time one arises.

Our proposed solution, which we call the HARMOS[3] decision support system, enables an airport operator to deploy its resources—people (knowledge), data and information, and tools—more efficiently, resulting in an improved understanding of the airport system, its problems, and potential strategies for airport development, while explicitly facilitating the involvement of stakeholders in the planning process. A graphical representation of HARMOS, and how it is positioned in the decision environment, is shown in Figure 5.

The HARMOS DSS is the centrepiece of the planning effort. HARMOS provides *coordination* of the data and tools, so that consistent and *relevant information* for planning and decision making is obtained.

As such, HARMOS significantly reduces the huge coordination effort that currently needs to be taken by airport staff and consultants. Instead of spending their time on this coordination effort, planners and experts can use their valuable time to more extensively explore planning problems and the potential strategies that solve those problems.

The uncertain future can be adequately addressed by using the DSS to develop multiple scenarios. Functionality for developing scenarios provides a direct means to actively engage stakeholders [34].

HARMOS enables airport staff *and* stakeholders to effectively share information and work together on their problems so that they gain an understanding of each other's perspectives and objectives. Only when there is a mutual understanding is it possible to look

---

[3]HARMOS is the Greek root for harmony and the act of bringing people, concepts and objects together. Asian philosophy calls this the *Aiki* principle, which is the key principle of the Japanese martial art Aikido (practiced by the first author).

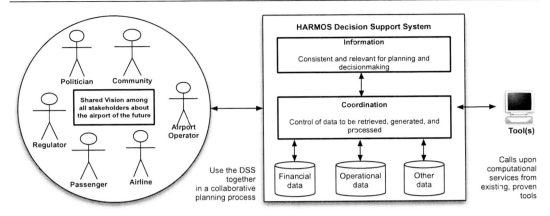

Figure 5. HARMOS, bringing people together.

for strategies that are satisfactory to all parties involved (see the left side of Figure 5). As a result, an airport operator and its stakeholders can create a *shared vision* for the future development of the airport.

## 3.4.    Design Principles of the HARMOS DSS

Our solution, the HARMOS Decision Support System, has the potential to improve the practice of airport strategic planning. However, the envisioned DSS needs to be designed and implemented, which is not a trivial task.

Many DSS development projects do not deliver enough value for the end-users and hence the delivered DSSs are not adopted by practioners [5, 16].

During our DSS design and development effort, we had to make sure we did not fall into this trap. In order to do that, two things were needed: (1) a set of key design principles; and (2) an appropriate DSS development process. The key design principles are briefly discussed here. The DSS development process is not further discussed [for more information, see 49].

The key principles drive the HARMOS design and implementation. These principles help to *formalize* the domain of airport strategic planning. Formalization of the domain is necessary for turning the conceptual solution, presented in Section 3.3., into a software system.

By adopting a set of design principles, we are able to effectively deal with the complexity of the airport strategic planning—the airport system and how it is affected by external factors and strategies, and the uncertain future—and capture this in a consistent *Domain Model* [49, Chapter 7]. A Domain Model is a *system of abstractions* that describes *selected* aspects of a domain and can be used to solve problems related to that domain [17]. The key design principles for designing the Domain Model (and hence the DSS) are:

**Policy Analysis.** The policy analysis approach, according to **(author?)** [45], is used to design the problem solving functionality of the DSS. Policy analysis is a systematic, well-defined, complete, and comprehensive approach for problem solving and decision making.

The approach according to Walker defines a framework for structuring planning problems and a process with seven steps to go through the problem solving. These steps are:

**Step 1: Identify the problem.** Identify the planning problems (this also cover a need to identify new opportunites), clarify constraints on possible strategies, identify the airport stakeholders, and discover the major operative factors.

**Step 2: Identify objectives.** Identify objectives from the airport operator, and the objectives of other stakeholders, so that later it can be determined if (1) a strategy solves the problem identified or seizes the opportunity, and (2) how a strategy affects the various stakeholders.

**Step 3: Decide on outcome indicators.** Identify the consequences of a strategy that can be estimated (quantitatively or qualitatively) and that are directly related to the objectives.

**Step 4: Develop scenarios.** Define the future contexts within which the problems are to be analyzed and the strategies will have to function. In this step, several plausible scenarios are developed.

**Step 5: Identify strategies.** Specify the strategies, in terms of structural, operational, and managerial changes to the system, whose consequences are to be estimated.

**Step 6: Analyze strategies.** Determine the consequences that are likely to follow if the strategy is actually implemented in each of the scenarios, where the consequences are measured in terms of the outcome indicators chosen in Step 3.

**Step 7: Compare strategies.** Examine the strategies in terms of their estimated outcomes for each of the scenarios, making tradeoffs among them, and choosing a preferred strategy (or combination of strategies), which is robust across multiple futures.

If none of the strategies examined so far is good enough to be implemented (or if new aspects of the problem have been found, or the analysis has led to new strategies), return to Step 1, 4, or 5.

Steps 1–3 are related to problem *formulation*, steps 4–6 are related to *analysis*, and step 7 is about *interpretation*. Strategies are designed to change the system such that the airport's performance (measured in terms of the outcomes of interest) meets the decisionmaker's objectives. The objectives of the decisionmakers are explicitly identified early on in the policy analysis process (Step 3). This evokes strategic thinking about planning problems and the potential strategies that might be able to address them.

Policy analysis explicitly recognizes that problems caused by systems affect many stakeholders, and hence finding solutions needs to be done by involving those stakeholders. Policy analysis also recognizes that there is uncertainty about the future and provides different methods to deal with uncertainty.

The majority of problems in airport planning are due to the lack of stakeholder involvement and the absence of a method to account for an uncertain future. Policy analysis is therefore ideally suited for investigating airport strategic planning problems.

The DSS is thus based on a well-defined and systematic methodology for problem solving, which is an important requirement for software to support strategic planning at the management level [44].

**Integration.** As already pointed out, the fundamental cause of the problems in current airport planning is a dispersion of data, tools, information, and knowledge within the organization of the airport operator and its stakeholders.

An integrative approach toward the deployment of people, data/information, and tools is needed to address these problems.

These principles have already been described in detail in **(author?)** [48] and are therefore not further discussed here. Besides these principles, the HARMOS design and implementation is driven directly by user requirements, which are described in the next section.

# 4. User Functionality of the DSS

In order to define the user-specific HARMOS functionality, *use cases* have been written. Writing use cases is a very effective method for identifying the actors, and identifying and specifying the functional requirements of a software system [11]. Use cases describe the *interaction* between a software system and its actors and are *goal-oriented*.

## 4.1. Identifying the DSS Users

The first step in the DSS development process is to analyze the business activities, in order to identify the scope and users for the software system. For a software system, typically three categories of actors (or users) can be distinguished: Primary, supporting, and off-stage actors. The primary actors are those actors that have their goals fulfilled through using services of the system. They need to be identified because through them the user goals, which drive the use cases, are found. The primary actors follow directly from the conceptual model presented in Figure 6.

This figure shows the roles of the people involved in an airport strategic planning effort, including the main sources of information that people with these roles use or have available. This is a very schematic representation. In reality, each of the roles and sources of information is interlinked with one another. Also, strategies come not only from the decisionmaker, but can be put forward by people with any of the other roles as well.

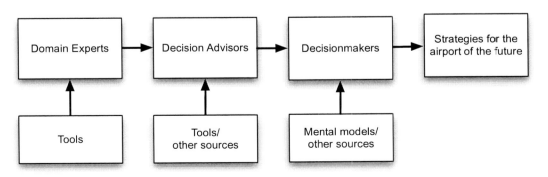

Figure 6. Roles of the people involved and their information.

With regard to the airport organization, there are three major roles in the planning process, which are performed by one or more persons, depending on the size of the airport operator's organization:

**Decision Makers.** The persons that have the decision power to develop and implement strategies for the airport's development, operation, and management.

Strategies are developed such that they meet the business goals associated with the vision about the airport of the future. Decisionmakers usually do not make direct use of (analytical) computer tools. The sources these people use are very diverse (e.g., newspapers, meetings with airport staff and stakeholders, and their intuition) and include their own mental models and input from their advisors.

**Decision Advisors.** The persons that advise the people that make the actual decisions.

Decision advisors explore the strategies that could be implemented for meeting the goals set by the decisionmakers. In order to accomplish this task, they hire external consultants, use in-house computer tools, and consult domain experts.

**Domain Experts.** The persons that have specific knowledge of the airport system (e.g. of the airside, landside, ground access infrastructure) and its operation.

Domain experts use various tools to provide quantitative information about the (future) airport performance (e.g. capacity and delay, environmental impacts, and financial results).

A supporting actor provides a service to the system. This is often a computer system, but it can also be an organization. The most important supporting actors for HARMOS are the tools for airport performance analysis.

An off-stage actor is an actor that has an interest in the software system, but is not directly using it. Depending on the organizational structure of an airport operator, a decision maker could actually be an off-stage actor.

As pointed out, in order to be successful as an organization, airport strategic planning should be a collective effort of both the people within the airport operator's organization and its stakeholders. Therefore, both groups should be able to use the DSS.

In order to meet the different needs of people with the above roles, the design of the DSS' functionality starts with identifying *functional* requirements, based on the goals of the users. The most important goals of the primary actors that we identified are listed in Table 2.

The collection of use cases is called a Use Case Model. The use case diagram shown in Figure 7 is a graphical presentation of the Use Case Model [11, p.128]. However, a use case diagram provides only a high-level overview of the functionality; it is not that useful for requirements analysis, because a diagram cannot capture the user-DSS interactions in enough detail. The next sections briefly present a number of the use cases in textual form.

## 4.2.   Define Decisionmaking Context

Airport management needs to revisit its strategies continually in order to evaluate whether the strategies are still adding value to the company, its customers, and its stakeholders. In

**Table 2. Actor-goal list**

| Actor | Goal |
|---|---|
| Decision Maker | Define Decisionmaking Context |
|  | Compare Strategies |
| Decision Advisor | Define Decisionmaking Context |
|  | Develop Scenario |
|  | Define Strategy |
|  | Evaluate Strategy |
| Domain Expert | Calibrate Study (not further discussed) |
|  | Specify System Model (not further discussed) |
|  | Execute Performance Analysis (not further discussed) |
|  | Develop Scenario |

order to do that, the effect of the strategies on the airport's performance need to be assessed against multiple plausible futures and compared to the objectives of the decisionmakers from the airport operator and its stakeholders.

Although there is a constant need to revisit strategies, the actual assessment of strategies is done within a specific decision making context. Decisionmakers from the airport operator and its stakeholders discuss this context. More specifically, the *problem* at hand or *opportunity* to be seized is tentatively defined, the *objectives* of the decisionmakers from the airport operator and its stakeholders are identified, and the *outcome indicators* to be used for quantifying the effects of the strategies.

Based on the results of the discussion among decisionmakers, the decision advisors create and set up a new *study* within the HARMOS DSS. Within the newly created study, a decision advisor: (1) Defines the planning period; (2) documents the problem or opportunity; (3) specifies the objectives of the airport operator and its stakeholders; and (4) selects the outcome indicators to be used for the assessment of strategies.

The functionality described in this section supports the formulation phase of problem solving and is directly related to Steps 1–3 of the policy analysis process—identify the problem, identify objectives, and decide on criteria.

## 4.3.  Develop Scenarios

Scenarios are to be used to test the strength and robustness of the strategies. Building scenarios is not directly supported by HARMOS because it is a creative and interactive process among decisionmakers and scenario planners that cannot and should not be automated [41].

A decision advisor (experienced in scenario planning) facilitates the creative process of building the scenarios. The steps, according to **(author?)** [42], of the scenario building process are: (1) Identify the major uncertainties the decisionmakers are facing in the context of the planning study; (2) identify the driving forces (and their impacts) within the (business) environment (3) organize the driving forces in higher level clusters; (4) position the clusters within the so-called uncertainty/relevance matrix; (5) take the two clusters that are

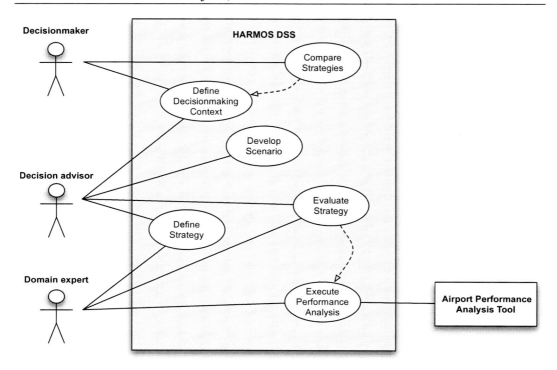

Figure 7. Functional View of the HARMOS architecture.

most relevant and uncertain to define the dimensions of the scenario space; (6) define the scenario space (four scenarios), which are characterized using extreme states of the driving forces; (7) name the scenarios uniquely and write the storylines. Decision advisors store the information generated during each of these steps within the DSS, so that it is available for later use.

Next, the decision advisors and domain experts quantify each of the scenarios. Decision advisors use the data used for calibration of the study as a starting point for quantifying the external factors for each of the four scenarios. The following information is combined consistently into a specific scenario: (i) economic developments that drive traffic demand; (ii) technological developments affecting ATM system performance, aircraft performance, noise and emissions, and aircraft accident rates; (iii) demographic developments, specifying the density and distribution of people living in the vicinity of the airport; (iv) regulatory developments, imposing constraints on some of the aspects of an airport's operation.

The functionality described in this section is directly related to Step 4 of the policy analysis process—developing scenarios.

## 4.4. Define Strategy

Implementing strategies that add value to the organization as well as its stakeholders is essential for any business. Strategies that might be identified typically fall in one of these three categories:

**Expand Capacity.** e.g. extend a runway or build a new runway, or improve the performance of the Air Traffic Management (ATM) system.

**Manage demand.** e.g. set curfews, ban noisy carriers, introduce pricing policies, or prohibit night flights.

**Revisit operations.** e.g. introduce noise abatement procedures, use alternative fuels for ground support equipment, redesign take-off and landing procedures, or change the use of runway configurations.

So, there are many strategies to choose from. Each specific strategy will have a different effect on the airport's performance, and hence be more or less satisfying to a particular stakeholder. It is therefore important to explore as many strategies as possible.

After having identified strategies, decision advisors use HARMOS to specify those strategies so that their effect on airport performance can be evaluated (described in the next section) for each of the scenarios that have been developed (see previous section).

The decision advisors define a strategy within the DSS by giving it a unique name and specifying how it affects the airport's infrastructure, operations, and management. Domain experts might help with specifying the details of a strategy.

For example: Suppose a decision advisor identifies a strategy *build new runway*. Domain experts specify the characteristics of the new runway (location, tracks, type of landing system used, etc.) and its planned operational use.

Decision advisors also specify all the necessary details related to the strategy's implementation. The most important detail is obviously the specific point of time within the planning period when the changes to the system as defined by the strategy come into effect (e.g. the new runway becomes operational on August 31, 2015). Besides that, the financial plan related to the strategy needs to be specified, detailing the cost recovery elements and revenue generating potential of the investments associated with the strategy (e.g. the additional capacity made available through a new runway could be partially financed by an increase in landing fees).

One strategy that is included by default by HARMOS is the *business as usual* strategy. This strategy defines changes to the system for the entire planning period according to a strategy that is not fundamentally different from the airport's current strategy. The business as usual strategy is used as a reference for assessing new strategies.

The functionality described in this section is directly related to Step 5 of the policy analysis process—define strategies.

## 4.5.  Evaluate Strategy

This step is about generating the appropriate information for discussion and negotiation among the airport operator and stakeholders.

Each strategy defined within a study (described in the previous section) needs to be evaluated for all the scenarios (see Section 4.3.). Without such an evaluation, the airport operator and its stakeholders cannot truly make reasonable assessments about the effectiveness of a strategy in addressing a problem or seizing an opportunity.

The lack of quantification of specific strategies proposed by either an airport operator or one of its stakeholders often causes gridlock during the implementation of a chosen strategy.

Airport stakeholders usually oppose a strategy whose results have not been discussed with them. In such a case, its effects cannot be valued in terms of their objectives.

Decision advisors, therefore, evaluate each strategy defined within the study against all of the scenarios that have been developed. For each strategy, the decision advisor selects the appropriate outcomes of interest—capacity, delay, noise, emissions, third-party risk, and finance.

The decision advisor selects specific periods of interest (either a year or a day) within the planning period and runs a performance analysis for each of the outcomes of interest. The HARMOS DSS executes the specific performance analysis, calling upon the computational services of the appropriate tools for the airport performance analysis.

The functionality described in this section is directly related to Step 6 of the policy analysis process—evaluate strategies.


## 4.6.  Compare Strategies

Once all of the strategies have been evaluated for all of the scenarios (see Section 4.5.), the results need to be presented to the decision makers. The numerous and diverse effects of a strategy on the airport's performance need to be summarized and presented in a way that facilitates the comparison and ranking of the strategies.

HARMOS uses a disaggregate approach to presenting its results, in which the effects of the strategies are presented in the form of tables called *scorecards* [32]. An example of a scorecard is shown in Figure 8.

Each column of a scorecard represents an effect and each row represents a strategy. An entire row shows all of the effects of a single strategy; an entire column shows each strategy's value for a single effect. Numbers or words appear in each cell of the scorecard to convey whatever is known about the size and direction of the impact without comparison among cells. Colors are used for the cells to indicate to what extent a specific strategy meets the objectives of the airport operator and its stakeholders (e.g. red: objective for none of the stakeholders is met; green: objective is met for all stakeholders; no color: objective is met for most of the stakeholders).

In comparing the strategies, each stakeholder and decisionmaker can assign whatever weight he/she deems appropriate to each effect. Explicit consideration of weighting thus becomes central to the decision process itself, as it should be (Walker, 2000).

HARMOS generates a scorecard for each scenario presenting the effects on the airport's performance for each of the strategies. The scorecards are then used as a means for discussion between the decisionmakers of the airport operator and its stakeholders in order to make a choice for the preferred strategy or strategies to be implemented. The decisionmakers might also decide to ask for more analysis, either because none of the strategies that have been evaluated can satisfactorily meet their objectives or there is the need to evaluate strategies not thought of before.

This functionality is directly related to Step 7 of the policy analysis process—compare strategies.

| Strategy | Airport performance indicators | | | | |
|---|---|---|---|---|---|
| | Average delay [min] | Noise [houses] | Emission [tons] | 3rd party risk [houses] | Profit [euro] |
| Business as usual | 7.5 | 20,000 | 7,500 | 2,500 | 170 mln |
| Build new runway | 4.1 | 17,500 | 9,000 | 3,000 | 160 mln |
| Noise abatement | 4.8 | 10,000 | 8,000 | 2,500 | 140 mln |
| Manage demand | 3.5 | 16,000 | 6,500 | 2,000 | 120 mln |

Figure 8. Example of a scorecard for comparing strategies.

## 4.7. The Graphical User Interface

The complexity of the airport domain and the business activity of strategic planning motivated the use of a Domain Model (mentioned previously in Section 3.4.) as the heart of the HARMOS DSS. The Domain Model is the most sophisticated form of a Domain Logic pattern [20, p.26 and p.116]. We argue that without it, it is not possible to realize the functional requirements described in the previous sections and thus adequately support airport strategic planning. As previously mentioned, a detailed description of the Domain Model can be found in (author?) [49, Chapter 7].

The GUI presented in this section discusses how the functionality of the Domain Model is *exposed* to the DSS users. The current GUI is composed of a number of different components, each related to a different part of the functionality of the Domain Model.

**Study Manager.** Exposes the Domain Model functionality related to: (1) creating new studies, opening studies, and deleting studies; and (2) organizing the strategic planning problem and the decisionmaking context being subject of study.

As such, the Study Manager implements that part of the GUI that exposes the functionality described in Section 4.2.—define decisionmaking context. The Study Manager also provides the functionality to partly address the third problem area (Section 2.1.3.)—involvement of the stakeholders—by providing a means to document the problem perspectives and objectives of the airport operator and its stakeholders.

**Scenario Builder.** Exposes the functionality for developing scenarios. As such, the Scenario Builder implements that part of the GUI that exposes the functionality described in Section 4.3.—develop scenario.

The Scenario Builder addresses the second problem area (Section 2.1.2.)—modeling the (uncertain) future.

**Strategy Builder.** Exposes the functionality for specifying strategies. As such, the Strategy Builder implements that part of the GUI that exposes the functionality described in Section 4.4.—define strategy.

**Strategy Evaluator.** Exposes the functionality for evaluating the effects of a strategy on the airport's performance for one or more scenario. As such, the Strategy Evaluator implements that part of the GUI that exposes the functionality described in Section 4.5.—evaluate strategy.

The Strategy Evaluator is a major part of the DSS that exposes the functionality to addresss the first problem area (Section 2.1.1.)—the efficiency of problem solving—by providing the means to integrally evaluate the effects of strategies for particular periods of interest within the planning period.

**Strategy Comparator.** Exposes the functionality for comparing one strategy versus another for each of the scenarios. As such, the Strategy Comparator implements that part of the GUI that exposes the functionality described in Section 4.5.—compare strategies.

The Strategy Comparator exposes the functionality to partly address the third problem area (Section 2.1.3.)—involvement of the stakeholders—by providing a means to present different strategies to the airport operator and its stakeholders. Using information about specific strategies, a constructive discussion about which strategies are collectively preferred for implementation, can take place.

So, the GUI components logically follow from the functional requirements. The components are available to each type of user—decision maker, decision advisor, and domain expert—although the actual use of the components will vary per type of user. Most of the components are directly accessible from the Study Manager. Besides that, a menu structure is provided to access the components. The menu structure is not further discussed here.

The users can navigate through the HARMOS GUI whatever way they like. This idea of *non-linear navigation* was also the basis for an earlier strategic planning tool, the Airport Business Suite, which we worked on [46]. During the planning effort, the users are not constrained to a predefined way of using the GUI. The users are in control.

Only at the start of the planning effort, during the so-called calibration of the study, is it required to follow steps in a predefined sequence (enforced by the DSS) in order to make sure that everything is set up correctly.

## 5.   Conclusion

This chapter started with describing the problem situation that airport operators face when preparing plans for the future development of the airport (Section 1.1.). Also, the economic and social aspects of an airport's performance were discussed, resulting in the conclusion that the appropriate balance between them is needed for long-term, sustainable airport development (Section 1.2.). Strategies need to be implemented that not only satisfy an airport operator's objectives, but also those of all their stakeholders.

Strategic planning is therefore essential for airport operators. However, current airport strategic planning has to overcome a number of problem areas: (1) the efficiency of problem solving, (2) modeling the (uncertain) future, and (3) involvement of the stakeholders (Section 2.1.). The currently available approaches to airport strategic planning (Section 2.2.) do not address these problem areas concurrently (Section 2.3.).

Master Planning, the most widely used approach to airport strategic planning, still results in strategic plans that are either not capable of dealing with changes within the airport's operators business environment, or are strongly opposed by some of the stakeholders, or even both.

The proposed new approaches are well equiped to deal with the uncertain future, but they do not provide a meaningful way to involve the stakeholders. These approaches also assume that the appropriate use of computer-based tools will be taken care of by the people involved in a strategic planning effort.

The analysis of the resources involved in a strategic planning effort (Section 2.4.) brings us to the conclusion that the coordination of these resources is at the root of the problems with current airport strategic planning. Coordination of people (knowledge), data and information, and tools is very time-consuming and leaves little time for strategic thinking about the planning problem at hand.

The huge effort related to tools led to many projects designing and developing computer-based systems (Section 2.5.). However, these computer-based systems are strongly focused on integrating tools for airport performance analysis. Therefore, these systems lack functionality for problem formulation and interpretation, and have therefore not been adopted by airport operators.

Maintaining a balance between economic and social performance requires strategies that reduce an airport's environmental impact while maintaining or improving its financial success. These strategies can be better found if the airport operator and its stakeholders are provided decision support that quantifies the effect of wide range of strategies on the airport's performance for multiple scenarios representing the many plausible futures that might unfold.

The HARMOS decision support system has been proposed to help an airport operator and their stakeholders to strategically think about their future, and identify, evaluate, and implement strategies that realize a shared vision about the airport's long-term development (Section 3.3.).

The different functionalities provided by the HARMOS DSS have been discussed, showing how the current problems with airport strategic planning are addressed (Section 4.). The next section concludes to what extent the generic decision making needs, as identified by Zachary, are met. Finally, Section 5.2. draws conclusions about using the HARMOS DSS as compared to Master Planning.

## 5.1.   Meeting Decision Making Needs

The design of the HARMOS DSS has been driven by the need to deal with the problems discussed in Section 2.1., as revisited by the problem statement presented in Section 3.2. The GUI design reflects this as well (Section 4.7.) The functionality exposed through the GUI shows how the needs identified by **(author?)** [51] (as mentioned in the introduction of Section 3.) as satisfied:

1. The Scenario Builder meets Zachary's first need, i.e. project into the future despite uncertainty;

2. The Strategy Evaluator supports the first part of Zachary's second need: It provides functionality to evaluate different alternatives. The second part of Zachary's second need — comparing alternatives and making trade-offs among competing goals—is supported by the Strategy Comparator;

3. The design of the Domain Model (not discussed in detail), based on a policy analysis approach as the means to structure the planning problem and the problem solving process, meets the third need, i.e. managing large amounts of information simultaneously. The Strategy Evaluator organizes information related to individual strategies. The Strategy Comparator organizes information (albeit at a higher level of aggregation) related to all strategies that have been evaluated in the study;

4. The DSS as a whole meets Zachary's fourth need: Analyzing complex situations within constraints on time and resources;

5. The GUI as a whole fulfills Zachary's fifth need—visualizing and manipulating those visualizations—as it presents the relevant information for decision making in a graphical way;

6. The Strategy Comparator supports the sixth need: making heuristic judgments, even if they are only qualitative. The DSS users are able to test strategies against multiple futures, learn from the results they obtain, and try other strategies and scenarios.

We mentioned that previous and current projects mainly focus on computer-based systems for airport performance analysis (Section 2.5.). Functionality for problem formulation or interpretation is not explicitly provided. HARMOS provides functionality for each phase of the problem solving process, and this is reflected through the components of the GUI. Within each of the phases, the GUI components are used as follows:

**Formulation.** The Study Manager is used to start a new strategic planning effort. The Study Manager is used to capture information about the planning problem, the airport operator and its stakeholders, and their objectives.

**Analysis.** The Scenario Builder is used for quantitatively developing scenarios. The Strategy Builder is used for defining strategies. The Strategy Evaluator is used to evaluate the strategies against the scenarios in terms of the outcomes of interest.

**Table 3. Master Planning versus HARMOS' functionality.**

| Master Planning | HARMOS' Functionality |
| --- | --- |
| Pre-planning | Study Manager |
| Public Involvement | Study Manager, Strategy Comparator |
| Existing Conditions | Calibrator (has not been discussed) |
| Aviation Forecasts | Scenario Builder |
| Facility Requirements | Strategy Evaluator for Business as Usual |
| Alternatives Development and Evaluation | Strategy Builder, Strategy Evaluator |
| Environmental considerations | Strategy Evaluator |
| Financial Feasibility | Strategy Evaluator, Strategy Comparator |

**Interpretation.** The Strategy Comparator is used to compare strategies within a collaborative setting involving decisionmakers from the airport operator and its stakeholders.

So, the HARMOS DSS addresses the problem areas with current airport strategic planning (Section 2.1.), meets the generic needs for a DSS defined by Zachary, and supports the entire problem solving process, from formulation, through analysis, to interpretation. By doing so, we believe to have covered the high-level needs of the people involved in airport strategic planning studies.

## 5.2.   Compatibility with Master Planning

As discussed in Section 2.2.1., the dominant approach to airport strategic planning is Master Planning. Although the HARMOS DSS has been primarily designed to deal with all problem areas of current airport strategic planning—the efficiency of problem solving, modeling the future, and stakeholder involvement—it actually encompasses the activities defined within Master Planning as well. This is not surprising because policy analysis evolved from systems analysis, which is used as the analytical framework for Master Planning.

Table 3 presents a comparison of the Master Planning activities (see also Section 2.2.1.) and specific HARMOS functionality. Master Planning starts with identifying the need for a Master Plan. The need for a planning study could be based on existing or potential shortcomings in the existing plan or airport, or be driven by the Vision or Business Plan for the airport.

We think that in today's rapidly changing world, there is a continuous need for an airport operator to monitor and revise its strategies. At any time, the HARMOS Study Manager can be used for creating a new planning study to investigate a problem or opportunity.

Public involvement is directly facilitated by HARMOS through the functionality for defining the decision making context (Section 4.2.), which is exposed to the users by the Study Manager. The ease with which different strategies can be defined and evaluated makes it possible to assess strategies proposed by each of the stakeholders. The HARMOS DSS eliminates the coordination effort related to data and information, and tools, so that the time that becomes available can be used to interact more meaningfully with the stakeholders. Obviously, there still needs to be the willingness to invite the stakeholders to participate in a planning study, and vice versa.

The evaluation of existing conditions at an airport is taken care of by the (required) use of the Calibrator (not discussed here) after creating a new study.

Aviation forecasts are covered by the Scenario Builder, which in addition offers a way to deal with more external factors than demand alone.

Facility requirements are dealt with through the use of the Strategy Evaluator for the 'business as usual' strategy. The evaluation of that strategy does not provide the requirements for the airport facilities per se; it merely shows which airport facilities become bottlenecks at some point in the future.

The development of alternatives is done with the Strategy Builder; their evaluation is covered by the Strategy Evaluator. Environmental considerations do not have to be separately assessed, because the Strategy Evaluator provides the functionality to integrally assess the outcomes of interest—capacity and delay, noise, emissions, and third-party risk. For the same reason, the assessment of the financial feasibility of a strategy is covered by the Strategy Evaluator.

In addition, the Strategy Comparator provides the means to provide financial information at a higher level of aggregation than when using the Strategy Evaluator (e.g. the return on investment, payback period), needed to be able to compare the financial feasibility of different strategies.

So, using the HARMOS DSS does not violate current airport planning practice. The DSS actually incorpates the procedures, tasks, and activities of Master Plannnig into a broader framework for problem solving and decision making, to overcome the problems with current airport strategic planning.

# References

[1] Paul Achleitner, Igor Ansoff, and Gay Haskins. The firm: Meeting the legitimacy challenge. *European Management Journal*, **2**(1):19–27, 1983.

[2] Anthony. *Planning and Control Systems: A Framework for Analysis.* Harvard University Press, 1965.

[3] William Ascher. *Forecasting: an appraisal for policy-makers and planners.* Johns Hopkins University Press, Baltimore, 1978.

[4] Simon Bishop and Tony Grayling. *The Sky's the Limit. Policies for Sustainable Aviation.* Institute for Public Policy Research, United Kingdom, 2003.

[5] Rex V. Brown. Planning decision research with usefulness in mind: Toward quantitative evaluation. In *Creativity and Innovation in Decision Making and Decision Support*, London, UK, 2006. Volume I.

[6] John M. Bryson. *Strategic Planning for the Public and Nonprofit Organizations.* Jossey-Bass, 1995.

[7] John M. Bryson. Strategic Planning. In *International Encyclopedia of the Social and Behavioral Sciences*. Elsevier, 2004.

[8] Guillaume Burghouwt. *Airline Network Development in Europe and its Implications for Airport Planning*. Ashgate Publishing, Hampshire, England, 2007.

[9] Guillaume Burghouwt and Menno Huys. Deregulation and the consequences for airport planning in europe. *DISP*, **145**(3):37–45, 2003.

[10] Robert E. Caves and Geoffrey D. Gosling. *Strategic Airport Planning*. Pergamon, Oxford, 1999.

[11] Alistair Cockburn. *Writing Effective Use Cases*. Addison-Wesley Professional, 2001.

[12] Richard de Neufville. Strategic planning for airport systems: An appreciation of Australia's process for Sydney. *Australian Planner*, **29**(4):174–180, dec 1991.

[13] Richard de Neufville. Dynamic strategic planning for technology policy. *International Journal of Technology Management*, **19**:225–245, 2000.

[14] Richard de Neufville and Amedeo Odoni. *Airport Systems: Planning, Design, and Management*. McGraw-Hill Professional, New York, 2003.

[15] Stephen Dempsey. *Airport Development and Planning Handbook: A Global Survey*. McGraw-Hill Professional, New York, 1999.

[16] Gemma Dodson, David Arnott, and Graham Pervan. The client and user in decision support systems: Review and research agenda. In *Creativity and Innovation in Decision Making and Decision Support*, 2006. Volume I.

[17] Eric Evans. *Domain Driven Design*. Addison-Wesley, 2004.

[18] FAA. Advisory Circular 150/5070-6, 1985.

[19] FAA. Advisory Circular 150/5070-6, 2005.

[20] Martin Fowler. *Patterns of Enterprise Application Architecture*. Addison-Wesley, 2003.

[21] Paul Freathy. The commercialization of European airports: successful strategies in a decade of turbulence? *Journal of Air Transport Management*, **10**:191–197, 2004.

[22] Paul Freathy and Frank O'Connel. Planning for profit: the commercialization of European airports. *Long Range Planning*, **32**:587–597, 1999.

[23] Andrew R. Goetz and Joseph S. Szyliowicz. Revisiting transportation planning and decision making theory: The case of Denver International Airport. *Transportation Research Part A*, **31**:263–280, 1997.

[24] ICAO. *Airport Planning Manual Doc 9184*. International Civil Aviation Organization, Montreal, Canada, 2nd edition, 1987. Reprinted July 2004.

[25] David Jarach. The evolution of airport management practices: towards a multi-point, multi-service, marketing-driven firm. *Journal of Air Transport Management,* 7:119–125, 2001.

[26] Joakim Karlsson. Dynamic strategic planning in practice: Pease international airport. `faculty.dwc.edu/karlsson/Karlsson_AMERC2003.pdf`, 2003. Accessed August 4, 2008.

[27] Jurek Keur and Warren Walker. The Airport Business Suite project. Presentation at the kickoff meeting of the ABS project. Delft Airport Development Center. Delft University of Technology., 2003.

[28] Ans Kolk and Mark van der Veen. Dilemmas of balancing organizational and public interests: How environment affects strategy in Dutch Main Ports. *European Management Journal,* **20**:45–54, 2002.

[29] Jan H. Kwakkel, Warren E. Walker, and Vincent A.W.J. Marchau. Dealing with uncertainty in airport strategic planning. In *Proceedings of the ATRS 2007 Conference,* 2007.

[30] Murray May and Stuart B. Hill. Canberra. *Journal of Transport Geography,* **14**:437–450, 2006.

[31] Henry Mintzberg. Rethinking strategic planning Part I: Pitfalls and fallacies. *Long Range Planning,* **27**(3):12–21, 1994.

[32] Hugh J. Miser and Edward S. Quade. *Handbook of Systems Analysis: Craft Issues and Procedural Choices.* John Wiley and Sons, Ltd., 1988.

[33] Amedeo R. Odoni. Existing and required modeling capabilities for evaluating ATM systems and concepts. Technical report, National Aeronautics and Space Administration, March 1997. AATT Program, Grant No. NAG2-997.

[34] M. Patel, K. Kok, and D.S. Rotman. Participatory scenario construction in land use analysis: An insight into the experiences created by stakeholder involvement in the Northern Mediterranean. *Land Use Policy,* **24**:546–561, 2007.

[35] Michael Porter. The state of strategic thinking. The Economist. May 23. pp.19–23, 1987.

[36] Schiphol Group. Annual report 2006. `http://www.schipholgroup.nl`, 2006.

[37] Schiphol Group. Long term vision (in dutch). `http://www.schiphol.nl`, 2007.

[38] Linda Soneryd. Public involvement in the planning process: EIA and lessons from the Sorebro airport extension, Sweden. *Environmental Science & Policy,* **7**(1):59–68, February 2004.

[39] SPADE Consortium. Project plan. Technical report, European Commission, December 2003.

[40] E. Turban. *Decision support and expert systems: management support systems.* Prentice Hall, Englewood Cliffs, N.J., 1995.

[41] Kees van der Heijden. *Scenarios: The art of strategic conversation.* John Wiley & Sons, 1999.

[42] Kees van der Heijden, Ron Bradfield, George Burt, George Cairns, and George Wright. *The Sixth Sense.* John Wiley and Sons, 2002.

[43] Dries Visser, Warren E. Walker, Jurek Keur, Jan Veldhuis, Roland Wijnen, Uta Kohse, and Niels Lang. The Airport Business Suite: A Decision Support System for Airport Strategic Exploration. In *Proceedings of the 3rd AIAA Aviation Technology, Integration, and Operations Symposium,* Denver, Colorado, U.S.A., 2003.

[44] Christian Wagner. Enterprise strategy management systems: current and next generation. *Journal of Strategic Information Systems,* 13:105–128, 2004.

[45] Warren E. Walker. Policy analysis: A systematic approach to supporting policymaking in the public sector. *Journal of Multicriteria Decision Analysis,* 9(1-3):11–27, 2000.

[46] W.E. Walker, N.A. Lang, J. Keur, H.G. Visser, R.A.A. Wijnen, U. Kohse, J. Veldhuis, and A.R.C. De Haan. An organizational decision support system for airport strategic exploration. In Tung Bui, Henryk Sroka, Stanislaw Stanek, and Jerzy Goluchowski, editors, *DSS in the Uncertainty of the Internet Age,* pages 435–452, Katowice, Poland, 2003. Karol Adamiecki University of Economics.

[47] Alexander T. Wells and Seth B. Young. *Airport Planning & Management.* McGraw-Hill, New York, 5th edition, 2004.

[48] Roland A. A. Wijnen, Warren E. Walker, and Jan H. Kwakkel. Decision support for airport strategic planning. *Transportation Planning and Technology,* 31(1):11–34, 2008.

[49] Roland A.A. Wijnen. *Decision support for airport strategic planning.* PhD thesis, Faculty of Aerospace Engineering, Delft University of Technology, forthcoming.

[50] Ian Wilson. Strategic planning isn't dead - it changed. *Long Range Planning,* 27(4):12–24, 1994.

[51] Wayne Zachary. Decision support systems: Designing to extend the cognitive limits. In Martin G. Helander, editor, *Handbook of Human-Computer Interaction.* Elsevier Science Publishers, 1998.

[52] Konstantinos Zografos, Michel van Eenige, and Rosa Valdes. Integrated airport performance analysis through the use of the OPAL platform. *Air Traffic Control Quarterly,* 13(4):357–386, 2005.

In: Airports: Performance, Risks, and Problems
Editors: P.B. Larauge et al, pp. 105-121

ISBN: 978-1-60692-393-1
© 2009 Nova Science Publishers, Inc.

*Chapter 5*

# OCCUPATIONAL EXPOSURE IN AIRPORT PERSONNEL: HEALTH RISKS

## *Delia Cavallo, Cinzia Lucia Ursini and Sergio Iavicoli*

Department of Occupational Medicine, ISPESL- National Institute for Occupational
Safety and Prevention, Italy

## Abstract

Occupational exposure in airport personnel is very complex and still poorly characterized and includes either chemical pollutants (influenced by environmental factors associated to different climatic and meteorologic conditions), or physical agents such as microwaves-radiofrequency radiations and noise pollution. Airport ground personnel performs different tasks such as aircraft fuel tank, aircraft routine maintenance procedures, airplane parking/towing, baggage charge/discharge, that can induce exposure to complex chemical mixtures including several polycyclic aromatic hydrocarbons (PAHs) produced by vapours or combustion of commercial Jet A-A1 fuels and by combustion of diesel/gasoline engines of runway shuttles and baggage trolleys operating in the vicinity of the planes. Although the airport workers are exposed to low levels of PAHs there is a possibility of long-term health effects following chronic exposure by inhalation or skin contamination. The most available studies on health effects of airport pollution concern military aviation that employs a different kind of jet propulsion fuel in respect to civil aviation and report some genotoxic and carcinogenic effects. For civil aviation only a few data are available on PAHs levels in airports, biological monitoring of occupational exposure and on health risks for airport personnel. In particular genotoxic and oxidative DNA damage, neurotoxic, respiratory, irritant and reproductive effects have been reported by biomonitoring and epidemiological studies. In addition to scarcity of data on health effects of airport pollution on workers there are not enough studies on health risks for populations living and working in surrounding of the airport. This paper will present the most important studies actually available on health risks of airport occupational exposure giving prominence to effects of chemical pollution.

## Introduction

Occupational exposure of airport workers (ground and flight personnel) is very complex and still poorly characterized and includes either chemical pollutants (PAHs, aliphatic hydrocarbons, Volatile organic compounds (Vocs), metals, ozone) influenced by environmental factors associated to different climatic and meteorological conditions, and physical agents such as microwaves-radiofrequency radiations, cosmic radiations, ultraviolet radiations, electromagnetic fields and noise pollution.

Few data are in general available on health effects of airport pollution on workers and populations living and working in surrounding of the airport [Passchier et al. 2000].

The studies on airport workers report low back pain [Froom et al. 1996] and neurotoxic [Knave et al. 1976], genotoxic and oxidative [Pitarque et al. 1999, Cavallo et al. 2002, 2006], respiratory [Yang 2003, Tunnicliffe et al. 1999], auditory [Chen et al 1992, Hong and Kim 2001; Thakur et al. 2004], reproductive and irritant effects [Lemasters et al. 1999, Yang 2003]. Moreover some studies on air traffic controllers report cardiovascular and stress related diseases associated to their work [Costa et al. 2000, 2004, Zeier 1994].

While in people living near large airports hypertension [Rosenlund et al. 2001; Jarup et al. 2005; Eriksson et al. 2007] sleep loss, fatigue, concentration failure [Health Council of Netherland 1999] or effects on auditory system [Chen et al. 1997] related to aircraft noise are reported.

Airport ground personnel performs different tasks such as aircraft fuel tank, aircraft routine maintenance procedures, airplane parking/towing, baggage charge/discharge, that induce exposure to complex chemical mixtures including several polycyclic aromatic hydrocarbons (PAHs) produced by vapours or combustion of commercial Jet A-A1 fuels and by combustion of diesel/gasoline engines of runway shuttles and baggage trolleys operating in the vicinity of the planes.

Flight personnel, including flight attendants and pilots, are occupationally exposed to cosmic radiations (during long-haul intercontinental flights), airborne pollutants such as the combustion products of jet propulsion or other volatile substances released from aircraft construction materials, ozone, ultraviolet radiations, electromagnetic fields and life-style that could potentially induce health hazardous effects such as cancer [Rafnsson et al. 2000].

Airport pollutants such as ionizing radiation, UV-light, polycyclic aromatic hydrocarbons (PAHs) have been identified to compromise genetic stability by inducing different type of DNA damage either directly or after metabolic conversion to reactive intermediates or by ROS induction.

Although the airport ground workers are exposed to low levels of PAHs there is a possibility of long-term health effects following chronic exposure by inhalation or skin contamination such as genotoxic and oxidative damage [Cavallo et al. 2006]. Moreover flight personnel, especially those employed on long haul routes, chronically exposed to ionizing cosmic radiations are potentially exposed to genotoxic and carcinogenic risk [Cavallo et al. 2002].

In this review we resume the main chemical and physical airport pollutants, describe the principal occupational risks related to exposure to such agents and present the most important studies actually available on health effects of airport occupational exposure giving prominence to effects of chemical pollution. Moreover, we report the main available studies concerning health impact of airport pollution on people living near large airports.

# Occupational Exposure of Airport Personnel

## Chemical Pollutants

Airports are source of air pollution that results from the fuel combustion in aircraft engines, ground service vehicles, airport-associated traffic. Combustion of aviation fuels results in $CO_2$, CO, $NO_x$, particles, and a great number of organic compounds such PAHs, among which a number of carcinogens [Tesseraux 2004]. Monitoring data of air pollutants are available for many airports, but they are mostly restricted to classical pollutants like $SO_2$, $NO_x$, CO, particles and a few others in special monitoring programs [Tesseraux 2004].

A study on air quality of the area around the Amsterdam airport Schiphol monitored the levels of some chemical airport pollutants such as $NO_2$, CO, $O_3$, PM10, black smoke, benzo[a]pyrene and did not find differences with the background urban air quality [Meijer and De Jonge 2003].

Another study reporting data on the exposure to airport pollutants from jet and diesel engine exhaust of a population living around a large airport didn't show higher levels of air pollution than those of a typical urban environment, however while the toxic emissions from cars are being reduced by better fuels and engines, much less attention is paid on aircraft emission [Tesseraux 2004].

The potential human exposure to PAHs from aircraft exhaust, evaluated in a military aviation base, showed a prevalence of naphthalene, alkyl- naphthalenes in the vapour phase and particle-bound PAHs such as fluoranthene, pyrene and benzo(a)pyrene [Childers et al. 2000].

Airport ground personnel of large civil airports is occupationally exposed to several polycyclic aromatic hydrocarbons (PAHs) produced by vapours or combustion of commercial Jet A-A1 fuels and by combustion of diesel/gasoline engines of runway shuttles and baggage trolleys operating in the vicinity of the planes. Fuel Jet-A is a kerosene-based fuel containing approximately 81% aliphatic hydrocarbons (butane, dodecane, undecane, hexane, heptane, octane, nonane, pentane, trichloroethane), 18% aromatic hydrocarbons (benzene, toluene, styrene, xilene) and less than 1% olefins [Riviere et al. 1999, Pleil et al. 2000]. The exposure to the complex chemical mixtures including PAHs can occurs through dermal contact with raw fuel and/or aerosol; dermal contact with clothing and gloves saturated with fuel; inhalation of jet-A vapours or exhaust and diesel combustion. The exposure conditions are highly variable since influenced by environmental factors (wind, heat etc.) associated to different climatic and meteorological conditions.

Few data are available on PAHs levels in civil airports [Iavicoli et al. 2006, 2007]. These data are related to mixed exhaust from both motor vehicles and jet engines and show that naphthalene and methylnaphthalenes are the main components of the airborne PAHs mixture. In particular a prevalence of 2-ringed PAHs was found with total naphthalene concentrations ranged from 130 to 13.050 $ng/m^3$, 1-methylnaphtalene from 24 to 35.000 $ng/m^3$, 2-methylnaphtalene from 93 to 28.500 $ng/m^3$ and biphenyl ranged from 24 to 1.610 $ng/m^3$. Concentrations of three or more ringed PAHs were considerably lower. However all found PAHs levels were below the occupational exposure limits established by Occupational Safety and Health Administration (OSHA), American Conference of Governmental Industrial Hygienists (ACGIH) and The National Institute for Occupational and Safety Health (NIOSH).

## Physical Agents

Airport workers can be exposed in airport or during long-haul flights to several physical agents such as noise pollution, cosmic radiations and non-ionizing radiations (microwaves-radiofrequency radiations, ultraviolet radiations, ELF electromagnetic fields).

### Noise Pollution

A few data are available on the assessment of noise levels in airports. Two studies on occupational exposure to noise in airport workers report an association between noise-exposure levels and hearing deficiencies [Abel Moneim 1995; Hong and Kim 2001].

More studies are available on noise pollution in areas around large airports. A recent study that examines noise pollution in the community around LaGuardia Airport in New York City [Cohen et al. 2008] demonstrates that residences at airport area were exposed to noise exceeding the limit established by U.S. EPA in 1974 to protect health and welfare [U.S. EPA 1974]. In fact this study revealed that at the homes near the airport the day-night noise levels were higher (from 54.9 to 73.5 dB(A)) than those found in the comparison homes (38.5 dB(A)). However, since the homes near the airport were near major highways and busy streets that caused traffic noise, the authors of the study believe that the term airport-related noise, rather than aircraft noise should be used to describe noise impacts for the specific studied communities. Other studies performed in areas around large airports find a relationship between noise exposure levels of people living in these areas and health effects such as hypertension [Eriksson et al. 2007; Haralabidis et al. 2008], annoyance [van Kamp et al. 2004; Lim et al. 2008], or impairment of cognitive performance in children [Stansfeld et al. 2005].

### Cosmic Radiations

Flight personnel are occupationally exposed to significantly higher levels of ionizing radiation of cosmic origin (protons, neutrons and gamma radiation) than at ground level. On intercontinental flight routes, at an altitude around 10.000 m, it has been estimated that the mean cumulative dose of exposure for flight personnel in civil aviation is 2-3 mSv/year, with values ranging from 1-10 mSv/year [Bagshaw et al. 1996].

### Non-ionizing Radiations

Occupational exposure to microwaves-radiofrequency radiations in airport involves air traffic controllers for which long-term health effects such as nervous, ophthalmic and haematological-immunological disorders, psycophysiological and stress response or reproductive impairment [Goldoni et al 1993; Costa 1993; Zeier 1994; Liu et al. 2003, Ding et al. 2004; Jauchem 2008] have been reported.

Airport workers could be also exposed to ELF electromagnetic fields generated by electrical and electronic appliances and to ultraviolet radiations during outdoor activities.

# Health Effects of Airport Pollution

The main airport pollutants with the relative health effects are reported in Table 1.

## Table 1. Airport pollutants and related health effects

| Airport pollutants | Health effects |
|---|---|
| ***Chemical agents*** | |
| PAHs | Genotoxicity, oxidative damage, carcinogenicity |
| Aliphatic hydrocarbons, aldehydes | Eye and respiratory irritations, liver toxicity |
| Volatile Organic Compounds VOCs | Irritative, respiratory- pulmonary effects, carcinogenicity |
| Heavy metals | Genotoxicity, oxidative damage, reproductive disorders, carcinogenicity |
| Ozone | Irritative, respiratory and pulmonary effects |
| NOx, CO, SO$_2$ | Eye and respiratory-pulmonary irritations |
| ***Physical agents*** | |
| Microwaves-radiofrequency radiations | Nervous, ophthalmic, haematological-immunological, cardiovascular disorders, reproductive impairment |
| Cosmic radiations | Genotoxicity, carcinogenicity |
| Ultraviolet radiations | Genotoxic, oxidative, carcinogenic |
| Noise pollution | Hearing loss, hypertension, sleep loss, fatigue, concentration failure, cardiovascular and neuropsychological disorders, annoyance |

## Table 2. Studies on health effects of airport chemical pollutant and cosmic radiations

| Exposure | Exposed population | Observed effects | References |
|---|---|---|---|
| PAHs | Airport ground personnel | Higher SCE frequency and increase of Chromosomal Aberrations and Oxidative DNA damage | Cavallo et al. 2006 |
| PAHs | Airport ground personnel | Slight DNA damage | Pitarque et al. 1999 |
| Jet fuel exhaust and solvents | Aircraft maintenance workers | Statistically significant increase of SCE frequency | Lemasters et al. 1997 |
| Jet fuel exhaust | Airport ground workers | Respiratory effects | Tunnicliffe et al. 1999 |

## Table 2. Continued

| Exposure | Exposed population | Observed effects | References |
|---|---|---|---|
| Jet fuel exhaust | Airport ground workers | Adverse respiratory and irritant effects | Yang et al. 2003 |
| Petroleum-distilled fuel | Aircraft factory workers | Nervous system effects | Knave et al. 1976 |
| Jet fuel exhaust and solvents | Aircraft maintenance workers | Male reproductive effects (decrease of sperm motility) | Lemasters et al. 1999 |
| Cosmic radiations | Civil aviation pilots and crew members | Increased frequency of dicentric and ring chromosomes | Romano et al. 1997 |
| Cosmic radiations | Concorde pilots | Increase of dicentric chromosomes and MN frequency | Heimers et al. 2000 |
| Cosmic radiations | Airline pilots with many years of flight experience | Significant increase of traslocations | Cavallo et al. 2002 ; Nicholas et al. 2003 |
| Cosmic radiations | Female cabine attendants | No increase of dicentric frequency | Wolf et al. 1999 |
| Cosmic radiations | Flight engineers | No increase of dicentric frequency | Zwinmann et al. 1998 |

## Table 3. Studies on health effects of noise pollution and microwaves-radiations

| Exposure | Exposed population | Observed effects | References |
|---|---|---|---|
| Aircraft Noise | Airport ground personnel | Hearing loss particularly in the groups of maintenance workers and firemen | Chen et al. 1992 |
| Aircraft Noise | Airport ground personnel | Hearing defects | Abel Moneim 1995 |
| Aircraft Noise | Airport ground personnel | Hearing loss | Hong and Kim 2001 |
| Aircraft Noise | Ground crew employees | Hearing loss | Thakur et al. 2004 |
| Residential Aircraft Noise | Populations living at different distances from the airport | Reduction of hearing ability in individuals living near the airport | Chen et al. 1997 |
| Residential aircraft noise | Population living near the airport | Hypertension risk | Rosenlund et al. 2001; Eriksson et al. 2007 |
| Residential aircraft noise | Populations living near six European airports (HYENA project) | Increase of blood pressure and cardiovascular disease | Jarup et al. 2005, 2008; Haralabidis et al. 2008 |

## Table 3. Continued

| Exposure | Exposed population | Observed effects | References |
|---|---|---|---|
| Residential aircraft noise | Population living near the airport | Annoyance | van Kamp et al. 2004; Lim et al. 2008 |
| Residential aircraft noise | Population living near the airport | Cardiovascular and neuropsychological disorders (sleep loss, fatigue, concentration failure) | Health Council of the Netherlands 1999 |
| Residential aircraft noise | Population living near the airport | Impairment of cognitive performance in children | Stansfeld et al. 2005 |
| microwaves and radiofrequency radiation | Radar operators | Nervous, ophthalmic and haematological-immunological effects | Goldoni et al. 1993 |
| microwaves and radiofrequency radiation | Radar operators | Immunological disorders | Moszczynski et al. 1999 |
| microwaves and radiofrequency radiation | Personnel working at a civil aircraft radar-tracking system | Cardiovascular disease | Tikhonova et al. 2003 |
| microwaves and radiofrequency radiation | Radar operators | Decreased sperm mobility and viability | Liu et al. 2003 |
| microwaves and radiofrequency radiation | Radar operators | Increase of sperm dysmorphia | Ding et al. 2004 |

No many studies are in general available on health effects of airport pollution on workers and populations living and working in surrounding of the airport.

The principal published studies on the effects induced by exposure to chemical and physical airport pollutants are reported in Table 2 and Table 3.

Some studies on airport workers report genotoxic and oxidative [Pitarque et al. 1999; Cavallo et al. 2002, 2006], neurotoxic [Knave et al. 1976], respiratory [Yang 2003; Tunnicliffe et al. 1999], auditory [Chen et al. 1992; Hong and Kim 2001; Thakur et al. 2004] reproductive and irritant effects [Lemasters et al. 1999; Yang 2003]. Two studies relative to cancer induction by exposure to airport pollution did not show significant increase of such disease on airport ground personnel or airport neighbours [Froom et al. 1996; Visser et al. 2005].

While in people living near large airports hypertension [Rosenlund et al. 2001; Jarup L. et al. 2005; Eriksson et al. 2007] sleep loss, fatigue, concentration failure [Health Council of Netherland 1999] cardiovascular and neuropsychological disorders [Pisani et al. 2003; Jarup et al. 2005] or effects on auditory system [Chen et al. 1997] related to aircraft noise are reported.

## Genotoxic Effects

Genotoxic effects of jet fuel exposure in military aviation that employs specific kind of jet propulsion fuels (JP-4, JP-5, JP-8) have been shown. In particular in a study on aircraft maintenance workers exposed to JP-4, a small but statistically significant increase of SCE frequency after 30 weeks of exposure was found for sheet metal workers exposed to the highest total solvent and fuel breath exposure levels [Lemasters et al. 1997].

For civil aviation that uses principally jet A fuel, a few data are actually available on genotoxic effects of Jet A exposure. A study of Pitarque et al. 1999 performed on airport ground personnel at Barcelona airport measured Sister Chromatide Exchanges (SCE), Micronuclei (MN) and DNA damage. No increase of SCE and MN were found while a slight DNA damage evaluated by comet test was observed [Pitarque et al. 1999]. A recent study performed on airport ground personnel of a large civil airport in Italy reports that chronic exposure to airport pollutants can induce genotoxic and oxidative effect on airport personnel [Cavallo et al. 2006]. In particular the study evaluates the occupational exposure to PAHs and their genotoxic and oxidative effects by Chromosomal Aberrations (CA), SCE, MN and formamidopyrimidine glycosylase (Fpg)-modified comet assay. Environmental monitoring of exposure was carried out analysing 23 PAHs on air samples collected from airport apron, airport building and terminal/office area during 5 working days. Biological monitoring of exposure was performed measuring urinary 1-Hydroxy-pyrene (1-OHP). Total PAHs level in airport apron was significantly higher than in the other monitored areas. Urinary OH-pyrene didn't show differences between exposed and controls. The exposed group showed an higher mean value of SCE and of total structural CA in particular breaks and fragments whereas there were no differences for MN frequency. Comet assay evidenced a direct and oxidative DNA damage.

This study furnished an useful contribution to the characterization of civil airport exposure and suggest the use of comet assay on exfoliated buccal cells to assess the occupational exposure to mixtures of inhalable pollutants at low doses since these cells represent the target tissue for this exposure and are obtained by non-invasive procedure.

Several studies are available on genotoxic effects of exposure to cosmic radiations in flight personnel. In these studies chromosomal aberrations are investigated and an increase of unstable aberrations such as dicentric and ring chromosomes in civil aviation pilots and crew members [Romano et al. 1997] and dicentric chromosomes and MN frequency in Concorde pilots [Heimers et al. 2000] were found while no increase of dicentric frequency was shown in female cabine attendants [Wolf et al. 1999] and flight engineers [Zwinmann et al. 1998]. In other studies evaluating stable chromosomal aberrations, particularly those induced by chronic low-dose exposure (traslocations), a significant increase of these aberrations were found in airline pilots with many years of flight experience [Cavallo et al. 2002; Nicholas et al. 2003] and a cumulative dose within 26 to 72 mSV range.

## Other Health Effects

### Airport Workers

Health effects such as eye and respiratory irritations due to aldehydes after occupational exposure to jet engine emissions, have been reported [Kobayashi and Kikukawa 2000]. An association between occupational exposure to aviation fuel or jet steam exhaust and some respiratory effects was also reported by Tunnicliffe et al. [1999] in UK airport ground workers. Adverse respiratory and irritant effects of airport pollution has been also found in airport workers in Taiwan [Yang 2003]. In these exposed workers, chronic respiratory symptoms such as cough and dyspnea were significantly more common in respect to control group of unexposed subjects and a prevalence of acute irritative symptoms although not statistically significant was also found.

Long-term exposure to petroleum-distilled fuels can also produce deleterious changes in the nervous system. Employees working with jet fuel in an aircraft factory were examined by Knave et al. [1976] to investigate the possible effect of long-term exposure on the nervous system. The exposed workers were divided in heavily exposed and less heavily exposed groups and all the first group and 7 of the 16 subjects of the second group presented repeatedly acute symptoms (dizziness, respiratory tract symptoms, palpitations, pressure on the chest, nausea, headache). A high rate of symptoms indicative of neurasthenia and psychasthenia and symptoms and signs indicative of polyneuropathy were observed in both groups.

In a prospective study Lemasters et al. evaluated male reproductive effects of solvent and fuel exposure during aircraft maintenance [Lemasters et al. 1999]. This study demonstrated that the paint shop group of workers had a significant decline in sperm motility of 19,5% after 30 weeks of exposure.

The negative effects of aircraft noise on auditory function of airport workers were evidenced by several studies reporting hearing loss related to occupational exposure [Chen et al. 1992; Hong and Kim 2001; Thakur et al. 2004]. Audiometry and brainstem auditory evoked potentials were measured in 112 airport employees (maintenance workers, firemen, policemen, airline ground staff and civil servants) to study the effects of aircraft noise on hearing and auditory pathway function [Chen et al. 1992]. In this study the authors found that the incidences of noise-induced hearing loss were highest in the groups of maintenance workers and firemen, who are almost continuously exposed to aircraft noise. The degree of auditory damage coincided with job patterns.

A study performed at the Alexandria airport that assessed noise levels and measured hearing acuity of working personnel, revealed significant hearing defects especially in workers exposed to noise aircraft and other airport activities at the exterior of the airport building [Abel Moneim 1995]. Thakur et al. [2004] performed a study on auditory evoked functions in the ground crew employees working in Mumbay airport to evaluate the effects of continuous exposure to high level of noise of the surroundings of the airport. The exposed group showed hearing loss at different frequencies. The exposure to the high level of noise caused considerable decline in the auditory conduction up to the level of the brainstem with no significant change in conduction in the midbrain, sub cortical areas, auditory cortex and associated areas [Thakur et al. 2004].

Another health effect of airport work, reported by a study evaluating the frequencies of most common medical problems in airport ground personnel, is the low back pain that resulted to be the most common disease [Froom et al. 1996].

Long-term health effects such as nervous, ophthalmic and haematological-immunological disorders, psycophysiological and stress response or reproductive impairment [Goldoni et al. 1993; Costa 1993, 2000; Zeier 1994; Liu et al 2003, Ding et al. 2004; Jauchem 2008] have been evidenced in air traffic controllers in association with occupational exposure to microwaves-radiofrequency radiations, ELF electromagnetic fields or workload. In particular Moszczynski et al. [1999] found that radar operators exhibited elevated IgM and decreased total T8 lymphocytes, Liu et al. [2003] found decreased sperm mobility and viability and Ding et al. 2004 noted an increase of sperm dysmorphia in radar operators.

## People Living Around Airport

There are strong evidences that support a correlation between noise and cardiovascular disease, but it has also been supposed a relationship between noise and other physiological disorders. A review concerning the noise and health literature affirms: "Exposure to noise constitutes a health risk" [Passchier-Vermeer and Passchier 2000]. Excessive noise from highways, railroads, and airports have long been regarded as hazardous to health and well being [USEPA 1978].

Aircraft noise exposure of people living around airports has been linked to various physiological and psychological effects, such as sleep disturbances, electroencephalographic changes and annoyance [Morrell and Taylor 1997].

In a Swedish study a strong association between annoyance and measures of maximum aircraft noise levels compared with energy averaged levels was found [Björkman et al 1992].

Other more recent studies found a relationship between noise exposure levels of people living in areas close to large airport and annoyance [van Kamp et al. 2004; Lim et al. 2008], or impairment of cognitive performance in children [Stansfeld et al. 2005]. Some studies report an association between aircraft noise and hypertension [Rosenlund et al. 2001; Eriksson et al. 2007; Jarup et al. 2008, Haralabidis et al. 2008]. Other studies found cardiovascular and neuropsychological disorders such as sleep loss, fatigue, concentration failure (Health Council of the Netherlands 1999) or effects on auditory system in residents surrounding large airports [Pisani et al. 2003, Jarup et al. 2005; Chen et al. 1997]. In particular audiometry measurements, performed on two groups of individuals who lived in two communities located at different distances from the airport, indicated that hearing ability was reduced significantly in individuals who lived near the airport and who were exposed frequently to aircraft noise [Chen et al. 1997].

## Epidemiological Studies

### Chemical Airport Pollution

The most widely quoted studies on carcinogenic effects of jet fuels were conducted by Selden and Ahlborg (1986, 1987) on a cohort of 2182 Swedish military personnel and others exposed to JP4 or jet A1-like fuels with mean jet fuel vapour concentrations often exceeding 350 mg/m$^3$ and didn't show higher incidence of cancers or death during a follow-up of six years [Selden and Ahlborg 1986, 1987].

A study relative to cancer induction by exposure to airport pollution did not show significant increase of such disease on airport ground personnel in respect to other workers [Froom et al. 1996].

The incidence of cancer during 1988-2003 was estimated in the area around Amsterdam airport Schipol in a population-based study using the regional cancer registry [Visser et al. 2005]. In this study total cancer incidence in the area around the airport was almost equal to the national cancer incidence (standardize incidence ratio (SIR) 1.02). An association was found between residence in the airport area and incidence of haematological malignancies, especially non-Hodgkin lymphoma and acute lymphoblastic leukaemia, while the incidence of cancer of the respiratory system was statistically decreased.

**Cosmic Radiations**

Particular attention has been focused on the cancer risk linked to cosmic radiations exposure of flight personnel. Since the early 1990s, several epidemiological studies have been published on cancer incidence and mortality among aircrew indicating increased risk for different cancer types [Salisbury et al. 1991; Irvine et al. 1992; Ballard et al. 2000]. A meta-analysis evaluating the results of six cancer incidence cohort studies to investigate cancer incidence in pilots, evidenced a significant incidence for acute mieloid leukemia (AML) (combined relative risk $RR_c$ 4.63), non melanoma skin tumors ($RR_c$ 2.82), prostate cancer ($RR_c$ 1.37) and testicular cancer ($RR_c$ 1.71). The main finding is the increased incidence of AML (tumor associated to exposure to ionizing radiation) particularly in jet pilots with more flight hours [Marinaccio et al. 2001]. More recent studies did not find significant increase of cancer risk linked to cosmic radiation exposure in commercial airline pilots or cabin attendants [Zeeb et al. 2002; Langner et al. 2004; Kojo et al. 2005]. In particular in a cohort study on 6.061 male cockpit personnel of two German airlines, that were traced for the period 1960-1997, a lack of increased cancer risk in association to individual radiation dose was found [Zeeb et al. 2002]. Moreover Langner et al. [2004] in a large European cohort study (ESCAPE) investigated cancer mortality on the basis of individual effective dose and did not find any increase of cancer mortality due to cosmic radiations.

**Noise**

In a cross-sectional epidemiological study performed on 255 high noise-exposed full-time male workers at an airport in Korea, Hong and Kim [2001] found that both occupational noise exposure (noise exposure level and years of noise exposure) and personal risk factors such as non-occupational noise exposure, history of ear disease, ototoxic drug use, cigarette smoking, hypertension, and use of hearing protecting devices, were significantly associated with hearing loss [Hong and Kim 2001].

A cohort of 2754 men in 4 municipalities around Stockholm Arlanda airport was followed between 1992-1994 and 2002-2004 [Eriksson et al. 2007]. Residential aircraft noise exposure was assessed among those living near the airport. For subjects exposed to energy-averaged levels above 50 dB(A) the adjusted relative risk for hypertension was 1.19, similar to that found for men exposed above 70 dB(A) that was 1.20. However, stronger association was suggested for older subjects, those with normal glucose tolerance, non-smokers, and subjects not annoyed by noise from other sources. The European project (Hypertension and Exposure to Noise near Airports (HYENA)) involving six large airports in Germany, UK, Italy, the Netherland, Sweden and Greece aims to assess the impact of airport-related noise exposure on blood pressure and cardiovascular disease in people living near airport [Jarup et al. 2005]. The results of this project published by Jarup et al. [2008] and Haralabidis et al. [2008] indicate an excess risk of hypertension in relation to long-term noise exposure primarily for night-time aircraft noise and daily average road traffic noise.

## Microwave Radiation

There are a few data relative to the health effects of microwave radiation in man. The results of medical examinations of subjects exposed to microwaves and radiofrequency radiation was performed on 49 radar operators from the Zagreb air traffic control who were examined twice within a period of 18 months. The results of this follow-up study indicate that long-term occupational exposure to microwaves and radiofrequency may damage sensitive organic systems such as nervous, ophthalmic and haematological-immunological [Goldoni et al. 1993].

Garaj-Vrohac et al. [1993] examined six men accidentally exposed while repairing microwave devices used for air traffic control in Zagreb. The accidental exposure was greater than 1250-1350 MHz with power density of 10 μg/W to 20 mW/cm2 that represented the usual exposure conditions. The results of chromosome aberration analysis during 1984 to 1999 showed no increase in chromosomal abnormalities compared to control [Garaj-Vrohac et al. 1993].

Cardiovascular and immunological disorders [Tikhonova et al. 2003; Jauchem 2008] have been evidenced in air traffic controllers in association with occupational exposure to microwaves-radiofrequency radiations. Tikhonova et al. [2003] reported a high prevalence rate of cardiovascular disease in personnel working at a civil aircraft radar-tracking system.

## Workload

Interaction between workload and psycophysiological stress symptoms were studied in a population of 205 air traffic controllers in Zurich and Geneve airports by standardized questionnaires. About 10-15% of workers showed elevated values in psychological stress symptoms in association to workload [Zeier et al. 2004].

Psycophysiological, cardiopathy and stress response in air traffic controllers in association with workload were found in several Italian studies [Costa 1993, 2000, 2004]. In another Italian study evaluating burnout in 109 air traffic controllers by Rome Burnout Inventory, a closely and positively association between burnout syndrome and age, years spent in air traffic control, professional dissatisfaction and work stressors was found [Dell'Erba et al. 1994].

# Conclusion

Airport personnel is occupationally exposed to a very complex mixture of chemical and physical agents with potential negative health effects. The most available studies on health effect of airport pollution concern the aircraft noise-induced disturbs, represented by hearing loss in airport workers, and hypertension, cardiovascular and neuropsycological disorders in populations living near the airport. Other studies concern the health effects of microwaves-radiofrequency radiations (immunological and reproductive) and of workload (psycophysiological stress) in radar operators. Several studies on genotoxic effects of chronic exposure to cosmic radiations in flight personnel (working on long-haul flights) have been also published.

However, airport chemical pollution, due to several sources such as fuel combustion in aircraft engines, ground service vehicles, airport-associated traffic, represents for airport ground personnel the most critical hazard for health due to its potential carcinogenic effects. This exposure is very difficult to characterize due to the numerousness of substances that, although present at low concentrations, can interact each other and with other environmental factors such as solar radiation (UVA light), that could activate the chemical interaction between organic compounds and other PM components, or air $NO_x$, $O_2$ gases, inducing a possible synergistic biological effect. Therefore, it is very difficult to perform an accurate evaluation of the occupational exposure by environmental monitoring of all chemical pollutants. Among them PAHs represent the most hazardous since some of them are known carcinogens. Although the airport workers are exposed to low levels of PAHs, there is a possibility of long-term health effects following chronic exposure by inhalation or skin contamination, as reported in the few available studies on genotoxic effects of chemical air pollution in civil airport ground personnel [Pitarque et al. 1999; Cavallo et al. 2006]. There is a scarcity of data on PAHs monitoring in civil aviation airport probably due to inability of commonly used methods to measure trace amounts of each PAH [Bernabei et al. 2003]. However in the last years more sensitive methods for exposure assessment and evaluation of the induced genotoxic effects of PAHs have been developed. These methods could represent useful tools to monitor occupational exposure of airport workers and to furnish important indications in terms of risk assessment, prevention and management. The use of such sensitive tools to accurately evaluate occupational exposure and early biological effects in studies involving airport personnel from large airports in the world, are warmly desirable to clearly define health risk of airport pollution.

# References

Abel Moneim I. Do workers exposed to intermittent aircraft noise suffer from occupational deafness? A study in Alexandria airport. *J Egypt Public Health Assoc.* 1995, 70(5-6), 699-713.

Bagshaw M, Irvine D, Davies DM. Exposure to cosmic radiation of British Airways flying crew on oltralonghaul routes. *Occup Environ Med*, 1996, 53, 495-498.

Ballard T, Lagorio S, De Angelis G, Verdecchia A. Cancer incidence and mortality among flight personnel: a meta-analysis. *Aviat Space Environ Med*, 2000, 71(3), 216-224.

Bernabei M, Reda R, Galiero R, Bocchinfuso G. Determination of total and polycyclic aromatic hydrocarbons in aviation jet fuel. *J. Chromatograph. A,* 2003, 985, 197-203.

Björkman M, Åhrlin U, Rylander R. Aircraft noise annoyance and average versus maximum noise levels. *Arc Environ Health*, 1992, 47, 326-329.

Cavallo D, Marinaccio, Perniconi B, Tomao P, Pecoriello V, Moccaldi R, Iavicoli S. Chromosomal aberrations in long-haul air crew members. *Mutat Res*, 2002, 513/1-2, 11-15.

Cavallo D, Ursini CL, Carelli G, Iavicoli I, Ciervo A, Perniconi B, Rondinone B, Gismondi M, Iavicoli S. Occupational exposure in airport personnel: characterization and evaluation of genotoxic and oxidative effects. *Toxicology*, 2006, 223 (1-2), 26-35.

Chen TJ, Chiang HC, Chen SS. Effects of aircraft noise on hearing and auditory pathway function of airport employees. *J Occup Med*, 1992, 34(6), 613-619.

Chen TJ, Chen SS, Hsieh PY, Chiang HC. Auditory effects of aircraft noise on people living near airport. *Arch Environ Health*, 1997, 52(1), 45-50.

Childers JW, Witherspoon CL, Smith LB, Pleil J. Real-time and integrated measurements of potential human exposure to particle-bound polycyclic aromatic hydrocarbons (PAHs) from aircraft exhaust. *Environ. Health Perspect*, 2000, 108/9, 853-862.

Cohen BS, Brozaft AL, Heikkinen M, Goodman J, Nadas A. Airport-Related air pollution and noise. *J Occup Environ Hyg*, 2008, 5, 119-129.

Costa G. Evaluation of workload in air traffic controllers. *Ergonomics*, 1993, 36(9), 1111-1120.

Costa G. Working and health conditions of Italian air traffic controllers. *Int J Occup Saf Ergon*, 2000, 6(3), 365-382.

Costa G. Cardiopathy and stress-inducing factors. *Med Lav*, 2004, 95(2), 133-139.

Dell'Erba G, Venturi P, Rizzo F, Porcù S, Pancheri P. Burnout and health status in Italian air traffic controllers. *Aviat Space Environ Med*, 1994, 65(4), 315-322.

Ding XP, Yan SW, Zhang N, Tang J, Lu HO, Wang XL, Tang Y. A cross-sectional study on nonionizing radiation to male fertility. *Zhonghua Liu Xing Bing Xue Za Zhi*, 2004, 25(1), 40-43.

Eriksson C, Roselund M, Pershagen G, Hilding A, Ostenson CG, Bluhm G. Aircraft noise and incidence of hypertension. *Epidemiology*, 2007, 18(6), 716-721.

Froom P, Cline B, Ribak J. Disease evaluated on return-to-work examinations: Aviation group personnel compared to other workers. *Aviation, Space, and Environmental Medicine*, 1996, 67(4), 361-363.

Garaj-Vrohac V, Fucic A, Pevalek-Kozlina B. The rate of elimination of chromosomal aberrations after accidental exposure to microwaves. *Bioelectrochem Bioenerg*, 1993, 30, 319-325.

Goldoni J, Durek M, Koren Z. Health status of personnel occupationally exposed to radiowaves. *Arh Hig Rada Toksikol*, 1993, 44, 223-228.

Haralabidis AS, Dimakopoulou K, Vigna-Taglianti F, Giampaolo M, Borgini A, Dudley ML, Pershagen G, Bluhm G, Houthuijs D, Babisch W, Velonakis M, Katsouyanni K, Jarup L. Acute effects of night-time noise exposure on blood pressure in populations living near airports. *Europ Hearth J,* 2008, 29, 658-664.

Health Council of the Netherlands. Committee on the Health Impact of Large Airports: public health impact of large airports. *The Hague*, 1999; 1999/14E:http://www.gr.nl/pdf.php?ID=19.

Heimers A, Schröder H, Lengfelder E., Schmitz-Feuer-hake I. Chromosome aberration analysis in aircrew members. *Radiat. Prot. Dosim*, 1995, 60, 171-175.

Hong OS and Kim MJ. Factor associated with hearing loss among workers of the airline industry in Korea. *ORL Head Neck Nurse*, 2001, 19(1), 7-13.

Iavicoli I, Carelli G, Bergamaschi A. Exposure evaluation to airborne polycyclic aromatic hydrocarbons in an Italian airport. *J Occup Env Med*, 2006, 48(8), 815-822.

Iavicoli I, Chiarotti M, Bergamaschi A, Marsili R, Carelli G. Determination of airborne polycyclic aromatic hydrocarbons at an airport by gas chromatography-mass spectrometry and evaluation of occupational exposure. *J Chromatogr A*, 2007, 1150(1-2), 226-235.

Irvine D, Davies DM. The mortality of British Airways pilots, 1966-1989: a proportional mortality study. *Aviat Space Environ Med*, 1992, 63(4), 276-279.

Jarup L, Dudley ML, Babisch W, Houthuijs D, Swart W, Pershagen G, Bluhm G, Katsouyanni K, Velonakis M, Cadum E, Vigna-Taglianti F. Hypertension and Exposure to Noise near Airports (HYENA): study design and noise exposure assessment. *Environ Health Perspect.*, 2005, 113(11), 1473-1482.

Jarup L, Babisch W, Houthuijs D, Pershagen G, Katsouyanni K, Cadum E, Dudley ML, Savigny P, Seiffert I, Swart W, Breugelmans O, Bluhm G, Selander J, Haralabidis A, Dimakopoulou K, Sourtzi P, Velonakis M, Vigna-Taglianti F. Hypertension and exposure to noise near airports: the HYENA study. *Environ Health Perspect.*, 2008, 116(3), 329-333.

Jauchem JR. Effects of low-level radio-frequency (3kHz to 300 GHz) energy on human cardiovascular, reproductive, immune, and other systems. A review of the recent literature. *Int J Hyg Env Health*, 2008, 211, 1-29.

Knave B, Persson HE, Goldberg JM, Westerholm P. Long-term exposure to jet fuel: an investigation on occupationally exposed workers with special reference to the nervous system. *Scand J Work Environ Health.* 1976, 2(3), 152-164.

Kojo K, Pukkala E, Auvinen A. Breast cancer risk among Finnish cabin attendants: a nested case-control study. *Occup Environ Med.* 2005, 62(7), 488-943.

Kobayashi A, Kikukawa A. Increased formaldehyde jet engine exhaust with changes to JP-8, lower temperature, and lower humidity irritates eyes and respiratory tract. *Aviation Space Environ Med.* 2000, 71, 396-399.

Langner I, Blettner M, Gundestrup M, Storm H, Aspholm R, Auvinen A, Pukkala E, Hammer GP, Zeeb H, Hrafnkelsson J, Rafnsson V, Tulinius H, De Angelis G, Verdecchia A, Haldorsen T, Tveten U, Eliasch H, Hammar N, Linnersjö A. Cosmic radiation and cancer mortality among airline pilots: results from a European cohort study (ESCAPE). *Radiat Environ Biophys*, 2004, 42(4), 247-256.

Lemasters GK, Livingston GK, Lockey JE, Olsen DM, Shukla R, New G, Selevan SG, Yiin JH. Genotoxic changes after low-level solvent and fuel exposure on aircraft maintenance personnel. *Mutagenesis*, 1997, 12(4), 237-243.

Lemasters GK, Olsen DM, Yiin JH, Lockey JE, Shukla R, Selevan SG, Schrader SM. Toth GP, Evenson DP, Huszar GB. Male reproductive effects of solvent and fuel exposure during aircraft maintenance. *Reprod Toxicol*, 1999, 13(3), 155-166.

Lim C, Kim J, Hong J, Lee S. Effect of background noise levels on community annoyance from aircraft noise. *J Acoust Soc Am*, 2008, 123(2), 766-771.

Liu X, Yan SW, Ding XP, Zhang N, Lu HO, Tang J. Evaluation of radiation damage to the sperm DNA of radar operator. *Zhonghua Nan Ke Xue,* 2003, 9(7), 494-496.

Marinaccio A, Perniconi B, Cavallo D, Scarselli A, Nesti M, Palmi S, Iavicoli S. Rischio cancerogeno per il personale di volo su rotte a lungo raggio. Una meta-analisi degli studi di coorte. *Prevenzione Oggi ,* 2001, 3, 71-80.

Meijer W, De Jonge D. *Datarapport Luchtkwaliteit Haarlemmermeer.* Resultaten 2002. (Air quality Haarlemmermeer; results 2002). Haarlem: Provincie Noord-Holland, 2003.

Morrell S and Taylor R. A review of health effects of aircraft noise. *Aust N Z J Public Health,* 1997, 21, 221-236.

Moszczyński P, Lisiewicz J, Dmoch A, Zabiński Z, Bergier L, Rucińska M, Sasiadek U. The effect of various occupational exposures to microwave radiation on the concentrations of immunoglobulins and T lymphocyte subsets. *Wiad Lek,* 1999, 52(1-2), 30-34.

Nicholas JS, Butler GC, Davis S, Bryant E, Hoel DG, Mohr LC Jr. Stable chromosome aberrations and ionizing radiation in airline pilots. Aviat Space Environ Med, 2003, 74(9), 953-956.

Passchier W, Knottnerus A, Albering H, Walda I. Public health impact of large airports. *Rev Environ Health,* 2000, 15(1-2), 83-96.

Passchier-Vermeer W and Passchier WF. Noise exposure and public health. *Environ Health Perspect,* 2000, 108 (suppl 1), 123-131.

Pisani S, Bonarrigo D, Gambino M, Macchi L, Banfi F, Verri AM, Degli Stefani C, Cislaghi C, Bossi A, Cortinovis I. Epidemiologic study Salus domestica: evaluation of health damage in a sample of women living near the Malpensa 2000 airport. *Epidemiol Prev.* 2003, 27(4), 234-241.

Pitarque M, Creus A, Marcos R, Hughes JA, Anderson D. Examination of various biomarkers measuring genotoxic endpoints from Barcelona airport personnel. *Mutat. Res,* 1999, 440, 195-204.

Pleil JD, Smith LB, Zelnick SD. Personal exposure to JP-8 jet fuel vapours and exhaust at Air Force bases. *Environ. Health Perspect,* 2000, 108, 183-192.

Rafnsson V, Hrafnkelsson J, Tulinius H. Incidence of cancer among commercial airline pilots, *Occup Environ Med,* 2000, 57, 175-179.

Riviere JE, Brooks JD, Monteiro-Riviere NA, Budsaba K, Smith CE. Dermal absorption and distribution of topically dosed jet fuels Jet-A, JP-8, and JP-8(100). *Toxicol. Appl. Pharmacol,* 1999, 160, 60-75.

Romano E, Ferraci L, Nicolai F, Derme V, De Stefano GF. Increase of chromosomal aberrations induced by ionising radiation in peripheral blood lymphocytes of civil aviation pilots and crew members. *Mutat. Res,* 1997, 377, 89-93.

Rosenlund M, Berglind N, Pershagen G, Järup L, Bluhm G. Increased prevalence of hypertension in a population exposed to aircraft noise. *Occup Environ Med,* 2001, 58, 769-773.

Salisbury DA, Band PR, Threlfall WJ, Gallagher RP. Mortality among British Columbia pilots. *Aviat Space Environ Med,* 1991, 62(4), 351-352.

Selden A and Ahlborg G. Jr. *Causes of death and cancer morbidity at exposure to aviation fuels in the Swedish armed forces.* ASF Project 84-0308. Department of Occupational Medicine, Orebro, Sweden 1986.

Selden A and Ahlborg G. Jr. *Causes of death and cancer morbidity at exposure to aviation fuels in the Swedish armed forces*. An update. Department of Occupational Medicine, Orebro, Sweden 1987.

Stansfeld SA, Berglund B, Clark C, Lopez-Barrio I, Fischer P, Ohrström E, Haines MM, Head J, Hygge S, van Kamp I, Berry BF; RANCH study team. Aircraft and road traffic noise and children's cognition and health: a cross-national study. *Lancet*, 2005, 365(9475), 1942-1949.

Tesseraux I. Risk factors of jet fuel combustion products. *Toxicology Lett*, 2004, 149, 295-300.

Thakur L, Anand JP, Banerjee PK. Auditory evoked functions in ground crew working in high noise environment of Mumbay airport. *Indian J Physiol Pharmacol*, 2004, 48(4), 453-460.

Tikhonova GI. Epidemiological risk assessment of pathology development in occupational exposure to radiofrequency electromagnetic fields. *Radiats Biol Radioecol*, 2003, 43(5), 559-564.

Tunnicliffe WS, O'Hickey SP, Fletcher TJ, Mile JF, Burge PS, Ayres JG. Pulmonary function and respiratory symptoms in a population of airport workers. *Occup Environ Med*, 1999, 56, 118-123.

U.S. Environmental Protection Agency (EPA). Information on levels of environmental noise requisite to protect public health and welfare with an adequate margin of safety (EOA/ONAC Report 550/9-74-004). Washington D.C.: USEPA. 1974.

U.S. Environmental Protection Agency (USEPA). Noise : A Health Problem. Washington, D.C.: USEPA, Office of Noise Abatement and Control. 1978.

van Kamp I, Job RF, Hatfield J, Haines M, Stellato RK, Stansfeld SA. The role of noise sensitivity in the noise-response relation: a comparison of three international airport studies. *J Acoust Soc Am*, 2004, 116(6), 3471-3479.

Visser O, van Wijnen JH, van Leeuwen FE. Incidence of cancer in the area around Amsterdam airport Schiphol in 1988-2003: a population-based ecological study. BMC Public Health, 2005, 5/127, 1-10.

Wolf G, Pieper R, Obe G. Chromosomal alterations in peripheral lymphocytes of female cabin attendants. *Int J Radiat Biol* , 1999, 75, 829-836

Yang CY. Adverse respiratory and irritant health effects in airport workers in Taiwan. *Journal of Toxicology and Environmental Healt A,* 2003, 66, 799-806.

Zeier H. Workload and psychophysiological stress reactions in air traffic controlles. *Ergonomics*, 1994, 37(3), 525-539.

Zeeb H, Blettner M, Hammer GP, Langner I. Cohort mortality study of German cockpit crew, 1960-1997. *Epidemiology*, 2002, 13(6), 693-699.

Zwingmann H, Welle IJ, van Herwijnen M, Engelen JJM, Schilderman PAEL, Smid TJ, Kleinjans JCS. Oxidative DNA damage and cytogenetic effects in flight engineers exposed to cosmic radiation. *Environ Mol Mut,* 1998, 32, 121-129.

In: Airports: Performance, Risks, and Problems
Editors: P.B. Larauge et al, pp. 123-145

ISBN: 978-1-60692-393-1
© 2009 Nova Science Publishers, Inc.

*Chapter 6*

# CAPACITY ANALYSIS OF CHECK-IN UNITS IN AIRPORTS USING FUZZY LOGIC AND ARTIFICIAL NEURAL NETWORK APPROACHES

## *Recep Koray Kiyildi[1]*

Niğde University, Department of Civil Engineering, 51245 Niğde,Turkey

## Abstract

An airport is like a complicated factory. Any problem that may happen in any situation can directly be a restrictive factor for the airport capacity. It is necessary to develop a reasonable model in which the time is considered between the plane lands and passengers get out of the airport. One of the most important issues in the capacity analysis of airports is check-in unit capacity analysis. Any airport must have enough number of check-in counters providing necessary and facilitated transportation that takes passengers and their luggage into account. In the literature there is limited work available including the capacity analysis of check-in units in airports to obtain a relation applicable to actual problem. In this work, two different approaches will be presented for the capacity analysis of check-in units of airports which includes many passengers intensively. One is artificial neural network (ANN) method and the other is fuzzy logic approach.

ANN is an efficient method for the analysis of a broad range of engineering problems. In the current problem, an ANN structure predicts the functional time depending on the number of passengers and luggage affecting the capacity. Proposed ANN model is a dynamic model and is a new approach in capacity analysis of airports. A method of relationship is improved to be used in the check-in department with neural network education. Different ANN models have been used and a number of results have been obtained.

Fuzzy logic approach is also extensively used in the analysis of many engineering problems in different disciplines. In the control mechanisms of events linguistic uncertainties may play a significant role. Fuzzy approach considers this role as in the key elements in human thinking. Besides ANN approach, this study also considers the capacity analysis of a check-in department in an airport with the view of those linguistic variables of number of passengers and their luggage adopted.

Both ANN and Fuzzy Logic methods for the capacity analysis of check-in units in airports are used for the check-in unit analysis of a national airport (Antalya Airport). The

---

[1] E-mail address: rkoray@nigde.edu.tr

results have shown both methods work well and as a result, required number of counters in the airport can be determined to provide passengers suitable and facilitated transportation.

# 1. Introduction

An airport is a field which includes many structures built for passengers and plane traffic and much infrastructure equipment for preparing planes for landing and taking off. The most important components of an airport are passengers that are carried by planes, the department for cargo and establishments like taxi, apron and many runways. A reasonable design and healthy operation of an airport require determination of optimum airport capacity, and well management in order to satisfy the airport users and efficient transportation.

The most significant factor that slows down the airport transportation is the deficiency in the airport capacity. The main reason of the deficiency in the airport capacity is the increase in demand which cannot be predicted on time. Hence, necessary actions may not be taken. As a result of this problem, the crowd can increase and possible delays can occur. Consequently, the fly cost and the number of dissatisfied airport users may also increase, and the quality of the service may be deteriorated. Especially in small airports in which limited number of check-in units exists, the terminal capacity mainly determine the airport capacity.

Therefore, the airport capacity must be properly determined. There are number of studies concerning with design and operation of an airport. Lemer (1992) developed some measures of performance for decision making concerning for planning and design or operational airport passenger terminal buildings and how data analysis method and computer based method could be effectively used in yielding these measures. Odoni and Neufville (1992) presented practical procedures for terminal design, based on airports. Hamzawi (1992) considered lack of airport capacity in his study and proposed alternative solutions to the problem. Seneviratne and Martel (1991, 1994 and 1995) determined service quality in airport terminals in order to cover the need of airport users in their studies. Jerynolds and Button (1999) made an assessment of the capacity and congestion levels at European airports. They examined the current capacity of the EU's airport infrastructure and main factors determining that capacity.

Considerable amount of work has been completed in the direction of evaluation of airport performance an airline service quality. Humphreys, Fry and Francis (1995) studied on international survey of performance measurement in airports. Most of important performance evaluation studies are performed with performance measures relating to the airport operating and management such as airline services Adler and Berechman (2001), financial performance Vasigh and Hamzaee (1998). Yeh and Kuo (2003) presented a fuzzy multi-attribute decision making approach for determination passenger service quality of 14 major Asia-Pacific international airport via surveys. Doganis (1992) pointed out to be relatively inelastic the passenger demand for airport services. Measuring quality of passenger services provided by international airports. The mainstream research on service quality has been conducted based on the nation that the quality level of services is perceived and evaluated by customers Gronroos (1990 and 1993). Humphreys and Francis (2000) studied on airport performance evaluation using data envelopment analysis (DEA) and total factor productivity (TFP). Fernandes and Pachece (2002) analyzed the capacity of 35 Brazilin domestic airport using DEA with wives point to defining the efficiency in terms of the number of passengers operated. Pels, Nijkamp and Rietveld (2001) used DEA to determine relative efficiency ratios for European airports. Martin and Roman (2001) applied DEA to measure the efficiency of Spanish Airports prior to privatization. Operational efficiency Sarkis (2000) and productivity Gillen and Lal (1997) and airport passenger terminal operations analysis and modeling Tosic (1992) are displayed. Bauerle, Engelhardt and Kolonko (2007) examined a model for the landing procedure of aircrafts at an airport and computed bounds on the waiting times by comparison to simpler queuing systems. Minaenko and Orekhov (2006) used statistical simulation, the conventional and their proposed methods to control air traffic when airport resources are expected to be reduced. Gilbo (1997) proposed a new technique for improvement of air traffic flow management at airports which takes into account the interaction between runway capacity and capacities of fixes to optimize the traffic flow through the airport system. Huttig, Busch and Gronak (1994) analyzed trends of future air traffic demand and described the capacity problems of the main Germany airports. Yan, Tang and Chen (2004) developed an integer programming model to assist airport authotorities to assign common use in check-in counters. They used heuristic approach to solve the model. Wei and Hansen (2006) developed an aggregate demand model for air passenger traffic in a hub-and-spoke network considering the roles of airline service variables. Bianco, Dell'Olmo and Giordani (2006) proposed a job-shop scheduling model with sequence dependent set-up times with relying the dates to coordinate both in-bound and out-bond traffic flows on all the prefixed routes of an airport terminal area and all aircraft operations at the runway complex. Janic (2005) developed a model including estimating congestion and flight delays, the cost of these delays and the efficiency of particular flights following the introduction of a congestion charge. Ignaccolo (2003) outlined the limits of the analytical approach and shows how to build a simulation procedure. Janic (2004) discussed the long term matching of capacity to demand at London Heathrow Airport in England and provided an analysis including predicting airport demand relative to annual number of air craft movement and number of passengers, designing solutions for provided capacity and generating scenarios for long term matching of capacity to demand. Cao, Chen and Zhou (2005) developed the analytical capacity of an airport with two runways system and analyzed the yielded theoretical capacity curves. There are also some airport capacity related articles employing genetic algorithms. Tzeng and Chen (1999), Hu, Chen and Di Paolo (2007), Hu, Chen (2005), Hu, Wu and Ju (2004) applied genetic algorithm technique for solving airport capacity related problems. Liang, Han and Chou (2005) presented a fuzzy quality function deployment model to achieve service quality assurance before implementing the service actions. They constructed a fuzzy relation matrix for linking service management requirements to customer needs on the basis of cross functional expertise. Yeh and Kuo (2003) presented a fuzzy multi-attribute decision making approach for determination passenger service quality of 14 major Asia-Pacific international airport via surveys. Kiyildi and Karasahin (2008) have used fuzzy logic approach successfully for the capacity analysis of check-in units and total capacity of check-in gates in airports.

In this work, first Fuzzy Logic and ANN models for the check-in unit capacity analysis of an airport are developed and then capacity analyses of an international airport (Antalya Airport) are performed with respect to measurements from the same airport. Antalya is approximately at the center of many tourism regions in the south and southwest of Turkey. Hence a very dense passenger flow is occurring in that airport. As a result, capacity management of Antalya airport is very important for Turkey. Proposed models are applied to the Antalya airport and capacity analyses are carried out considering both passengers and their luggage which are the main effects influencing the capacity of the airports. And these studies given above are related to the testing (scoring) of some departments of the airport for serving efficiently to the passengers and plane traffic. Moreover, they are linked with the identification of delays that can occur in some stages of the demand beforehand. Besides, the expected efficiency can not be taken from some airports because of constructing without taking opinions of the passengers or with unsuitable plans.

This study presents a successful application of artificial neural network and fuzzy logic approaches for developing models to analyze the airport capacity problems.

## 2. General Information on Airports

### 2.1. Airport Capacity

An airport system must use the demand in a logical and economical way and it must have additional facilities for additional requirements. Since the establishment of additional buildings require more time, the available capacity can be improved with new re-arrangements.

As it comes to the airport capacity, the first thing that comes to mind is the capacity of available runways. The capacity of runways is related with its coping with the plane traffic in a certain time (hour, day and year). If the demand is near the capacity, the services are become getting slower and delays can be possible. The fully-functioning of the runways reminds of the efficiency of the airport and services. The problem here is that with the fully-functioning of the runways, the number of the passengers increase. In such a situation, the circumstances for serving shouldn't be kept deteriorated. This situation brings up the capacity of the airport landside component and especially passenger terminal building.

### 2.2. Passenger Terminal Building

Landside components performs functions related to the activities about transportation of the passengers and their luggage from passenger terminal building to the plane, and transportation of commutation passengers and their luggage between flights. A passenger terminal building should be well-equipped to provide a relaxing atmosphere for both passenger and its staff. The kind and sizes of passenger buildings and their components are determined from the activity forecast and field studies. The most crucial aim at the design of a passenger terminal is to keep the expense at optimum level. Furthermore, the buildings should be founded with taking the future requirements into consideration. In order to provide the passengers with well-designed transportation, the directions should be simple and comprehensible.

In these kinds of buildings there should be enough number of car-parks and aprons. If the passenger movement slows down, the optimum rate, additional buildings should be provided. The opportunities for future needs should be provided and; flexible and enlargeable accommodation opportunities should be available. Passenger movement plan should be taken into consideration for proposing and designing components of the terminal building. Besides, the course of luggage is as important as the course of passengers. However, luggage movement can be arranged simpler when compared to the passenger movement.

## 2.3. The Capacity of the Passenger Terminal Building

The capacity of a passenger terminal building is divided into three as its ability of it to serve for passengers, planes and cargo. In order to identify whole terminal capacity, one should evaluate all units in a terminal field (Wells, 2000). The main function of an airport building is to provide the transportation between the air part and the land part. The functions in terminal building are very significant in the evaluation of the quality of the service for each passenger (Morlok, 1973).

## 2.4. Check-in Capacity

The number of required check-in counter is a function of the average speed of passenger flow through check-in points and average time period to serve a passenger. Average check-in capacity time period varies with destination and type of traffic. Based on the process time period, an acceptable check-in speed can be identified and the capacity required for each check-in point can be determined (FAA, 1988). Density within hour occurs as in unloading ground vehicles and time unit for measuring flow speed is obtained from research measures (USHT, 1987). Processes of passengers coming before the last closing hour for check-in must be carried out without any delay. Required number and type of counters are determined by considering staff criteria, luggage and passenger policy of airline companies.

Other factors which affects check-in capacity are number of airline companies, their share in traffic, process frequency and situation of the position of check-in. Provided that these numbers are used homogeneously, the number of required facilities will be minimized and any passengers can check in through any check-in points for any flights (USHT, 1987). The use of required capacity and facilities will be depending on whether some points are allocated for special purposes. (For instance, different check-in points for domestic flights and international flights). If extra entrance check in capacity is required, it depends on the decisions of airline operators and airport officials. Using all check in positions homogeneously provides comfort for passengers and ground vehicles operate for unloading easily. As using the above mentioned facilities for special purposes increases, providing a balanced capacity distribution becomes more difficult and passenger flows may become disorganized rather than being in line.

## 2.5. Check-in Systems

Check-in systems used by airline companies and operators have important effects on planning of entrance check-in systems. In most of small airports, manual ticket check, weighing luggage and labeling are still carried out. On the contrary, in big airports, computerized entrance check-in systems are widely used. Since, additional place for check-in positions are needed for new operational systems, they can affect planning of passenger buildings. These systems may increase the check-in position capacity significantly (flow speed) since they reduce service duration unit for a passenger. However, manual check-in systems is expected to be used for following years.

Capacity provided in any parts of destinations of passenger flow must be in harmony with those in other parts. In other case, it will cause disorder in parts that have lower capacity or successive delays or decline in output in parts that have bigger capacity. Modifications to be done in entrance check-in system also affects location orders and usage of these systems. Operators are consulted in view of local conditions by airport official to determine how many entrance check-in counters are needed and where to locate these systems.

# 3. Methods of Analysis

## 3.1. Fuzzy Logic Approach

Fuzzy logic concept was first presented by Zadeh L.A. (Zadeh, 1967). Previously two-valued Aristotelian logic (1 or 0, exist or not exist) had been the only valid approach in dealing with logical statements. However, in the control mechanisms of events linguistic uncertainties may play a significant role. Fuzzy approach considers this role as in the key elements in human thinking. The uncertainties are not probabilistic or stochastic type. Zadeh in his study observed that every linguistic word could be represented by means of a fuzzy subset. This study considers the capacity analysis of a check-in department in a national airport (Antalya Airport) with the view of those linguistic variables of number of passengers and their luggage adopted. The fuzzy logic approach is for tailored for the capacity model in a similar way for the use of fuzzy logic control of dynamic systems, which is named shortly as fuzzy logic control.

In this approach, fuzzy propositions i.e. IF-THEN statements are used for the characterization of the model considered, and the true value of statements is a measure of good match between the description and the state of system. Fuzzy logic has been developing rapidly in the world-wide, especially in Japan where it is now being used for the automatic control of commercial products such as robotics. There are many textbooks on the concepts of fuzzy logic approach (Klir and Fogel 1988; Kosko 1992; Zadeh and Kacprzyk 1992; Kosko 1993, McNeill and Thro 1994). The basic idea of the method is the allowance to belong different subsets partially, instead of belonging to a single set. Partial belonging is taken into account by means of a membership function assuming values between 0 and 1.

There is a huge amount of literature about assigning membership functions to fuzzy variables. Intuitions, inference, rank ordering, angular fuzzy sets, neural networks, genetic algorithms, inductive reasoning are most used methods for this process. Intuition includes contextual and schematic knowledge about an issue; linguistic truth about this knowledge is also involved (Zadeh and Kacprzyk 1992). Although the measurement seems to be crisp quantities; they can be fuzzyfied. If uncertainty form seems to have happened due to impression, ambiguity or vagueness, the variable is said to be fuzzy and can be represented by a membership function. Membership functions are assumed as linear in practical applications for the simplification of calculations. The objective then may be described as maximizing the minimum membership value. This operation has the effect of balancing the degree to that the objective is attained.

Fuzzy sets can be used to constitute rules in the following (3.1) forms:

R: IF the value of variable $X_1$ is "large" and variable $X_2$ is "medium" THEN the result

$$Y \text{ is "small"} \tag{3.1}$$

This statement resembles more closely to human thinking than any explicit mathematical rules. Therefore, fuzzy control rules can be used for modeling the behavior of human expert.

The interval representing word or expression which is processed by fuzzy logic is formed by qualified persons about the expression and; then membership functions are constructed according to them.

Membership function is such a curve changing its shape with respect to set member's values. If the most important members are represented by 1, the others are changing between 0 and 1. As a result, the items of membership function have a membership level with respect to their importance level. Membership functions generally are used as triangles or trapezoids. Membership levels of membership functions are determined by means of different methods. Among them mostly used methods are neural network and genetic algorithm (Sen, 1998).

Figure 3.1 shows a fuzzy system in which fuzzification and defuzzification process on input and output units are represented as boxes. A fuzzification unit is added for the numerical inputs and defuzzification unit for the fuzzy outputs which are to be transformed into numerical values.

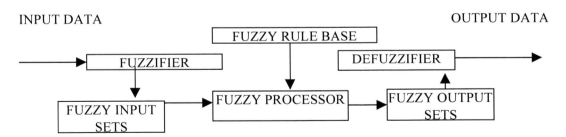

Figure 3.1. Fuzzy system with fuzzification-defuzzification unit.

One of the most important properties of a fuzzy system is the transformation of multiple inputs to a single output. Fuzzy system detects the system response transforming the nonlinear input variables into output variables. Hence; it is possible to control the system considered to reach the required results by making a transformation to the nonlinear data base (Sen, 2004).

For the applications, outputs can not be used directly and must be transformed into a single value. To make this operation, defuzzification process must be employed which is the inverse of fuzzification. There are 7 methods for defuzzification. One can be decided, for use of appropriate method for the case under consideration (Sen, 2004).

Main defuzzification methods are: Defuzzification with respect to maximum membership degree method, Defuzzification with respect to centroid method, Defuzzification with respect to weighted average method.

## 3.2. Artificial Neural Network Approach

The ANN methodology has been used in various communicates traffic and transportation engineering related problems in the last decade. Artificial neural network is a kind of programming technique which is developed depending on the working mechanism of the human brain. In this method, human brain functioning is realized in a computer atmosphere. In other words the ANN is an artificial intellience technique which is developed for finding solutions to the problems which are complicated or the problems whose relationships are not known. The algorithm works like a brain, can decide, can come to a conclusion, can deduce knowledge from an unknown or available data, can accept permanent data entrance, can learn and remember.

The structure of ANN is modeled in relationship with human brain. Although this simulation has many effects on the development of ANN, there is not actual similarity between them. The ANN has lots of features such as learning about input data, generalizing the knowledge, abbreviating, working like a human brain. In order to make the best modelling, it is necessary to identify all biological structure and functions of human brain. Even though we don't have enough knowledge about the methodology of human brain, we have enough knowledge to develop ANN models.

The studies about ANN first started in the 1940's. In an ANN model, there are input, hidden and output layers. Each unit composed of many neuron cells and they are linked to each other with weights. The style of linking and the number of neuron cells may be different. It is forbidden to have any communication between the neurons that are in the same layer. The neurons have the input from either from the beginning input or mid value relations.

There are three main layers in ANN structure; a set of input nodes, one or more layers of hidden nodes, and a set of output nodes. Each layer basically contains a number of neurons working as an independent processing element and densely interconnected with each other. The neurons using the parallel computation algorithms are simply compiled with an adjustable connection weights, summation function and transfer function. A simple ANN architecture with one neuron is illustrated in Figure 3.2.

The methodology of ANNs is based on the learning procedure from the data set presented it from the input layer and testing with other data set for the validation. A network is trained by using a special learning function and learning rule. In the learning stage, network initially starts by randomly assigning the adjustable weights and threshold values for each connection between the neurons in accordance with selected ANNs model. After the weighted inputs are summed and added the threshold values, they are passed through a differentiable non-linear function defined as a transfer function. This process is continued, until a particular input captures to their output (i.e., target) or as far as the lowest possible error can be obtained by using an error criterion. In other words the network training is the determination of the weights and the biases (Basma and Kallas, 2004; Moosavi, Yazdanpanah and Doostmohammadi, 2006). An ANNs model can be differently composed in terms of architecture, learning rule and self organization. The most widely used ANNs are the feed-forward, multilayer perceptrons trained by back-propagation algorithms based on gradient descent method (FFBP). This algorithm can provide approximating to any continuous function from one finite-dimensional space to another for any desired degree of accuracy. The superiority of FFBP is that it sensitively assigns the initial weights values very sensitively and therefore it may yield closer results than the each other. It is also easy to implement and the training duration is short.

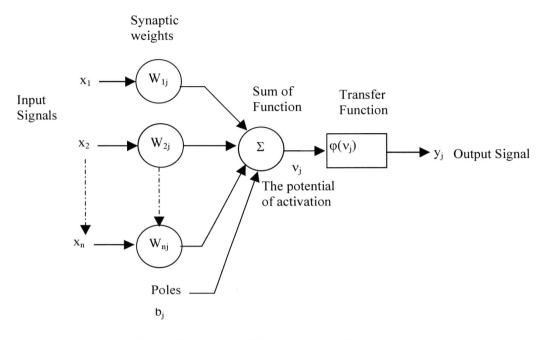

Figure 3.2. A simple ANN architecture with one neuron.

The back propagation is a learning algorithm most widely used in ANNs. The main characteristic of this paradigm is that it works by sending inputs forward and then propagating errors calculated by using certain error criteria backwards. In this algorithm, the learning is based on supervised rule and the training of network model is continued by adjusting the weights until the minimal error is obtained. A feed forward network configuration is plotted in Figure 3.3.

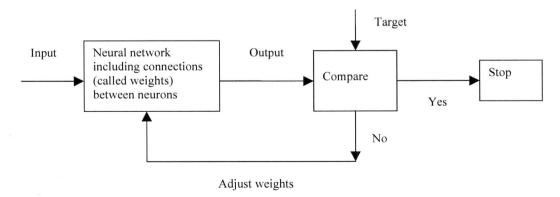

Figure 3.3. Basic principles of a feed forward back-propagation network configuration.

The back propagation process of error is performed by two steps; the first step is a feed forward phase in which the output from the any node is calculated by propagating the input value given from the input nodes. The second step is a backward phase in which connection weights values is corrected by using error criteria. An output value for any neuron in the hidden layer is computed as following equations;

$$Y_j = f\left[\sum_{i=1}^{n} X_i w_{ij} + q_j\right], \qquad i=1,\ldots\ldots,n \qquad j=1,\ldots\ldots,m \qquad (3.2)$$

Where, $Y_j$ is the output value of any neuron in the hidden layer, $X_i=\{X_1,X_2\ldots\ldots X_n\}$ is the input vector, $w_{ij}$ is the weights from the $i^{th}$ neuron to $j^{th}$ neuron. $q_j$ is a threshold value (bias value). $f$ is the transfer function or activation function. n and m is the number of neuron in the input and hidden layer, respectively. The output value of the any output neuron is computed as follow;

$$Y_t = f\left[\sum_{j=1}^{m} Y_{jt} w_{ij} + q_t\right] \qquad t=1,\ldots\ldots,k \qquad (3.3)$$

where k is the number of the neuron in the output layer.

ANNs includes the various transfer function used to establish a relationship between the input and output at each neuron layer. Log sigmoid and tangent sigmoid shown below are most commonly utilized as the transfer functions. The networks would be able to map nonlinear input-output relation by means of nonlinearity of the transfer functions.

$$f(x,w) = \frac{1}{(1+e^{\sum X\ w+q})} \qquad \text{Log-Sigmoid} \qquad (3.4)$$

$$f(x,w) = \frac{(1-e^{\sum X\ w+q})}{(1+e^{\sum X\ w+q})} \qquad \text{Tan-Sigmoid} \qquad (3.5)$$

$$f(x) = x \qquad \text{Purelin} \qquad (3.6)$$

The network propagates the inputs or outputs mapping by using connection weights as far as the lowest possible error can be obtained by using an error criteria. The error is the differences between the calculated output and the target value. The sample Mean square error (MSE) for all input patterns is computed from the following equation.

$$MSE = \frac{1}{N}\sum_{s=1}^{N}\sum_{t=1}^{k}\left(T_{st} - Y_{st}\right)^2 \qquad (3.7)$$

where N is the number of data set pattern. $T_{st}$ is actual value or target value for the $s^{th}$ pattern, $Y_{st}$ is the neural network output value for the $s^{th}$ pattern.

The back propagation algorithm provides to iteratively minimize error. According to gradient descent method, the back propagation paradigm adjusts the weights by calculating the gradient ($\delta_t$) for each neuron on the output layer with the following equations;

$$\delta_t=Y_t(1-Y_t)\ (T_t-Y_t) \qquad (3.8)$$

The error gradient $\delta_j$ is then recursively determined for the hidden layers by computing the weighted sum of the errors at the previous layer.

$$\delta_j=Y_j(1-Y_j)\sum_{t=1}^{k}\delta_t w_{jt} \qquad (3.9)$$

The change in connection weights is updated by using error gradients Eq. (3.9) as shown below.

$$\Delta w_{ij}(r)=-\eta\frac{\partial E}{\partial w_{ij}}=\eta\delta_j x_i \qquad (3.10)$$

$$w_{ji}(r+1)=w_{ji}(r)+\Delta w_{ji}(r) \qquad (3.11)$$

The weigth change after the the $t^{th}$ data presentation is;

$$\Delta w_{ji}(r)=\eta\delta_j x_i+\alpha\Delta w_{ji}(r-1) \qquad (3.12)$$

Where, $\eta$ is the learning rate, $\alpha$ is the momentum rate and r is the iteration number. Back propagation can converge to local minimum some times and therefore global minimum may not reached. To overcome this problem, the momentum rate is used. The other problem in the training stage is overfitting happening during the learning. Although the error of the training may be very small value, however when the new data is evaluated by using the same network, the error may be relatively high. The network memorizes the training data, but it does not generalize new case. To improve the generalization, a method called Bayesian regularization is used. This method use a performance function modified by adding a term that consists of the mean of the sum of squares of the network weights and biases as follow.

$$MSE_{reg} = \beta MSE + \alpha MSw \qquad (3.13)$$

Where MSE is the mean sum of squares of the network errors, MSw is the sum of squares of the networks weights, $\beta$ and $\alpha$ are the performance function parameter (Foresee and

Hagan, 1997). The one of effective way to avoid overfitting is to have as much data as possible. For this purpose one of the criteria is that number of the training case should be at least 30 times of the weights in the networks. Furthermore model selection and early stopping can be used to improve the generalization.

This method has been applied for several kinds of engineering branches. There are a lot of studies, in which ANN is used, in civil engineering. In these studies, Feed-forward back propagation learning algorithm has been used for several times (Sanad and Saka, 2001), (Kartam, Flood and Garrett ,1997), (Waszczyszyn, 1996) and it has given good results. Each neuron has an activation values which is the total of input that comes from other neurons. Input layer support ANN with input from outside. Moreover, output layer gives estimation of ANN. Hidden layers connect input layers and output layers. Optimum number of hidden layers and neuron number of each hidden layer is a specific problem. Accordingly, adequate number of hidden layer and number of neuron for each layer has been found; doing some trials (Sanad and Saka, 2001), (Kartam, Flood and Garrett, 1997), (Waszczyszyn, 1996) (Flood and Kartam, 1994), (MathWork, 1999). The ANN can perform a good generalization according to data. Education is done with application of a group of input and output data on ANN. While data moves into the network, it is processed by neurons and bonds between neurons. Network does iterations for obtaining target exit to balance the weight of each neuron. The duration of balancing neuron weight goes on until the network fault is minimized to a specific rate. After ANN is being trained and tested enough, exit rate forecast can be done for an unknown data by using the developed ANN (Kartam, Flood and Garrett ,1997), (Refiq, Bugman and Easterbrook, 2001), (MathWork, 1999).

There are a lot of techniques and methods for training the network. Back propagation is the most successful and the most general of these. In this method, input data spreads from input layer to output layer along hidden layer. Afterwards, network fault does back propagation from output layer to input layer where connection coefficient is arranged. This duration is repeated until the fault is minimized at a specific level (Kartam, Flood and Garrett ,1997), (Flood and Kartam, 1994), (Haykin, 1994). This learning alghoritm is called as feed-forward back propagation.

The neurons in hidden layer are bonded with each of the neurons in input layer. This bond is evaluated according to the weight of connection from inputs. The data that are transferred to each neuron in hidden layer are added and this signal triggers the activation function. This function gives an output that is above a specific rate. The neurons in output layer collect the data from each neuron in hidden layer according to the weight coefficient. These data are resulted as an output with activation function. If these data, which is found as output, is suitable according to the real output data, the result can be acceptable. If not, the difference is accepted as fault and it is used to correct the weight coefficient. However, this time the procedure is from end to start. This procedure is repeated until the data reach the acceptable rate (Haykin, 1994).

The ANN model, which is used in this study, is given in Figure 4.9 Feed-forward back propagation is used as a learning algorithm in this study. This model is composed of an input layer, a (or more than one) hidden layer and an output layer. Layers are connected with links, which is shown in Figure 4.9. The hidden layer is composed of processor units which are called as neurons. The rates of bonds between neurons are expressed with numerical values which are called as weight.

# 4. Capacity of Check-In Units

The time data measurements used in this work were collected from Antalya Airport passenger terminal check-in unit. The number of family members in the passengers, their luggage numbers and the time they spent for check-in operation have been measured in the passengers for the model proposed in this study. The database is divided into two parts. The first part having 128 subgroups is the training data and the other part having 42 subgroups is the predicting data.

Queues are formed in different areas of airport passenger terminal due to density of passenger movement. To handle this issue, capacity analysis of airport must be done. In this study, this problem whose practical solution is not available is analyzed using both artificial neural network and fuzzy logic methods. In the following sections analyses using both methods are presented.

## 4.1. Analysis Using Fuzzy Logic Approach

After the investigations, the variables affecting the capacity have been determined and their member functions are constructed to begin the analysis using fuzzy logic method. Proposed fuzzy logic model in terms of number of luggage variable and number of person variable are developed as shown in Figure 4.1. In this model output are each family's luggage and their check-in times. In the modelling, member functions are produced using the measurements done in related airport. The results obtained from proposed fuzzy logic model are tested using the field data to check the validity of the model.

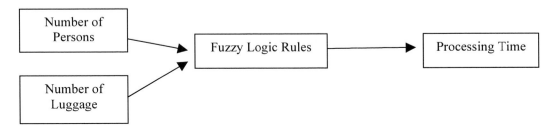

Figure 4.1. General structure of fuzzy logic model.

In the model, firstly, possible number of the passenger number of luggage combinations is determined. Number of passengers and luggage were selected randomly by using a computer program written previously. Random selection flowchart is given in Figure 4.2.

In each execution, input values are selected randomly and processed in the fuzzy logic model to obtain the results. Flow chart of the proposed fuzzy logic model is seen in Figure 4.3. Two different fuzzy logic methods are used in the analyses. Each data is processed using both methods. Analysis is continued until the cumulative time reaches 3600 sec. (1 hour). Obtained results are 1 hour working capacity of one check-in unit. This number is multiplied by total number of check-in units to obtain total capacity of check-in unit per hour.

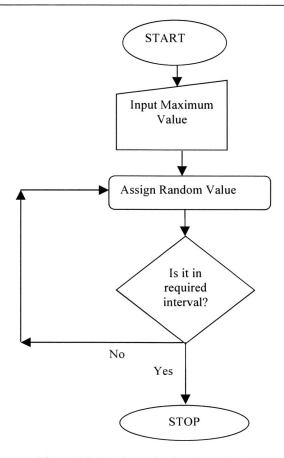

Figure 4.2. Random selection flow chart.

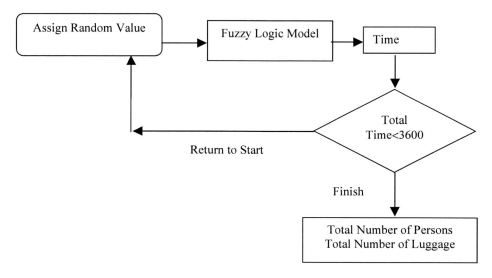

Figure 4.3. Flow chart of capacity analysis model.

Relation of predicted values from the proposed capacity analysis model with real values is graphically presented and correlation is determined between the real and predicted values. Both analyses with fuzzy logic approach give good results as seen from the graphs.

In Figures 4.4 and 4.5 member functions used in the capacity analysis are shown. Membership functions are constructed using the data obtained from Antalya Airport. Output membership functions are shown Figure 4.6.

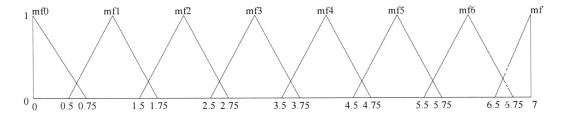

Figure 4.4. Number of luggage member functions.

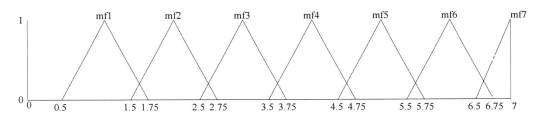

Figure 4.5. Number of passenger member functions.

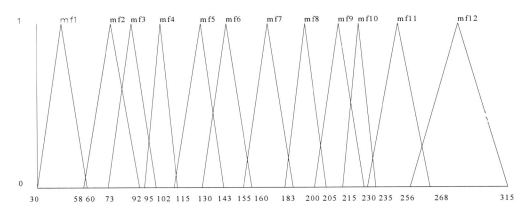

Figure 4.6. Operation time number member functions.

The values from randomly selected input values are processed using two different fuzzy logic approaches. Analyses are stopped when the cumulative time reaches 3600 sec. (1 hour) Validity of the proposed model is tested by comparing the results from the analysis and the field data. The results obtained from capacity analysis model for Antalya Airport are given in Table 4.1. In this table real values and the results from both fuzzy logic models are compared.

**Table 4.1. Results obtained from capacity analysis model for Antalya Airport check-in department**

| Number of Luggage | Number of Persons | Real time (second) | Centroid | Mom |
|:---:|:---:|:---:|:---:|:---:|
| 0 | 1 | 31 | 45 | 44 |
| 0 | 2 | 49 | 75 | 76 |
| 1 | 1 | 37 | 45 | 44 |
| 1 | 2 | 73 | 75 | 76 |
| 1 | 3 | 126 | 130 | 130 |
| 1 | 4 | 134 | 130 | 130 |
| 2 | 1 | 68 | 75 | 76 |
| 2 | 2 | 71 | 87 | 87 |
| 2 | 3 | 137 | 130 | 130 |
| 2 | 4 | 162 | 145 | 144 |
| 3 | 2 | 111 | 105 | 104 |
| 3 | 3 | 141 | 145 | 144 |
| 3 | 4 | 230 | 213 | 215 |
| 3 | 5 | 273 | 250 | 252 |
| 4 | 2 | 103 | 105 | 104 |
| 4 | 3 | 112 | 105 | 104 |
| 4 | 5 | 136 | 145 | 144 |
| 5 | 5 | 209 | 193 | 195 |

Relations between proposed capacity analysis model and real values are graphically given with $R^2$ values in Figures 4.7 and 4.8. Results have shown that both of the different fuzzy logic methods have given good results.

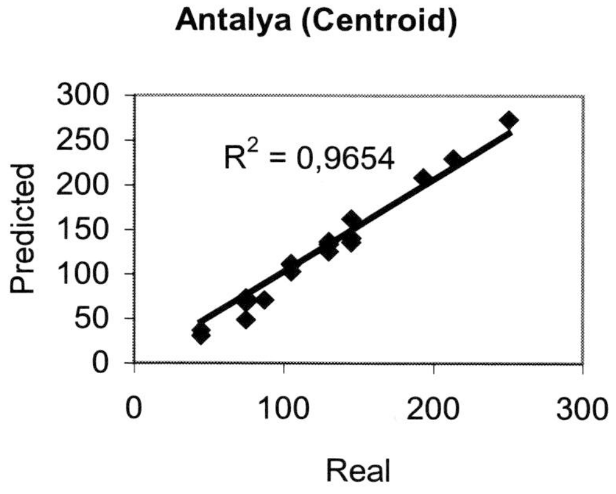

**Antalya (Centroid)**

$R^2 = 0,9654$

Figure 4.7. Relation between real time values and centroid fuzzy logic model results.

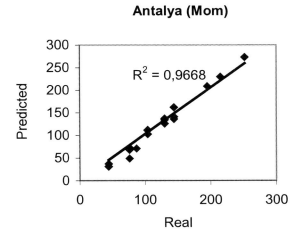

Figure 4.8. Relation between real time values and mom fuzzy logic model results.

**Table 4.2. Calculated hourly capacity for Antalya Airport passenger terminal check-in unit**

| Number of Luggage Randomly Chosen | Number of Passenger Randomly Chosen | Fuzzy Logic Processing Time (sec.) |
|---|---|---|
| 6 | 1 | 105 |
| 5 | 1 | 87 |
| 5 | 3 | 130 |
| 3 | 2 | 105 |
| 3 | 3 | 130 |
| 6 | 4 | 168 |
| 0 | 2 | 75 |
| 4 | 3 | 130 |
| 7 | 1 | 130 |
| 6 | 5 | 193 |
| 4 | 1 | 87 |
| 7 | 5 | 212 |
| 0 | 2 | 75 |
| 4 | 1 | 87 |
| 6 | 4 | 168 |
| 5 | 1 | 87 |
| 5 | 3 | 130 |
| 3 | 3 | 130 |
| 3 | 1 | 87 |
| 3 | 2 | 105 |
| 6 | 7 | 224 |
| 6 | 6 | 212 |
| 4 | 1 | 87 |
| 5 | 1 | 89 |
| 1 | 3 | 130 |

**Table 4.2. Continued**

| Number of Luggage Randomly Chosen | Number of Passenger Randomly Chosen | Fuzzy Logic Processing Time (sec.) |
|---|---|---|
| 5 | 3 | 175 |
| 0 | 2 | 75 |
| 3 | 3 | 130 |
| 3 | 2 | 105 |
| Σ=118 | Σ=76 | Σ=3648 |

According to the results obtained from capacity analysis model, 76 passengers pass with 118 luggages from one check-in counters per hour. Since total number of check-in counters is 59, 1 hour check-in capacity becomes 4484 passengers with 6962 luggage, if all check-in counters are open.

## 4.2. Analysis Using Artifical Neural Network Approach

In the ANN analysis of the problem, optimum architectural structure, which has a minimum error, has been chosen. This network testing and results are shown in Table 4.3. In this table, it is shown as (4*2*1), and these numbers show input number, neuron number in hidden layer and output layer, respectively. In this architecture, feed-forward back propagation was used as a learning algorithm. Although (4*3*1) structure gave the minimum MSE, the regression coefficient for (4*2*1) structure was higher then the (4*3*1) structure. Therefore, Tangent sigmoid and purelin transfer function was used as a transfer function. (4*2*1) was chosen, because it gave the most acceptable mean square error (MSE) rate (0.0041). This rate is within the acceptable limits.

**Table 4.3. The used ANN modelling for forecast of operation time about Antalya airport check-in department**

| ANN network architecture | Learning algorithm | Activation function | MSE | $R^2$ Training | $R^2$ Testing |
|---|---|---|---|---|---|
| 3*2*1 | Feed-forward back propagation | Tansig-Purelin | 0.00588 | 0.85 | 0.68 |
| 4*2*1 | Feed-forward back propagation | Tansig-Purelin | 0.00419 | 0.89 | 0,62 |
| 4*3*1 | Feed-forward back propagation | Tansig-Purelin | 0.00572 | 0.86 | 0,70 |
| 2*3*1 | Feed-forward back propagation | Tansig-Purelin | 0.0078 | 0.81 | 0,71 |
| 2*4*1 | Feed-forward back propagation | Tansig-Purelin | 0.0078 | 0.81 | 0,71 |
| 2*5*1 | Feed-forward back propagation | Tansig-Purelin | 0.0072 | 0.82 | 0,48 |

In the ANN training system, first, a result is found for all input vectors. After the produced result is close enough to the last input vector, error update is finished, which means that the weights have been recalculated about the error. Finding the results of all input vectors is called as 'one-iteration training to network'. In this study, 500-iterations were observed as enough number of iterations. Here, the fault is root MSE and it is given in the equation (4.1)

$$\text{Root MSE} = \sqrt{\frac{\sum_{i=1}^{N} \sqrt{(X_{Measurement} - X_{ANN})^2}}{N}} \qquad (4.1)$$

The Regression coefficient (R) is given in the equation (4.2)

$$R = \frac{n\sum(xy) - \sum x \sum y}{\sqrt{[n\sum(x^2) - (\sum x)^2][n\sum(y^2) - (\sum y)^2]}} \qquad (4.2)$$

The relationship between the test data and the data which were found from different ANN models are shown below in Table 4.3. Within these results, the second model which is ANN (4*2*1) model produced the best results. This ANN model is shown in Figure 4.9. Also, the graphical representation of the output obtained from this model is shown in Figure 4.10.

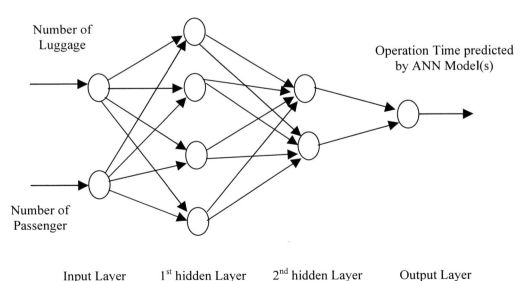

Figure 4.9. The improved ANN network for Antalya airport line service passenger terminal check-in department, (4*2*1).

In the ANN architecture shown in Figure 4.9, the network used includes 2 input data, four-neurons in hidden layer and one-output data.

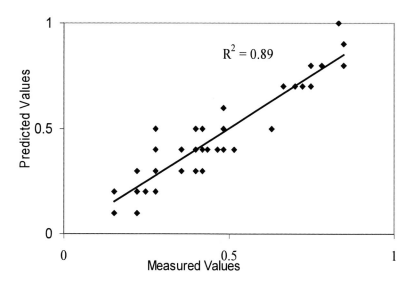

Figure 4.10. The relation between actual data obtained from field and the data which were produced from ANN model for Antalya airport check-in department

This scattering diagram of measured actual operation time and predicted ANN results for Antalya airport check-in department with respect to ANN (4*2*1) model which produces the best results. The ANN (4*2*1) model is tested with the data which is not used in training. Regression coefficient is found as $R^2 = 0,89$.

# 5. Conclusion

It is very important to conduct capacity analysis of check-in units in airports to prevent queues at different areas of airport passenger terminals. Since there are no available practical solutions to this problem, different capacity analyses models are developed in this study for Antalya Airport to analyze by using different methods, namely artificial neural network and fuzzy logic methods. Also, two different fuzzy logic methods and six different ANN structures are employed for the analyses and both methods give good results using proposed capacity analyses models. Results have shown that, proposed models give a fast and acceptable solution to the problem. Since, each airport has its own properties as management and passenger profiles, measurements must be done in the related airports for which the analyses are conducted.

According to the results obtained from these capacity analyses models, a management strategy may be developed to prevent queues in short and long-time periods. Hence; more comfortable service can be given for passengers in airport passenger terminals.

Another important conclusion which can be drawn from this work is both methods can also be used for the capacity analysis of any unit in the airport. From the results of this study it can also be concluded that, all of the units in an airport may be analyzed effectively by means off ANN and fuzzy logic methods and significant improvements can be supplied in the services provided in the airports based on the proposed methods oh analyses.

# References

Lemer, A.C., 1992. Measuring performance of airport passenger terminals, *Transportation Research Part A* **26A**(1), 37-45.

Odoni, A.R, Neufville R.D., 1992. Passenger terminal design, *Transportation Research Part A* **26**(1), 27-35.

Hamzawi, S. G., 1992. Lack of airport capacity: exploration of alternative solutions, *Transportation Research Part A* **26**(1). 47-58.

Seneviratne, P. N., Martel, N., 1991. Variables influencing performance of air terminal buildings. *Transportation Planning and Technology* 16 (1), 3-28.

Seneviratne, P. N., Martel, N., 1994. Criteria for evaluating quality of service in air terminal. *Transportation Research Record* **1461**, 24-30.

Seneviratne, P. N., Martel, N., 1995. Space standards for sizing air-terminal check-in areas, *Journal of Transportation Engineering*, **121**, 141-149.

Jerynolds, F. A., Button K.J., 1999. An assessment of the capacity and congestion levels at European Airports, *Journal of Air Transport Management* 5, 113-134.

Humphreys, I., Fry J., Francis, G., 1995. International survey of performance measurement in airports, *Journal of Transportation Engineering*, **121**, 101-105.

Adler, N., Berechman, J., 2001. Measurement airport quality from the airlines viewpoint: an application of data development analysis, *Transport Policy* **8**, 171-181.

Vasigh, B., Hamzaee, R.G., 1998. A comparative analysis of economic performance of US commercial airports. Journal of Air Transport Management 4, 209-216.

Yeh, C. H., Kuo, Y. L., 2003. Evaluating passenger services of Asia-Pacific International Airports, *Transportation Research Part E* **39**, 35-45.

Doganis, 1992. The Airport Business. Routledge, London

Gronroos, 1990. *Service Management and Marketing: Managing The Moments of Truth in Service Competition*. Free Pres, Lexington books, Lexington.

Gronroos, 1993. *Quality comes to service. in scheduling*, In:Cristoper, E.E., Cristoper, W.F. (Eds), The Service Quality Handbook, Amacom, New York, pp.17-24.

Humphreys, I., Francis, G., 2000. Traditional airport performance indicators a critical perspective. *Transportation Research Record* **1703**, 24-30.

Fernandes, E., Pacheco, R.R., 2002. Efficient use of airport capacity, *Transportation Research Part A* **36**, 225-238.

Pels, E., Nijkamp, P., Rietveld, P., 2001. Relative efficiency of European airports, *Transport Policy* **8**, pp: 183-192.

Martin, J.C., Roman, C., 2001. An application of DEA to measure the efficiency of Spanish Airports prior to privatization, *Journal of Air Transport Management* 7, 149-157.

Sarkis, J., 2000. An analysis of the operational efficiency of major airports in The United States. *Journal of Operation Management* **18**, 335–351.

Gillen, D., Lal, A., 1997. Developing measures of airport productivity and performance: An application of data envelopment analysis. *Transportation Research Part E* **33**, 261–273.

Tosic, V., 1992. A review of airport passenger terminal operations analysis and modelling, *Transportation Research Part A,* **26A** (1), 3-26.

Bauerle, N., Engelhardt-Funke, O., Kolonko, M., 2007. On the waiting time of arriving aircraft and the capacity of airports with one or two runways. *European Journal of Operational Research* **177** (2): 1180-1196.

Minaenko, V.N., Orekhov, M.O., 2006. Developing and analyzing optimal control methods of aircraft arrival flow when the capacity of the arrival airport is predicted to be reduced. *Journal of Computer and Systems Sciences International* **45**(5): 798-811.

Gilbo, E.P., 1997. Optimizing airport capacity utilization in air traffic flow management subject to constraints at arrival and departure fixes. *EEE Transactions on Control Systems Technology* **5**(5):490-503.

Hutting G., Busch, W., Gronak N., 1994. Growing demand and capacity of airports, *Transportation Research Part A-Policy and Practice* **28**(6): 501-509.

Yan, S., Tang, C., Chen, M., 2004. A model and a solution algorithm for airport common use check-in counter assignments. *Transportation Research Part A* **38** (2004) 101-125.

Wei, W., Hansen, M., 2006. An aggregate demand model for air passenger traffic in the hub-and-spoke network. *Transportation Research Part A-Policy and Practice* **40** (10): 841-851.

Bianco, L., Dell'Olmo, Giordani, S., 2006. Scheduling models for air traffic control interminal areas, *Journal of Scheduling* **9** (3): 223-252.

Janic, M., 2005. Modelling airport congestion charges. *Transportation planning and technology* **28**(1).

Ignaccolo, 2003. A simulation model for airport capacity and delay analysis. *Transportation planning and technology* **26**(2): 135-170.

Janic, M., 2004. Expansion of airport capacity at London heathrow airport, *Transportation Research Record* (**1888**) 7-14.

Cao, Y.H., Chen, Y., Zhou, Y., 2005. Studies of capacity estimation of the airport with two parallel runways. *Aeronautical Journal* **109** (1098):395-401.

Tzeng. G.H., Chen,Y.W., 1999. The optimal location of airport fire stations: A fuzzy multi-objective programming and revised genetic algorithm approach. *Transportation Planning and Technology* **23** (1):37-55.

Hu, X.B., Chen, W.H., Di Paolo E., 2007. Multi airport capacity management. Genetic algorithm with receding horizon, IEE Transactions of Inteligent *Transportation Systems* **8**(2):254-263.

Hu, X.B., Chen, W.H., 2005. Genetic algorithm based on receding horizon control for arrival sequencing and scheduling. *Engineering Applications of Artificial Intelligence* **18**(5): 633-642.

Hu, X.B., Wu, S.F., Ju, J., 2004. On line free-flight path optimization based on improved genetic algorithms, *Engineering Applications of artificial intelligence* **17**(8): 897-907.

Liang, G.S., Han, T.C., Chou, T.Y., 2005. Using a fuzzy quality function deployment model to identify improvement points in airport cargo terminal, Information Systems and *Technology Transportation Research Record* (**1935**) 130-140.

Yeh, C.H., Kuo, Y.L., 2003. Evaluating passenger services of Asia-Pacific International *Airports Transportation Research Part E* **39**: 35-45.

Kiyildi, R.K., Karasahin, M., 2008. The capacity analysis of the check-in unit of Antalya Airport using the fuzzy logic method, *Transportation Research Part A: Policy and Practice*, **42** (4), 610-619.

Wells, A.T., 2000. *Airport Planning and Management*, fourth ed. McGraw-Hill Inc..

Morlok, E.K., 1973. *Introduction to Transportation Engineering and Plannig*, McGraw-Hill Book Company, New York.

FAA, 1988. *Advisory Circular: Planning and desing guidelines for airport terminal facilities*, U.S. Department of Transportation, Federal Aviation Administration, AcNo:150/5360–13.

USHT, 1987. *Airport Plan Handbook. International Civil Aviation Organization*. Ministry of Transport Press (in Turkish).

Zadeh, L.A., 1967. Fuzzy Sets *Information and control 8*:38-53.

Klir, G.J., Fogel, T.A., 1988. *Fuzzy Sets, Uncertainty & Information*: Prentice Hall, New York.

Kosko, B., 1992. *Neural Networks Fuzzy Systems* Englewood Cliffs: Prentice hall.

Zadeh, L.A., Kacprzyk, J.,1992. *Fuzzy Logic for the Management of Uncertainty*

Kosko, B., 1993. *Fuzzy thinking: The New Science of Fuzzy Logic*. New York: Hyperion.

McNeill, F.M., Thro, E., 1994. *Fuzzy Logic: A Practical Approach*: AP Professional, Boston.

Sen, Z., 1998. Fuzzy Algorithm for estimation of solar irradiation from sunshine duration, *Solar Energy* **63**: (1), 39-49

Sen, Z., 2004. *The Principle of Modelling with Fuzzy Logic in Engineering*. Water Foundation Press, Istanbul (in Turkish)

Basma, A., Kalas, N., 2004. Modeling soil collapse by artificial neural networks, *Geotechnical and Geological Engineering*, **22**,(3), 427-438.

Moosavi, M., Yazdanpanah, M.J., Doostmohammadi, R., 2006. Modelling the cyclic swelling pressure of mudrock using artificial neural networks. *Engineering Geology* **87**, 178-194.

Foresee, F.D., Hagan, M.T., 1997. Gauss–Newton approximation to bayesian learning. *Proceedings of the International Joint Conference on Neural Networks*, 1930–5

Sanad, A., Saka, M.P., 2001. Prediction of ultimate shear strength of reinforced-concrete deep deams using neural networks. *J Struct Eng, ASCE* 2001; 127(7):818-38.

Kartam, N., Flood, I., Garrett, J.H., 1997. Artificial neural network for civil engineers: fundasmentals and applications. New York: *ASCDE*.

Waszczyszyn, Z., 1996. Some recent and current problems of neuro computing in civil and structural engineering. In: Topping BHV, editor. Advances in computational structures technology. Edinburg: Civil-Comp. Press: pp.43-58.

Flood, I., Kartam, N., 1994. Neural network in civil engineering I: principles and understandins. *J Comput Civil Eng, ASCE*; **6**(2):131-48.

MathWorks Inc. *MatLab the language of technical computing*. Natick, MA, USA: MathWorks Inc:1999. Version 6

Refiq, M.Y., Bugman, G., Easterbrook, D.J., 2001. Neural network design for engineering aplication. *Comput Struct;* **79**(17):1541-1552

Haykin, S., 1994. *Neural Networks, A Comprehensive Foundation*, Prentice Hall, Inc. A Simon&Schuster/A Viacom Company Upper Saddle River, New Jersey 07458.

In: Airports: Performance, Risks, and Problems
Editors: P.B. Larauge et al, pp. 147-163

ISBN 978-1-60692-393-1
© 2009 Nova Science Publishers, Inc.

*Chapter 7*

# REDUCING DELAYS BY OPTIMIZED RUNWAY ASSIGNMENT

### *Rainer Kiehne[1] and Michael Kolonko[2]*
[1]Air Transport and Airport Research,
German Aerospace Center, Köln, Germany
[2]Institut für Mathematik,
University of Technology Clausthal, Germany

### Abstract

During the last decades the limited capacity of runways has become an important source for delays on major airports. Particular safety regulations require asymmetric separation times for aircraft during their landing operations. If there are two or more runways available, aircraft can be assigned to runways in such a way that large separation times are avoided. This increases the actual throughput of the system and reduces additional delays.

We formulate the assignment problem as a mathematical optimization model. Though we cannot find optimal assignment strategies analytically, we can use the model as a framework for the simulation of strategies and as a tool for the heuristic optimization of strategies. We examine two classes of strategies that reduce the waiting times of arriving aircraft in simulations.

In particular, we can show that in realistic simulation scenario of a German airport, one of our strategies performs much better than the manual assignment as it is used by flight operators today. As our strategies are essentially simple look-up tables, they may well be incorporated into future flight assistance systems for airports.

## 1.  Introduction

During the last decades a significant growth of air traffic has been observed which has not been countered by an adequate increase of runway capacities at airports. Since runway capacity has been identified as a major source of delay, the efficient use of existing runway systems is necessary to meet the demand of commercial aviation.

In this article we present simple strategies to route arriving aircraft to runways in an efficient way such that for a given arrival rate of aircraft the waiting times are minimized or vice versa the arrival rate is maximized with waiting times below a given threshold.

A crucial point is the uncertainty concerning arrival times of approaching aircraft. If all details of future arrivals were known, the problem would be static and an optimal sequence could be determined by mathematical optimization. In reality however, the prediction of air traffic is often imprecise due to en-route delays or arrivals ahead of schedule. Thus a dynamic scheduling algorithm is needed that assigns incoming aircraft according to the information available at the time of arrival.

In this chapter, we restrict ourselves to a particular routing model: there are two runways available for landing aircraft (we do not consider any starts in the present set-up). Arriving aircraft are assigned to one of the runways as soon as they pass the threshold of the so-called terminal manoeuvring area (TMA) of the airport. We do not assume any knowledge about aircraft that are still beyond TMA, so the main information for the routing decision is the state of the runways. See [3] and the literature cited there for models that take into account additional information. If the assigned runway is not free at the time the aircraft is ready to land, it has to wait in a 'queue' which in this case is rather a loop. Each runway has its own queue, aircraft are not allowed to change the queue or their position within the queue once they are assigned to it. This restriction reflects the fact that assignments have to be fixed some time before the aircraft enters the final approach to ensure a safe trajectory to the runway.

If we look at the runways as servers and at the incoming aircraft as their customers, then the problem can be modeled as a simple queuing system with two parallel servers. The arrival times are random, often it is assumed that they form a Poisson process (see e. g. [7]) but we also consider more realistic arrival patterns in our simulation in Section 5.. The service time of an aircraft is the time a trailing aircraft has to wait until it can begin its landing operation. The aim is to find routing strategies that minimizes the average waiting time of a customer in the queue.

The characteristic feature here is that consecutive service times are *not* independent as it usually assumed in queuing systems. An aircraft causes air turbulences that endanger the stability of trailing aircraft. The required separation times between consecutive landings therefore depend on the size and weight of the two aircraft involved and on their order: a heavy aircraft may follow more closely on a light one than the other way round. Hence the service time of a landing aircraft, i. e. the separation time to its successor, also depends on the type of this successor and hence also on the following service time. This dependence of service times cannot be neglected as will be shown below.

We start in Section 2. by formulating a mathematical model for the problem sketched above. It turns out that determining an optimal routing strategy requires the solution of a complex stochastic optimization problem. Though the optimization problem seems intractable, a simulation of the performance of a given strategy is quite simple. We therefore try to find reasonable strategies by a combination of simulation and heuristic search. Using simulation for the evaluation of routing strategies also has the advantage that we can easily include any air traffic management procedures that depend heavily on the airport layout and airport specific regulations.

We identify two classes of simple and transparent strategies for which heuristic search provides good results. In the first case which is detailed in Section 3., the strategies are not allowed to use the full information of the system state, instead they must rely on a rough classification of the state into one of a few categories. Under this restriction good strategies can be derived by local search using ideas from neuro-dynamic programming, see e. g. [6].

In Section 4. we use strategies that are variations of the so-called join-the-shortest-queue principle. These strategies can easily be parameterized and good strategies, i. e. good parameter values can be determined by genetic algorithms and simulated annealing in combination with simulation.

In Section 5. we present results from simulation experiments for these two types of strategies with different scenarios. In a detailed study with realistic 24h data of a German airport we compare our strategies with the routing as it is performed by flight operators today. The results show that even though the mathematical model captures only part of the real problem, the strategies obtained have a significant potential for capacity improvements and delay reductions in real operations.

## 2.   Mathematical Models

In this section we sketch a mathematical model for the the runway assignment problem. For a single runway, a single server queue with dependent service times is an adequate model. Combined into a system of two (or more) runways this leads to a complex stochastic dynamic programming problem. Though we cannot solve this problem analytically to obtain an optimal strategy, we can use it as a framework for the simulation and evaluation of strategies in the Sections below.

### A Queuing Model

We start by analyzing a single runway without any routing. As indicated in the Introduction, aircraft are classified into three weight categories: heavy, medium and light. The separation times for consecutive aircraft are given in a $3 \times 3$ matrix

$$D := \begin{pmatrix} d(1,1) & d(1,2) & d(1,3) \\ d(2,1) & d(2,2) & d(2,3) \\ d(3,1) & d(3,2) & d(3,3) \end{pmatrix}. \tag{1}$$

Here $d(i,j)$ denotes the separation time an aircraft of type $j$ has to keep to a leading aircraft of type $i$ with $i, j \in \{1, 2, 3,\} = \{\text{heavy}, \text{medium}, \text{light}\}$.

In the most basic case, we assume that the arrivals are completely random. More precisely, this means that the arrival times of aircraft at the TMA form a Poisson process. The types of the arriving aircraft are selected according to a given 'type mix' $(p_1, p_2, p_3)$ which gives the average relative proportions of the three types. Here, $(p_1, p_2, p_3) = (0.23, 0.72, 0.05)$ e. g. means that 23% of the aircraft are of type 'heavy', 72% of type 'medium' and only 5% of type 'light'. Under these assumptions, a single runway can be modeled as an $M/SM/1$-queue, where '$SM$' stands for 'semi-Markov', a concept that allows for dependent service times as needed in our case, see [8] for more details.

An $M/SM/1$-system is slightly more complicated than the standard $M/G/1$-system with independent service times which is used as a model for a runway e. g. in [4]. In an $M/G/1$-system the average waiting time is easily determined as a function of the arrival rate and the first two moments of the service time distribution. The corresponding results for $S/SM/1$ are a little more involved, they include the effect the dependence of service times may have on the average (see [8], [1]). In [1] it is shown that the average waiting times obtained from the 'full' $M/SM/1$-models and the simplified $M/G/1$-models may be quite different and that the error becomes arbitrarily large as the arrival rate increases.

### Runway Assignment as Markovian Decision Process

We shall now turn to a system with two runways. If the 'local' arrivals of aircraft assigned to a runway form a Poisson process than we have a system of two separate $M/SM/1$-queues. But even if the outer arrival stream of aircraft at the airport (TMA) follows a Poisson process, the local arrival streams of aircraft after assignment will be Poisson only for very special assignment strategies, see [1] for more details on the so-called 'split-strategies'.

In general, an assignment decision influences the situation the next arriving aircraft will see on both runways so that they cannot be treated separately. Runway assignment is a typical *sequential* decision-making problem, it can be modeled using a discrete time Markovian decision process (MDP). We shall briefly describe the main ingredients of an MDP.

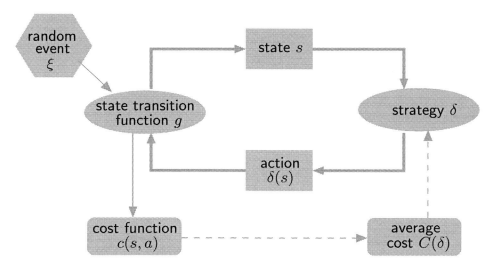

Figure 1. Markov Decision Process

In MDPs, decisions have to be made at certain points in time, in our case these are the arrival times of aircraft, denoted by $T_1, T_2, \ldots$. These may either form a Poisson process or result from an observation of a real arrival stream. The type of the $n$-th arriving aircraft is denoted by $J_n$ taking on one of the values $1, 2, 3$ for 'heavy','medium or 'light' as described earlier. The time that has elapsed since the last arrival and the type of the incoming aircraft together form a stochastic arrival *event*. If there are two runways named $I$ and $II$, the possible decisions or *actions* are simply $a = I$ or $a = II$.

The central part of the model is its *state* $s$. It has to comprise all information available about the future behavior of the system at the moment a decision has to be made, so that the decision may be based solely on the present state of the system. A decision *strategy* is then a function $\delta$ that in each state $s$ chooses an action $\delta(s)$. Once an action $a$ has been taken, the system state $s$ changes according to a *transition function* $g$ to the new state $s' = g(s, a, \xi)$

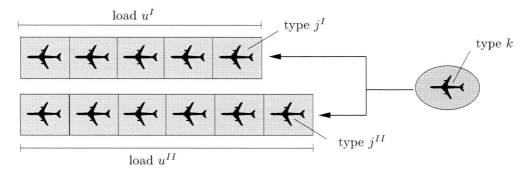

Figure 2. Elements of the system state

depending on $s, a$ and the *event* $\xi$ that represents the external random influence on the system. This transition incurs *one-step-costs* $c(s, a)$. A strategy $\delta$ can be evaluated e. g. by the average costs $C(\delta)$ resulting from applying $\delta$ to the system over a long time. This general scheme is depicted in Figure 1.

We must now define a 'state' appropriate for the runway assignment. As we assume that there is no knowledge about aircraft beyond TMA, the state consists of a description of the current load of the runways and the additional demand of the arriving aircraft. The *load* $u$ of a runway at a certain point in time is the remaining waiting time of the aircraft waiting at the tail of its queue. The load $u$ may be negative if there is no aircraft waiting and the last touch-down took place $-u$ time units ago. Beside the loads $u^I, u^{II}$ of the two runways, we also need the types of the aircraft involved in the assignment to be made. These are the types $j^I, j^{II}$ of the two aircraft waiting at the tail of the queue behind one of which the arriving aircraft has to queue and the type $k$ of the arriving aircraft itself, see Figure 2. For ease of presentation we assume for the moment that the aircraft do not need any additional time to proceed from the threshold TMA to the runways, so that if the assigned runway is free landing may start at once.

Hence the state of the system at the time of the arrival of an aircraft can be summarized as

$$s = (u^I, j^I, u^{II}, j^{II}; k), \qquad (2)$$

see Figure 2 for an example. Now assume, that the $n$-th aircraft arriving at time $T_n$ is of type $J_n = k$ and sees the state $s_n = (u^I, j^I, u^{II}, j^{II}; k)$ upon its arrival. If it is assigned to runway $I$ then its waiting time would be

$$[u^I + d(j^I, k)]^+$$

where $[t]^+ = \max\{t, 0\}$ is the positive part of a real number $t$. To see why this is the waiting time, note that the new aircraft first has to wait for $u^I$ time units until the aircraft (of type $j^I$) waiting in front of it begins its landing. In addition, it has to keep the separation time $d(j^I, k)$ to this predecessor resulting in $u^I + d(j^I, k)$. If this expression is positive it is the additional waiting time of the newly assigned aircraft in the queue. If it is negative or $0$, which may happen if the predecessor has landed a long time ago and $u^I$ is negative, then the additional waiting time of the aircraft is zero, it can start its landing operation immediately.

A similar argument applies for runway $II$, so that we can define the waiting time of the arriving aircraft of type $k$ when it is assigned to runway $a \in \{I, II\}$ as the one-step-costs

$$c(s, a) := \begin{cases} [u^I + d(j^I, k)]^+ & \text{if } a = I \\ [u^{II} + d(j^{II}, k)]^+ & \text{if } a = II \end{cases} = [u^a + d(j^a, k)]^+. \qquad (3)$$

Assume that the assignment was to runway $I$ and that the next aircraft is of type $J_{n+1} = l$ arriving $t$ time units later at $T_{n+1} := T_n + t$. Then the next arrival event is $\xi = (t, l)$ and the $n + 1$-st aircraft would see the load $[u^I + d(j^I, k)]^+ - t$ on runway $I$ and load $u^{II} - t$ on runway $II$ as $t$ time units have elapsed. Waiting at the end of queue $I$ is the newly assigned aircraft of type $k$, so that the new state, seen by the $n + 1$-st aircraft immediately before its own assignment is

$$s_{n+1} := ([u^I + d(j^I, k)]^+ - t, k, u^{II} - t, j^{II}; l).$$

Generally, the transition function from state $s = (u^I, j^I, u^{II}, j^{II}; k)$ when action $a$ was applied and the arrival event $\xi = (t, l)$ occurred is

$$g(s, a, (t, l)) := \begin{cases} ([u^I + d(j^I, k)]^+ - t, k, u^{II} - t, j^{II}; l) & \text{if } a = I \\ (u^I - t, j^I, [u^{II} + d(j^{II}, k)]^+ - t, k; l) & \text{if } a = II \end{cases}. \qquad (4)$$

Depending on the distribution of the arrival events, the sequence of states $s_1, s_2, \ldots$ becomes a stochastic process. If a strategy $\delta$ is applied, the $n$-th aircraft has waiting time $c(s_n, \delta(s_n))$ and we can define the expected average waiting time as

$$C(\delta) := \mathbf{E} \left( \lim_{N \to \infty} \frac{1}{N} \sum_{n=1}^{N} c(s_n, \delta(s_n)) \right). \qquad (5)$$

Finding a strategy $\delta$ that minimizes $C(\cdot)$ for a given event distribution (e.g. for a Poisson stream with a given type mix) requires the solution of a complex stochastic dynamic optimization problem, see [5] and [2] for more details about this. Nevertheless, the model sketched above can easily be used for simulation, see Section 5. below. We only need a source for the arrival events, then the state transitions and the determination of the waiting time can be performed as given in (4), (3).

Let us now discuss some simple strategies $\delta$ that could be used to assign the aircraft. First, the so-called round-robin strategy (also called 'stagger approach') simply switches between runway $I$ and $II$, so that all aircraft with an even number are on one runway and all with an odd number on the other. This strategy does not take into account the present state of the runway but simply tries to balance the loads. This can be done more efficiently by strategies of the type 'join-the-least-load' (JLL) (also called join-the-shortest-queue (JSQ)). In its most basic form, this strategy assigns an arriving aircraft to the shorter queue, i.e. to runway $I$ if $u^I \leq u^{II}$ for the present state $s = (u^i, j^I, u^{II}, j^{II}; k)$. As the types of the aircraft involved are known, it is more reasonable to route to runway $I$ if

$$[u^I + d(j^I, k)]^+ \leq [u^{II} + d(j^{II}, k)]^+ \qquad (6)$$

i. e., if the waiting time on runway $I$ would be less then on runway $II$. In terms of the MDP, this means that we choose that action (runway) $a$ that minimizes the one-step-costs $c(s, a)$.

Such a strategy does not take into account any long-term effects. In certain situations it may e.g. be reasonable to impose a larger waiting time on the present aircraft to keep a runway free for a heavy aircraft that may arrive next with high probability. Optimal solutions to the MDP balance the short-term and long-term effects of actions but, as was mentioned above, they are difficult to obtain due to the complexity of the state space. In the next two Sections we therefore study simpler strategies that do some balancing and perform much better than round-robin and JLL.

Before doing so let us shortly discuss a possible extension to our model. We can allow for an additional time $\tau$ that an aircraft needs to proceed from TMA to the runways. Then, the earliest landing time of an aircraft is its arrival time plus $\tau$. In reality, $\tau$ may depend on the aircraft, the runway it is assigned to and sometimes even on the size of the waiting queue of the runway it is not assigned to but which it must circumfly. If we restrict ourselves to the simple case where $\tau$ depends only on the arriving aircraft we may include $\tau$ into the arrival event $(t, l, \tau)$. We can then extend our model to the important case where aircraft may arrive at an airport from different directions, so that they have trajectories of different lengths to their runways or queues.

The waiting time on runway $I$ in (3) then changes to $[u^I - \tau + d(j^I, k)]^+$ as $u^i - \tau$ is the load the aircraft sees when it arrives at the runway. Its landing time is

$$[u^I - \tau + d(j^I, k)]^+ + \tau = \max\{\tau, [u^I + d(j^I, k)]^+\}.$$

Hence the load the next aircraft sees at its arrival as part of the next state $s_{n+1}$ is $\max\{\tau, [u^I + d(j^I, k)]^+\} - t$ on runway $I$ and $u^{II} - t$ on runway $II$.

However, for a runway system with high workload, a continuous occupancy of the runways without significant idle times can be expected. Thus it can be assumed that for most of the aircraft the earliest possible landing time is not of particular importance for the actual landing time. We shall therefore drop this feature from further discussions.

## 3. Optimal Strategies in a Reduced State Space

Formally, the state space $S$ for a model as sketched in Section 2. is very large, it contains all real numbers $u^I, u^{II}$ as possible loads of the runways. To derive optimal strategies becomes a very difficult task in this situation. Also, from a practical point of view, it seems unlikely that a routing strategy $\delta$ that takes on only two values can make full use of the detailed information contained in the state $s = (u^I, j^I, u^{II}, j^{II}; k)$.

Instead, it seems reasonable to assume that the routing decision for an incoming aircraft will mainly depend on the *difference* of the loads on the two runways and not so much on their absolute values. Hence one could replace the original state $s = (u^I, j^I, u^{II}, j^{II}; k)$ by $(\Delta, j^I, j^{II}; k)$ where $\Delta = u^I - u^{II}$. Moreover, one would expect that a good strategy does not change its values ($I$ or $II$) arbitrarily often as $\Delta$ varies. Hence, we may fix a few threshold values $x_1, \ldots, x_n$ and restrict ourselves to strategies $\hat\delta$ that change their values only at the thresholds. See Table 1 for an example with four thresholds.

Restricting the class of strategies may also be viewed as replacing the original state $s$ by a reduced state $\hat{s} := (d, j^I, j^{II}; k)$ where $d = 0, 1, \ldots, n$ denotes the *level* of the load difference determined by $x_d < u^I - u^{II} \leq x_{d+1}$ for $1 \leq d \leq n - 1$, $d = 0$ for

**Table 1. A simple threshold strategy with $n = 4$ symmetric thresholds**
$-120, -90, 90, 120.$

| $\Delta$ | $\Delta \leq -120$ | $-120 < \Delta \leq -90$ | $-90 < \Delta \leq 90$ | $90 < \Delta \leq 120$ | $120 < \Delta$ |
|---|---|---|---|---|---|
| level $d$ | 0 | 1 | 2 | 3 | 4 |

$u^I - u^{II} \leq x_1$ and $d = n$ for $x_n < u^I - u^{II}$, see Table 1. Note that our reduced state space $\hat{S}$ has only finitely many states, e.g. with four thresholds and three types of aircraft we have $5 \times 3^3 = 135$ reduced states in $\hat{S}$.

Our model has now become a special case of a so-called partially observable Markovian decision process (POMDP). These are generally used for systems in which the exact identification of the system state is impossible and only 'observations' of the true state are available to the decision maker. The structure of a POMDP is outlined in figure 3.

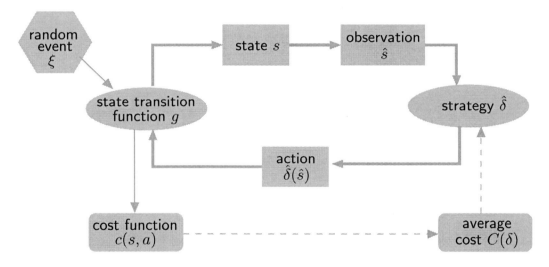

Figure 3. Partially Observable Markov Decision Process

Note that the restricted state space of observations is used for decision making only, the dynamics of the system still rely on the complete state $s$. In particular, when simulating the performance of a strategy $\hat{\delta}$, state transitions are as given in (4) but the action applied in state $s$ is $\hat{\delta}(\hat{s})$.

The advantage of this approach is that we may use the reduced state space for a simplified search for good strategies $\hat{\delta}$, whereas the quality of $\hat{\delta}$ is measured against the dynamic system with complete information. Of course, we still have to decide how the state space is reduced, i.e. we have to decide on the number and on the values of the thresholds to be used.

**Representation and Optimization of Threshold Strategies**

The finite state space $\hat{S} = \{\hat{s}_1, \ldots, \hat{s}_N\}$ allows for a representation of a strategy $\hat{\delta}$ as a vector of length $N$. Its $i$-th entry is $I$ if $\hat{\delta}(\hat{s}_i) = I$ and $II$ if $\hat{\delta}(\hat{s}_i) = II$ for $i = 1, \ldots, N$.

This vector is used as a look-up table to determine the action $\hat{\delta}(\hat{s})$ for each reduced state $\hat{s}$, see Table 2 for an example. Though the reduced state space is finite, the number of possible strategies is $2^N$ which still may be very large. Finding a good strategy $\hat{\delta}$ therefore remains a difficult task.

**Table 2. An example of a threshold strategy $\hat{\delta}$ with thresholds as in Table 1.**

| observation $\hat{s} = (d, j^I, j^{II}; k)$ | runway $\hat{\delta}(\hat{s})$ |
|:---:|:---:|
| (0,1,1;1) | I |
| (1,1,1;1) | I |
| (2,1,1;1) | II |
| (3,1,1;1) | II |
| (4,1,1;1) | II |
| (0,2,1;1) | I |
| (1,2,1;1) | I |
| (2,2,1;1) | I |
| (3,2,1;1) | II |
| $\vdots$ | $\vdots$ |

We have used local search for an iterative improvement of the strategies. Local search starts with an arbitrary solution and then randomly picks candidate solutions from the neighbourhood of the present solution. If the candidate is better, it becomes the new solution, otherwise a new candidate is picked.

If strategies are represented as vectors with entries $I$ and $II$, a natural neighbourhood of $\hat{\delta}$ for the local search is the set of all strategies (vectors) that differ in exactly one position from $\hat{\delta}$. This means that we have to compare $\hat{\delta}$ with a candidate strategy $\hat{\delta}'$ that chooses a different runway for exactly one reduced state $\hat{s}'$.

The strategies are compared with respect to the average waiting times. These waiting times are estimated by the following procedure: a certain number $H$ of arriving aircraft are simulated and their average waiting time over time horizon $H$ is recorded. This is repeated several times until we obtain a reliable estimator of the average waiting time for the strategy used. As the two strategies to be compared differ only in a single reduced state $\hat{s}'$ all waiting times are equal for the two strategies until the reduced state $\hat{s}'$ is hit for the first time. Therefore, we only need to simulate the system after it has gone through $\hat{s}'$. The simplest way to achieve this would be to start the simulation of the runway system in the reduced state $\hat{s}'$.

However, the problem here is that there is a huge class $S' \subset S$ of full states that may underly the observation of the reduced state $\hat{s}' = (d, j^I, j^{II}; k)$. In fact, these are all states $s'$ that have load differences on the level $d$. Starting with observation $\hat{s}'$ therefore means to select one of these states as starting state $s'$ of the runway simulation system. However, if the results are to representative, this choice of $s'$ must correspond to the frequency of the occurrence of $s'$ during operation or simulation. This is not known and will generally depend on the strategies used.

Nevertheless, we can simulate this unknown distribution by starting the simulation system in an arbitrary but fixed state $s_0 \in S$, e.g. with empty runways. The system is run and its reduced states $\hat{s}$ are observed until the particular reduced state $\hat{s}'$ occurs for the first time. Now, the average waiting time $w_1^H$ of the next $H$ aircraft is determined. After that, simulation is continued without recording of waiting times until $\hat{s}'$ appears again starting another observation sequence of $H$ aircraft resulting in average waiting time $w_2^H$. In this way average waiting times $w_1^H, \ldots, w_n^H$ with time horizon $H$ are sampled until the estimator

$$\frac{1}{n}(w_1^H + \cdots + w_n^H)$$

has a prescribed accuracy determined from the 95% confidence interval. If the particular reduced state $\hat{s}'$ reappears before a sequence of $H$ observations is finished, it is treated as an arbitrary state in order to keep the sampled sequences non-overlapping and independent.

Subsequently, the system is started again in state $s_0$ this time using the candidate strategy $\hat{\delta}'$. The estimated average waiting times over the finite horizon $H$ for the two strategies are then compared and $\hat{\delta}'$ is either accepted as new solution or rejected.

We cannot guarantee that the state process starting in $s_0$ will ever hit the reduced state $\hat{s}'$ or that it will return to it later. If $\hat{s}'$ has not (re-)occurred after a fixed number of steps (aircraft), we consider $\hat{s}'$ as irrelevant for the present strategy and pick a new candidate from its neighbourhood.

The characteristics of the solutions which are generated using the local search algorithm depend crucially on the simulation horizon $H$. For small values of $H$, the resulting strategies are greedy and short-sighted similar to join-the-least-load. In the extreme case where $H = 1$, a change of the routing decision is accepted only if it improves the waiting time of the next arriving aircraft. In our experiments we found best results with horizons $H$ between 5 and 10.

## 4.  Generalized JLL-Strategies

We shall now examine the join-the-least-load strategy and variants of it more closely.

In its simplest form, JLL routes an arriving aircraft to runway $I$ if $u^I \leq u^{II}$ in the present state $s = (u^I, j^I, u^{II}, j^{II}; k)$. If the waiting times are taken into account as in (6) we see that routing to runway $I$ occurs if either $[u^I + d(j^I, k)]^+ = 0$, i.e. runway $I$ is free, or if it is not free and

$$u^I \leq u^{II} + d(j^{II}, k) - d(j^I, k).$$

If we take $(u^I, u^{II})$ as a point in the two-dimensional plane, then these two strategies can be visualized as in Figure 4.

A more general class of strategies 'JLL++' is obtained if one allows any straight line $A + Bx$ with coefficients $A, B$ as a separator between the 'route to $I$' and 'route to $II$' regions as indicated in Figure 5. Moreover, these coefficients $A = A(j^I, j^{II}, k)$ and $B = B(j^I, j^{II}, k)$ may depend on the three types $j^I, j^{II}, k$ of aircraft contained in state $s$.

Finding good strategies in this class JLL++ means to determine $(3 \times 3 \times 3)$-matrices $A$ and $B$ such that the decision rule $\delta_{A,B}$ has low average waiting time where $\delta_{A,B}$ is defined by

$$\delta_{A,B}(s) = I \quad \Longleftrightarrow \quad u^I \leq A(j^I, j^{II}, k) + B(j^I, j^{II}, k) \cdot u^{II} \tag{7}$$

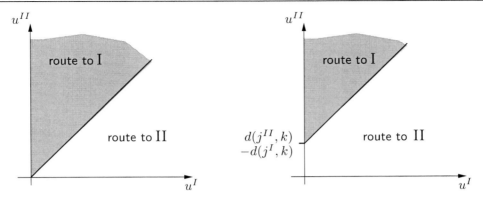

Figure 4. Simple JLL-strategies are characterized by a line parallel to the diagonal.

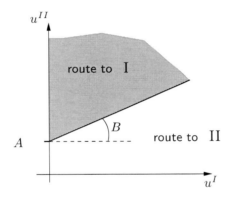

Figure 5. A generalized JLL-strategy, parameterized by $A = A(j^I, j^{II}, k)$ and $B = B(j^I, j^{II}, k)$.

with $s = (u^I, j^I, u^{II}, j^{II}; k)$. The average waiting time $C(\delta_{A,B})$ as defined in (5) has to be estimated for each pair $A, B$ from simulation.

   To find good parameters $A, B$ we used genetic algorithms, see e. g. [9] for a general outline of these algorithms. Genetic algorithms use a set of solutions, the *population*, which is iteratively improved by applying operations like crossover and mutation.

   In our case, the population consists of pairs of matrices $(A, B)$ as the *individuals*. A starting population is made up from randomly chosen matrices. A *crossover* creates a new pair $(A^+, B^+)$ from its two 'parents' $(A_1, B_1), (A_2, B_2)$ selected from the present population. $A^+$ could result from $A_1$ by exchanging part of the rows and columns with $A_2$ or by interpolation between $A_1$ and $A_2$ taken as points in the $3 \times 3 \times 3$-dimensional space. Similarly, $B^+$ is made up from $B_1, B_2$. The result $(A^+, B^+)$ hopefully inherits some of the good properties of its parents. It is then *mutated* by randomly changing some of the values in the matrices, typically by a small amount only.

   In this way, a number of new offspring individuals are produced enlarging the present population. Then the 'fittest' individuals from this extended population are selected to form the next population. Here 'fitness' of an individual $(A, B)$ is measured by the simulated average waiting time of the corresponding strategy $\delta_{A,B}$. The selection may be such that the best strategies only survive, but it is often more reasonable to randomize the selection and pick the individuals with a probability proportional to their average waiting times.

**Table 3. A solution $(A^*, B^*)$ for the generalized JLL++ strategy found by genetic algorithms.**

| | | $A^*(j^I, j^{II}, 1)$ | | | $A^*(j^I, j^{II}, 2)$ | | | $A^*(j^I, j^{II}, 3)$ | | |
|---|---|---|---|---|---|---|---|---|---|---|---|
| | | $j^{II}$ | | | $j^{II}$ | | | $j^{II}$ | | |
| | | 1 | 2 | 3 | 1 | 2 | 3 | 1 | 2 | 3 |
| | 1 | -0.423 | -0.307 | 0.814 | -0.953 | 0.489 | -0.864 | -0.253 | -12.576 | -45.014 |
| $j^I$ | 2 | 0.569 | -0.808 | -0.433 | 0.697 | 0.81 | -0.107 | 12.527 | -0.179 | -31.96 |
| | 3 | 0.121 | 0.658 | -0.827 | -0.591 | 0.917 | -0.617 | 44.515 | 31.935 | 0.22 |

| | | $B^*(j^I, j^{II}, 1)$ | | | $B^*(j^I, j^{II}, 2)$ | | | $B^*(j^I, j^{II}, 3)$ | | |
|---|---|---|---|---|---|---|---|---|---|---|---|
| | | $j^{II}$ | | | $j^{II}$ | | | $j^{II}$ | | |
| | | 1 | 2 | 3 | 1 | 2 | 3 | 1 | 2 | 3 |
| | 1 | 0.472 | 1.742 | 1.129 | 1.803 | 0.056 | 0.511 | 1.042 | 1.479 | 1.129 |
| $j^I$ | 2 | 0.928 | 0.695 | 1.3 | 1.682 | 0.304 | 0.885 | 1.755 | 0.957 | 1.076 |
| | 3 | 0.511 | 0.142 | 0.019 | 0.661 | 0.472 | 1.862 | 0.69 | 0.499 | 1.138 |

After several such 'generations', the population typically contains good solutions. The process can be improved if from time to time local optimization is applied to single individuals. This stops the genetic evolution for some time, but afterwards a new, often much improved individual is given back into the population. Its good 'genetic material' then improves the quality of the population during the next few generations.

Table 3 shows matrices $(A^*, B^*)$ obtained from optimization with genetic algorithms. The corresponding strategy $\delta_{A^*, B^*}$ works as follows: if e.g. an arriving aircraft of type $k = 1 = $'heavy' finds an aircraft of type $j^I = 3 = $ 'light' at the end of queue $I$ and $j^{II} = 2 = $ 'medium' at queue $II$ then it would be routed to runway $I$ if the load $u^I$ on this runway is less than or equal to

$$A(3, 2, 1) + B(3, 2, 1) \cdot u^{II} = 0.658 + 0.142 \cdot u^{II}.$$

## 5. Simulation Results

The simulation and optimization system we used were developed at UT Clausthal. The structure of the simulation tool is shown in Figure 6, it follows the structure of the Markov decision process as depicted in Figure 1. The arrival stream generator produces the random arrival events. They can be a truly random with inter-arrival times and types of aircraft selected according to some distribution but the events can also be derived from real arrival data of some airport. The central part of the system maintains the state of the runways and queues as formalized in (2). It uses a strategy $\delta$ for the routing decisions. Finally, the waiting times are recorded and averages and other statistical information from the simulation run are gathered.

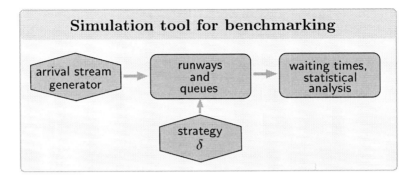

Figure 6. The structure of the simulation tool.

In this set-up, the tool is used for the simulation and benchmarking of given strategies. It may also be used as a subsystem for the heuristic optimization of strategies as indicated in Figure 7. Here the output of a simulation run (or part of it) is used for the evaluation of strategies during the iterative improvement by local search or genetic algorithms as described in the previous chapters.

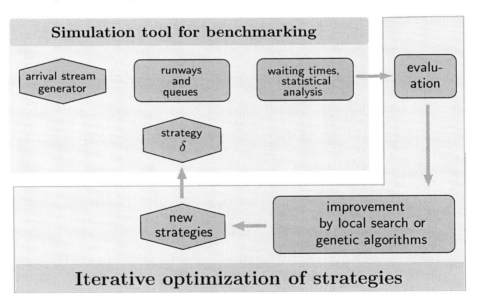

Figure 7. The interaction between optimization and simulation.

## Scenario Parameter

For the optimization and the comparison of different strategies we used a Poisson arrival stream where the inter-arrival times are independent and identically distributed according to an exponential distribution with different arrival rates $\lambda$. The weight class of arriving aircraft is determined randomly such that the arrival stream consists of 23% heavy, 72% medium and 5% of light aircraft. These are realistic data for larger airports.

The separation times that successive aircraft have to keep are determined by air traffic regulations. Table 4 shows data that were published for a major German hub. As the

### Table 4. Separation distances in nautical miles

|  |  | trailing | | |
|---|---|---|---|---|
|  |  | heavy | medium | light |
| leading | heavy | 4 | 5 | 6 |
|  | medium | 2,5 | 2,5 | 5 |
|  | light | 2,5 | 2,5 | 2,5 |

distances are typically given in nautical miles, we have to transform them into seconds. If we assume an average speed of 145kn for heavy aircraft, 140kn for medium sized and 130kn for light aircraft, the separation time at the runway threshold can be approximated by the times that are given in Table 5. These values were used for the separation matrix $D$ as given in (1).

### Table 5. Aircraft separation in seconds

|  |  | trailing | | |
|---|---|---|---|---|
|  |  | heavy | medium | light |
| leading | heavy | 124 | 153 | 191 |
|  | medium | 87 | 89 | 163 |
|  | light | 87 | 89 | 94 |

## Comparison of Different Strategies

We compared three different strategies. The first one is a threshold strategy of the reduced type described in Section 3.. It was determined using the local search algorithm with a Poisson arrival stream with arrival rate $\lambda = 69.23$ aircraft per hour. The second strategy is the generalized JLL strategy $\delta_{A^*B^*}$ as given in Table 3. It was obtained from optimization by genetic algorithm using a Poisson stream with $\lambda = 67.35$. Finally, we included as an additional benchmark the simple JLL strategy as described in (6).

We fed these strategies into our simulation tool and estimated the average waiting time for different arrival rates varying from about 45 aircraft per hour up to more than 70. For each arrival rate, the simulation was carried on until the relative error of the estimated values as determined by the 95% confidence interval was below 5%. Results are shown in Figure 8. Typically, the simulated average waiting times first grow moderately with increasing arrival rate. When the capacity of the system is reached the waiting times explode, the system becomes congested. The actual capacity, i.e. the arrival rate that still can be handled by the system, obviously depends on the routing strategy used.

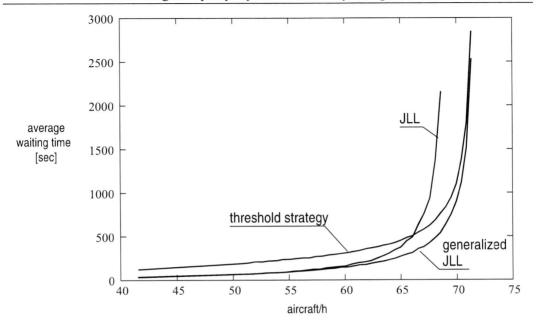

Figure 8. Average waiting times for increasing arrival rates.

Figure 8 shows that JLL performs well for low arrival rates where aircraft often find empty runways. In this situation the threshold strategy creates larger waiting times. This picture changes as the arrival rate gets beyond 65 aircraft per hour. Here both our optimized strategies are much better than JLL. In particular, the generalized JLL strategy seems to be very good under all arrival rates.

However, these are only simulations with an artificial scenario in which arrival rates and type mix are assumed to be constant during the simulation run. In realistic arrival data both arrival rates and type mix change drastically during a day. In Figure 9, the upper oscillating curve shows the typical pattern of the arrival rate over 24 hours.

We therefore performed an additional simulation study with the simulation tool Simmod$^{TM}$ that is often used for airport capacity analysis with more realistic scenarios. The data used originate from a major German airport, they also include starting aircraft that use the same runways as the arriving ones. Instead of JLL, we used as a benchmark an example of an actual manual routing as it was performed by a flight guidance. Figure 9 shows the additional delay for arriving aircraft as it occurred under the manual routing and under a strategy of the reduced threshold type which was optimized by local search with these arrival data. The waiting times here are moving averages over intervals of 15 minutes.

In this study, the threshold strategy was superior to the manual routing in practically all situations, the reduction of delay is significant. Not shown in the Figure are delays for departures which were included in the Simmod$^{TM}$ scenario. It turned out that these could also be reduced if landing aircraft were assigned by the threshold strategy.

At the time of writing, the corresponding results for the generalized JLL strategy were not yet available.

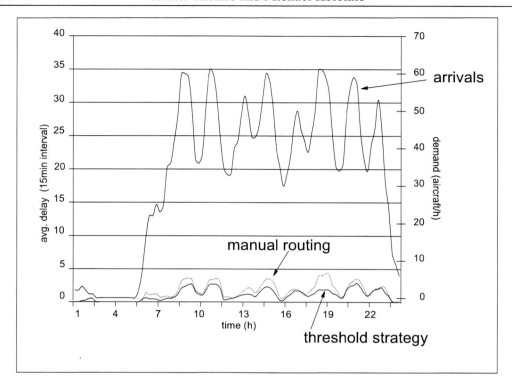

Figure 9. Comparison of delays under a manual routing and the routing according to a threshold strategy.

# 6.   Conclusion

We have have derived two types of dynamic strategies for the assignment of arriving aircraft to runways. Both offer significant potential for the reduction of delays occurring in heavy traffic situations. Due to their simple structure both type of strategies can be evaluated in real time and could be included into arrival management tools and decision support systems for air traffic management.

We restricted ourselves to an assignment of single aircraft in a first-come first-served fashion. These assignments can be made at an early stage of the arrival process so that air traffic management has enough time to calculate a safe trajectory to the assigned runway. Furthermore first-come first-served methods are considered as fair by the parties involved, especially the airlines, which is important for the acceptance of a computer based arrival management.

The simulation based approach used for the determination of our strategies also allows for an easy inclusion of additional constraints, e. g. dependencies between runways or additional weight classes.

Our future research will concentrate on strategies that adapt themselves to the changing arrival patterns as they appear in real operations. Further simulation studies under realistic scenarios have to be carried out.

# References

[1] Bäuerle, N., Engelhardt-Funke, O. and Kolonko M. (2007) On the Waiting Time of Arriving Aircrafts and the Capacity of Airports with One or Two Runways.*Europ. J. Operational Research*, **177**, 1180-1196.

[2] Bäuerle, N., Engelhardt-Funke, O. and Kolonko, M. (2004) Routing of Aircrafts to Two Runways: Monotonicity of Optimal Controls. *Probability in the Engineering and Informational Sciences* **18**, 533-560.

[3] Beasley, J.E., Krishnamoorty, M., Sharaiha, Y.M. and Abramson, D. (2000) Scheduling Aircraft Landings - The Static Case. *Transportation Science* **34**, p 180-197.

[4] Bolender, M.A. and Slater, G.L. (2000) Evaluation of Scheduling Methods for Multiple Runways. *Journal of Aircrafts* **37**, 410 - 416.

[5] Bertsekas, D. (1987) *Dynamic Programming: Deterministic and Stochastic Models.* Prentice Hall, Englewood Cliffs, N.J.

[6] Bertsekas, D. and Tsitsiklis, J. N. (1996) *Neuro-Dynamic Programming.* Prentice Hall, Englewood Cliffs, N.J.

[7] Horonjeff, R. and MCKelvey, F.X. (1994) *Planning and Design of Airports.* McGraw-Hill, 4. ed., Boston.

[8] Neuts, M.F. (1989) *Structured Stochastic Matrices of M/G/1 Type and Their Applications* Marcel Dekker, New York and Basel.

[9] Reeves, C. R. and Rowe, J. E. (2003) *Genetic Algorithms – Principles and Perspectives*, Kluwer Academic Publishers, Boston.

# SHORT COMMUNICATIONS

In: Airports: Performance, Risks, and Problems
Editors: P.B. Larauge et al, pp. 167-178

ISBN: 978-1-60692-393-1
© 2009 Nova Science Publishers, Inc.

# DOES AIRLINE MARKET POWER AFFECT AIRPORT PERFORMANCE?

*Carlos F. Alves[1] and Cristina Barbot[2,*]*
[1]CEMPRE, Faculdade de Economia, Universidade do Porto
[2]CETE, Faculdade de Economia, Universidade do Porto
Rua Dr. Roberto Frias, 4200-464 Porto, Portugal

## Abstract

In this paper, we first build a model that shows that a monopolist supplier's profits depend negatively on the market power in the buyers' industry. The model depicts an input market with Stackelberg competition and a market leader amongst buyers but with only one seller. We then proceed with an empirical study for airport and airline industries, and with the theoretical model we consistently get evidence that airports' financial performance depends negatively on the market power in the airline industry. Thus we conclude that airlines are able to extract rents from airports when they have a large market share.

## I. Introduction

The effect of market power on the seller's side in market structure and performance has become a standard theme in Industrial Organisation literature. Conversely, the effect of the market power of buyers has been analysed mainly in the extreme cases of monopsony and bilateral monopoly. Even the case of bilateral monopoly still only has two main literature contributions: the Nash bargaining solution (Nash, 1950) and Bowley (1928)'s model. But intermediate cases of a small number of buyers and sellers, or - in a broader context - of market power on both sides, have been scarcely dealt with. Among the few exceptions that have analysed this case, it is worth mentioning Horn and Wolinsky (1988), who apply the Nash bargaining solution to the case of two buyers and two sellers. This study aims to contribute to fill this gap.

* E-mail address: cbarbot@fep.up.pt; Telephone: + 351 225 571 100; Fax: + 351 225 505 050

In this paper we develop, theoretically and empirically, a model of a monopolist supplier and a small number of buyers, focusing on how supplier profits depend on the market power on the buyers' side. Our model is designed for a situation where there are $n+1$ firms selling a good or a service to consumers, and buying an input from a single firm. Competition amongst the $n+1$ firms is neither perfect (e.g., a large number of firms with no market power) nor symmetric (e.g., Cournot competition). Instead, we suppose that one of the $n+1$ firms is a quantity Stackelberg leader.

We illustrate and empirically test our model with one airport that sells its services to a finite number of airlines, but where one of them is a quantity leader, because this situation characterises well the market relationship between airline and airport industries, with major and often national airlines dominating airport traffic (European Commission, 2003; Consumer Federation of America, 2001). But the situation may apply to other cases. As examples, we may think of a monopoly that sells its goods or services to a certain number of small groceries and to a hypermarket, or of a telecommunications or an energy network monopolist supplying the network services to a large operator and to small ones.

We first build a theoretical model that shows how a monopolist airport's profits depend negatively on the market power in the airline industry. We then proceed with an empirical study to test this hypothesis, measuring the market power in the airline industry with the respective concentration ratio. We use a sample of 55 airports and we find support for our theoretical model. In particular, we get evidence that the higher the concentration ratio is for the three main airlines, the lower the financial performance of the airport company is measured by net earnings or net margin of revenues.

Airports' performance and profitability may depend on several factors, among which stand the efficiency of their operations, on the production side, ownership and governance structure, regulatory issues concerning the definition of aeronautical charges, and other variables concerning economic and financial management.

Oum et al. (2006) studied how the efficiency and profitability of airports depend on their governance structure and form of ownership. With a sample of 116 airports worldwide, these authors found that the ownership structure is a determinant of efficiency, and that partially privatised airports but with government majority are less efficient than others, even than those that are totally public. Moreover, airports with 100% private ownership are more profitable in Europe and Oceania, but no evidence confirms this result for the US. Also, Vasigh and Hamzaee (1998) have found a positive and significant correlation between airports' operating revenues and size.

With regard to airports' productivity, Oum et al. (2003a) found that it is positively correlated with size, thus suggesting the existence of economies of scale, and negatively correlated with the percentage of international traffic and with the share of aeronautical revenues.

But none of the studies mentioned above has dealt with what may be an important dimension of airports' profitability: their own market power and the market power of airlines that buy their services.

The paper contributes to theory and to policy, as it may enlighten the current debate between airports and airlines[1] as well as policy issues concerning concentration on the

---

[1] As it is known, airlines claim that airports' aeronautical charges are too high and airlines claim the opposite.

buyers' side. We conclude that airlines are able to extract rents from the airport whenever they have a large market share.

## II. Theoretical Model

Airport markets are often of imperfect competition. They may include more than one seller, when airports compete, and a limited number of buyers. Putting aside airport competition, we deal with the market between airlines and airports. Airlines buy airport aeronautical services, for which they pay a price, the so-called aeronautical charges, which include several items, such as landing and take-off charges, parking charges and others. Some of these charges are regulated, so the airport has only a limited interval of choice for these fees. But within the limits allowed by regulators, these charges depend on the buyers (airlines)' market power.

Our model is based on Bowley (1928)'s first case[2], in which the seller has more power than the buyer and so determines the input price, subject to the derived demand of the buyer. The choice of this case makes sense, as there is only one seller and a finite number of buyers. While Bowley (1928) used a bilateral monopoly situation, with one seller and one buyer, we use a finite number of buyers, one of them being a leader in the output market. The main point is that the largest buyer has market power, while the followers do not, but in a certain way they profit from the leader's market power, as the latter is in a strong position to negotiate the price of the input. Our concern is with the input market. The output market is only a standard Stackelberg situation. Our main purpose is to investigate whether leadership in the output market has any effect on the buyers' market power in the input market. In other words, we intend to find out whether the larger is the market power of the leader in the output market, the larger is the buyers' market power in the input market.

As a measure for the market power in the output market we use the leader's market share, $s_1$. Market power in the input market can be measured by the solution for the seller's profit: the higher the buyers' market power is, the smaller the seller's profit.

The game is developed in two stages. In the first stage, the seller chooses the input price, given its demand. In the second stage, the buyers choose the output quantity, given the input price.

### (i) The Final Product Market

In the output market there are $n+1$ firms competing in quantities. One of them, firm $1$, is a Stackelberg leader and all other $n$ firms are followers. Inverse demand is expressed by $p = a - Q$, where $p$ is the output price (the ticket fare) and $Q$ its total number of passengers.

For simplicity we assume that all the $n+1$ firms have constant marginal costs ($c$). They pay the price $P$ for one unit of the input. Also for simplicity, we suppose that the production function is $Q = X$, where $X$ denotes the input quantity. A standard result of the equal marginal costs assumption is that all the followers will produce the same quantity $q_j$, while the leader will produce $q_1$, $q_1 > q_j$.

---

[2] We follow Stahl (1978)'s formulation of Bowley (1928)'s model.

For any follower, for instance, for firm $i$, profits are represented by: $\pi_i = (a - q_1 - q_i - (n-1)q_j)q_i - (c + P)q_i$. Maximising profits, and making $q_j = q_i$, any

of the followers' best reply functions have the expression: $q_i = \dfrac{a - c - P - q_1}{n+1}$.

The leader then maximises its profits of $\pi_1 = (a - q_1 - n\dfrac{a - c - P - q_1}{n+1})q_1 - (c+P)q_1$.

Results for quantities are $Q = \dfrac{1}{2}\dfrac{(a - c - P)(2n+1)}{n+1}$, $q_1 = \dfrac{1}{2}(a - c - P)$,

$q_i = \dfrac{1}{2}\dfrac{a - c - P}{n+1}$ and $Q = q_1 + nq_i$, the derived demand for the input

is: $Q = \dfrac{1}{2}\dfrac{(a - c - P)(2n+1)}{n+1}$.

## (ii) The Input Market

The airport charges a price $P$, per passenger, for the aeronautical services it supplies to airlines. In addition to this, it gets revenues from the so-called concession activities[3]. We assume that each passenger spends $k$ euros on one item of concession activities so that the price of these goods or services is normalised to $k$ and that $k$ is exogenous. Notice that results do not change in their essential point (market power in the input market) if the seller is not an airport and does not perceive these revenues. We also assume that the airport (or the input firm) has only a fixed cost of $F$, variable costs being equal to zero. The seller's (airport's)

profits are then expressed by: $\pi_A = (P+k)(\dfrac{1}{2}(a-c-P)\dfrac{2n+1}{n+1}) - F$. Maximising its profits, the

airport has as the solution for $P$, $P = \dfrac{1}{2}(a - c - k)$ and for its profits

$\pi_A = \dfrac{1}{8}(a - c + k)^2 \dfrac{2n+1}{n+1} - F$.

## (iii) Interaction between Final and Input Markets

Finally, we can show that airports' profits depend on the share of the main airlines that use them. In fact:

Proposition: *The higher the market power in the output market, the lower the input supplier firm's profits.*

---

[3] These revenues are important for airports and should not be neglected. In fact, these non-airside (or concession) activities generated from 40% to 80% of all revenues in 50 major world airports in 1999 (Oum *et al.* 2003b). At Heathrow and Gatwick they account for about 60% of all airport revenues (Starkie, 2001).

Proof: To prove this proposition, consider the Stackelberg leader's market share, $s_1$, as a measure of the downstream market power. The expression of $s_1$ will be

$$s_1 = \frac{q_1}{Q} = \frac{\frac{1}{2}(a-c-P)}{\frac{1}{2}\frac{(a-c-P)(2n+1)}{n+1}} = \frac{n+1}{2n+1}$$ . Then the airport's profits expression may be written as:

$$\pi_A = (\frac{1}{8}(a-c-k)^2 \frac{1}{s_1} - F$$ . Now the derivative of $\pi_A$ in order to $s_1$ taken at both markets'

solutions is $\frac{\partial \pi_A}{\partial s_1} = -\frac{1}{8}\frac{(a-c+k)^2}{s_1^2}$, which is decreasing in $s_1$. The larger $s_1$ is, the lower $\pi_A$ will

be. Thus market power in the output market influences the solution of the input market. In particular, when a large firm is an output market leader, the input firm will have smaller profits.

# III. Empirical Study

## (*i*) Data

Our study started with data for the 100 biggest airports in 2005 according to Airline Business (June 2006). This data source includes the following variables: *i*) S1, S2 and S3, which are, respectively, the shares of the first, second and third major airlines; *ii*) PAX, which represents the number of passengers, in millions; *iii*) SI, which is the percentage of intercontinental flights in total flights for each airport; *iv*) SPF, which is the average number of seats per aircraft, considering all the aircraft that landed and took off at one airport. Based on major airlines' identification, we constructed three dummies: LCC1, LCC2 and LCC3, which take the value one, respectively, if the first, second and third largest airline in the airport is a low cost carrier and zero otherwise. Criteria to identify an airline as a low cost carrier was based on airlines' websites[4]. From Airline Business (December 2006), we collected the net earnings for 2004 and 2005, the revenues for 2004 and 2005 and the operating margin (OPM) for 2004. We searched airports' websites to get financial reports in order to fill gaps.

After merging Airline Business (June 2006)'s and Airline Business (December 2006)'s databases and filling in existing data lacking on websites, we got complete data for 55 airports, listed in the Annex. Airports are geographically distributed in the following way: 40% in Europe, 33% in the US, 15% in Asia, 5% in Latin America, 5% in Oceania and 2% in Africa.

Regressions were performed with EViews software.

## (*ii*) Variables

Dependent variables are net earnings and the ratio between net earnings and revenues (net margin of revenues). As mentioned above, explanatory variables are S1, S2 and S3, or a sum of three of them, which expresses concentration ratios. It is expected that, according to the

---

[4] Usually airlines define themselves as "budget" or "low cost". If not, the existence of free onboard service was a main criterion to classify an airline as "low cost".

previous section model, both dependent variables are negatively related to S1, S2 and S3, or to their sum. This is the main point of our study.

We added some control variables, also defined above: PAX, SI, SFP, OWN, LCC1, LCC2 and LCC3. PAX expresses the size of the airport. As mentioned in the Introduction, Vasigh and Hamzaee (1998) found a positive correlation between operating revenues and size. Also, Oum et al. (2003a) found the same positive correlation between size and productivity. Though productivity is by no means the only factor that accounts for profitability, it is expected that net earnings and the ratio between net earnings and revenues will increase with size. The variable OWN is a dummy that takes the value of zero if the airport has a majority of State ownership and of one otherwise. Oum et al (2006)'s study concludes that private ownership only leads to more efficiency in Europe and Oceania, and that the least efficient airports are those with private and public ownership, but with a majority of the latter. This result is about efficiency and not about profitability. As private ownership means a management aim of maximising profits, this variable is expected to have a positive sign.

SI intends to capture the airports' orientation, thus separating regional airports from those more oriented to international traffic. SPF measures the dimension of aircraft landing and taking off at the selected airports. Though it may seem that SI and SFP are correlated, as international traffic is performed with larger aircraft, this correlation is not very strong (correlation coefficient of 0.53). Thus there is no evidence of multicollinearity. Moreover, there is no *a priori* sign for a possible correlation between net earnings and these variables, internationally-oriented airports with larger aircraft being, *a priori*, no more or less profitable than those that handle mainly domestic flights.

Variables LCC1, LCC2 and LCC3 intend to capture the dominance of low cost airlines at airports. This purpose is two-fold. On one hand, airports that support low cost carriers' traffic should be efficient, as these airlines require quick and simple handling processes (Franke, 2004, Hansson et al., 2003). This higher efficiency could be turned into higher profits. On the other hand, low cost airlines seek to push down costs and so aeronautical fares, eventually making airports less profitable. The presence of these two effects, with opposite signs, does not allow us to suspect an *a priori* correlation between net revenues and LCC1, LCC2 or LCC3.

A lagged dependent variable is used to explain profits, accounting for the past history of airports' profitability. Correlation is obviously expected to be positive. Finally, lagged OPM (operating margin) may contribute to explaining net earnings and the expected sign is positive.

Table 1 shows some of theairports' statistics.

The average size is of 29 million passengers, with a higher value of 86 million at Atlanta Hartsfield and a lower value of 16 million at Portland. Mean and median values of SI, of about 20%, show that these airports deal mainly with domestic flights and use medium range aircraft with an average of 146 seats. The mean of the percentage of flights of the largest airline is high (38.1%), with a higher value (84%) at Houston George Bush and a lower value (11.6%) at New York LaGuardia. But the percentage of the largest three airlines (CR3) indicates that the industry is highly concentrated, with a mean and a median of 64%, and with a higher value of 95.4% for São Paulo Congonhas and a lower value of 33.2% for New York LaGuardia. Data for S1 and CR3 shows that airports are often dominated by one or a few airlines, supporting the hypothesis of our theoretical model. With regard to operational performance, data shows that, though the mean and median have similar values of, respectively, 22.3% and 22.6%, suggesting a symmetric distribution, dispersion is high, with a higher value of 56.6% and a lower value of -26.7%. Lagged operating margins are positive for 52 of the 55 airports, with a mean of 25% for positive margins, showing that the largest firms in this industry are performing well. Operational performance does not show a close relation with financial performance. Net results are negative in 9 of the 55 airports and have a higher value of 723 million dollars and a lower value representing losses of 164 million dollars.

**Table 1. Variables Statistics**

|  | Mean | Median | Higher Value | Lower value |
|---|---|---|---|---|
| PAX (millions) | 29.4 | 26.5 | 86 | 16 |
| SI | 20% | 19.4% | 62% | 0.1% |
| SPF | 146 | 136 | 282 | 90 |
| S1 | 38.1% | 37% | 84% | 11.6% |
| S2 | 17.7% | 17.1% | 40% | 3.7% |
| S3 | 8.6% | 8.5% | 17.7% | 2% |
| CR3 | 64.4% | 63.5% | 95.4% | 33.2% |
| Lagged OPM | 22.3% | 22.6% | 56.6% | -26.7% |
| NR05 (million $US) | 115.9 | 62 | 723 | -164 |

Obs.: *i*) PAX represents the number of passengers, in millions; *ii*) SI is the percentage of intercontinental flights in total flights at each airport; *iii*) SPF is the average number of seats per aircraft; *iv*) S1, S2 and S3 are, respectively, the shares of the first, second and third major airlines; *v*) CR3 is the sum of S1, S2 and S3; Lagged OPM is the operating margin for 2004; vi) NR05 is the net earnings for 2005.

Finally, variable OWN is not analysed in Table 1 as it is a binary variable. Concerning this data, it can be said that only 21.8% of the airports in our sample are totally private or have a majority of private capital.

## (*iii*) Results

Table 2 summarises our results. In all regressions, neither the share of intercontinental (usually long-haul) flights nor the average aircraft size are significant. Regional airports where smaller aircraft land and take off can perform as well as hub airports more dedicated to the long-haul intercontinental business.

None of the LCC variables are significant in any of the performed regressions, either. A large percentage of low cost airlines seem to have nothing to do with airports' net revenues. As stated above, this can happen as a result of the two opposite effects, namely the requirement of higher efficiency, pushing up revenues, and the pressure for low aeronautical charges, this time pushing revenues down. The sum of the two effects may make this variable's coefficient non-significant.

## Table 2. Regressions of Airport Earnings and Revenue Profitability

| | [1] Dependent Variable Net Earnings | | [2] Dependent Variable Net Earnings | | [3] Dependent Variable Net Earnings | | [4] Dependent Variable Net Margin of Revenues | |
|---|---|---|---|---|---|---|---|---|
| | Coef. | t-Stat. | Coef. | t-Stat. | Coef. | t-Stat. | Coef. | t-Stat. |
| C | 178.574 | 2.826 *** | 169.187 | 3.010 *** | 152.002 | 2.583 *** | 20.016 | 1.565 * |
| PAX | -0.658 | -0.878 | -0.671 | -0.908 | -0.267 | -0.352 | -0.239 | -1.529 * |
| SI | 2.085 | 0.224 | 2.274 | 0.248 | 9.869 | 1.092 | 2.994 | 0.153 |
| SPF | 0.216 | 0.650 | 0.227 | 0.695 | -0.047 | -0.146 | 0.047 | 0.617 |
| OWN | -31.859 | -1.206 | -31.296 | -1.202 | -30.457 | -1.108 | -2.116 | -0.384 |
| Lagged Dependent Variable | 0.726 | 15.820 *** | 0.726 | 16.019 *** | 0.737 | 15.484 *** | 0.351 | 1.557 * |
| Lagged OPM | -0.092 | -0.127 | -0.101 | -0.142 | -0.237 | -0.317 | 0.240 | 1.173 |
| S1 | -1.316 | -1.488 * | -1.202 | -1.487 * | | | | |
| S2 | -3.626 | -2.445 *** | | | | | | |
| S3 | -4.916 | -1.553 * | | | | | | |
| S2+S3 | | | -3.917 | -3.269 *** | | | | |
| S1+S2+S3 | | | | | -1.797 | -2.224 ** | -0.307 | -1.706 ** |
| LCC1+LCC2+LCC3 | -3.378 | -0.245 | -3.380 | -0.248 | -3.253 | -0.226 | 2.262 | 0.727 |
| R²/Adjusted R² | 0.919 | 0.896 | 0.919 | 0.899 | 0.907 | 0.887 | 0.449 | 0.323 |
| N | 47 | | 47 | | 47 | | 45 | |

Obs.: (*i*) The t-Stat in regression [4] is based on White's heteroskedasticity-consistent standard errors and covariance; (*ii*) The symbols ***, **, and * show statistical significance at the 1%, 5%, and 10% level respectively for one-sided statistical tests.

Also, variable OWN is not significant in any of the regressions. Its negative sign might suggest that public airports are more profitable than private ones. This does not confirm Oum et al (2006)'s findings about the poor performance of public/ private venture airports, when the majority of the capital is public. But the non-significance of OWN's coefficient does not support this conclusion[5].

Regressions 1, 2 and 3 clearly explain airports' net earnings, with an adjusted $R^2$ ranging from 0.92 to 0.90. In these regressions, the number of passengers and lagged operating margins are not significant. Net revenues are not influenced by airports' size, meaning that small airports are able to get high profits as well as large airports. Lagged operating margins also do not explain net earnings. Lagged net earnings (i.e., the net earnings of 2004) are obviously significant.

Regression 1 uses as explanatory variables the individual share of the first, second and third major airlines. It shows that the major airline's share, S1, isalways negative and significant. But while the influence of the share of the third major airline is less significant than the others', the share of the second one has a decisive importance.

But the important result is that the aggregated share of the first, second and third major airlines, or of groups of them, has a negative and significant coefficient. Regression 3 clearly shows that the sum of the shares of the three major airlines negatively influences airports' profits.

Therefore this empirical study confirms our model's results. The share of the largest airline has a negative and significant influence on airports' profits. The same happens with the share of the second major company, and, albeit to a lesser extent, with that of the third. Moreover, all this happens whether airports are oriented to international traffic or not, and whether low cost carriers are the main users or not. In other words, regardless of the type of airport and of the type of airlines that use it, its users' market power is negatively related to its profits.

In regression 4, net earnings are scaled by total revenues. Thus, here we use a relative indicator of performance (net margin of revenues). This margin is significantly influenced by the number of passengers, which means that bigger airports are less efficient in transforming revenues into net earnings. This explains why the biggest airports are not necessarily the most profitable (according to Regressions 1 to 3). Vasigh and Hamzaee (1998) found a positive correlation between operating revenues and size, which does not go against our result. Larger airports may get higher revenues, either from aeronautical or from concession activities[6], but these revenues are not transformed into higher net earnings.

# V. Conclusions

In this paper we develop a theoretical model that shows how a monopolist supplier's profits depend negatively on the market power in the buyers' industry. This model is built with Stackelberg competition and a market leader amongst buyers but with only one seller. This model's design is adequate to depict situations such as one airport selling its services to a

---

[5] Namely, these public/private ventures may contain a greater potential for conflict between public interests at the national level, public interest at the local level, and private interests.

[6] Usually large airports are hubs. In hubs passengers have to wait for connecting flights and spend more on concession activities items (bars and restaurants, shops).

finite number of airlines, but where one of them is a quantity leader. This situation clearly characterises the market relationship between airline and airport industries, with major and often national airlines dominating airports' traffic.

We test our model empirically using a sample of 55 airports. We find support for our theoretical model. Specifically, we get empirical evidence that airports' net earnings and net margins of revenue depend negatively on the market power in the airline industry.

Airports' performance depends on their efficiency but also on their market power towards airlines that use it. If much has been written on the first determinant (efficiency or productivity) there are no works that relate airports' performance to airlines' market power. This paper contributes to filling this gap in the literature. This paper also contributes to politics, as it may enlighten regulation topics, as well as the current debate between airports and airlines. As it is known, airlines claim that airports' aeronautical charges are too high and airports claim the opposite. We conclude that airlines are able to extract rents from airports when they have a large market share.

## Acknowledgements

CEMPRE and CETE are supported by FCT through POCTI of the QCAIII, which is financed by FEDER and Portuguese funds.

## Annex: List of Airports

| Ranking | | City | Airport | Code | Country |
|---|---|---|---|---|---|
| 2005 | 2004 | | | | |
| 1 | 1 | Atlanta | Hartsfield Int'l | ATL | USA |
| 3 | 3 | London | Heathrow | LHR | UK |
| 4 | 4 | Tokyo | Haneda | HND | Japan |
| 5 | 5 | Los Angeles | International | LAX | USA |
| 7 | 7 | Paris | Charles de Gaulle | CDG | France |
| 8 | 8 | Frankfurt | International | FRA | Germany |
| 9 | 11 | Las Vegas | McCarran | LAS | USA |
| 10 | 9 | Amsterdam | Schiphol | AMS | Netherlands |
| 11 | 10 | Denver | International | DEN | USA |
| 12 | 13 | Madrid | Barajas | MAD | Spain |
| 14 | 20 | Beijing | Capital | PEK | China |
| 15 | 15 | New York | JFK | JFK | USA |
| 16 | 17 | Hong Kong | Chek Lap Kok | HKG | China |
| 17 | 18 | Houston | George Bush | IAH | USA |
| 18 | 14 | Bangkok | International | BKK | Thailand |
| 20 | 19 | Detroit | Wayne Country | DTW | USA |
| 21 | 24 | Orlando | International | MCO | USA |

**Annex. Continued**

| Ranking | | City | Airport | Code | Country |
|---|---|---|---|---|---|
| 2005 | 2004 | | | | |
| 22 | 21 | San Francisco | International | SFO | USA |
| 23 | 22 | Newark | Liberty Int'l | EWR | USA |
| 24 | 23 | London | Gatwick | LGW | UK |
| 25 | 26 | Singapore | Changi | SIN | Singapore |
| 26 | 25 | Tokyo | Narita | NRT | Japan |
| 28 | 27 | Miami | International | MIA | USA |
| 31 | 31 | Sydney | Kingsford Smith | SYD | Australia |
| 32 | 32 | Rome | Fiumicino | FCO | Italy |
| 33 | 33 | Munich | Franz Joseph Strauss | MUC | Germany |
| 37 | 36 | Charlotte | Douglas | CLT | USA |
| 38 | 42 | Washington | Dulles International | IAD | USA |
| 39 | 39 | Seoul | Incheon International | ICN | S Korea |
| 40 | 38 | New York | La Guardia | LGA | USA |
| 41 | 40 | Paris | Orly | ORY | France |
| 43 | 41 | Mexico City | Benito Juarez International | MEX | Mexico |
| 46 | 46 | Kuala Lumpur | International | KUL | Malaysia |
| 48 | 44 | Manchester | International | MAN | UK |
| 50 | 61 | Salt Lake City | International | SLC | USA |
| 51 | 48 | London | Stansted | STN | UK |
| 53 | 51 | Palma | Palma de Mallorca | PMI | Spain |
| 54 | 53 | Melbourne | Tullamarine | MEL | Australia |
| 58 | 58 | Copenhagen | Kastrup | CPH | Denmark |
| 59 | 59 | Milan | Malpensa | MXP | Italy |
| 63 | 66 | Dublin | Dublin | DUB | Ireland |
| 65 | 65 | Zurich | Unique Zurich | ZRH | Switzerland |
| 66 | 70 | Washington | Ronald Reagan National DCA | DCA | USA |
| 69 | 67 | International | San Diego | SAN | USA |
| 71 | 68 | Stockholm | Arlanda | ARN | Sweden |
| 72 | 87 | Sao Paulo | Congonhas | CGH | Brazil |
| 73 | 84 | Sao Paulo | Guarulhos International | GRU | Brazil |
| 77 | 72 | Brisbane | International | BNE | Australia |
| 78 | 71 | Brussels | National | BRU | Belgium |
| 80 | 78 | Oslo | Gardermoen | OSL | Norway |
| 81 | 80 | Vienna | International | VIE | Austria |
| 83 | 86 | Johannesburg | International | JNB | South Africa |

**Annex. Continued**

| Ranking | | City | Airport | Code | Country |
|---|---|---|---|---|---|
| 2005 | 2004 | | | | |
| 84 | 73 | Dusseldorf | Rhein Ruhr | DUS | Germany |
| 88 | 88 | Athens | Eleftherios Venizelos | ATH | Greece |
| 91 | 90 | Portland | International | PDX | USA |

# References

Bowley, A. L., 1928. Bilateral monopoly. *The Economic Journal* **38**, 651-659.

Consumer Federation of America, 2001. *Mergers between major airlines: The anti-competitive and anti-consumer effects of the creation of a private cartel.*

European Commission, 2003. *Analysis of the European air transport industry - Final report.*

Franke, M., 2004. Competition between network carriers and low-cost carriers - retreat battle or breakthrough to a new level of efficiency? *Journal of Air Transport Management,* **10** (1), 15-22.

Hansson, T., J. Ringbeck, and M. Franke, 2003. Flight for survival: a new business model for the airline industry, *Strategy+Business,* **31**, 78-85.

Horn, H. and Wolinsky, A., 1988. Bilateral Monopolies and Incentives for Merger. *RAND Journal of Economics* **19**, 408-419.

Nash, J., 1950. The Bargaining Problem. *Econometrica* **18**, 155-162.

Oum, T. H., Yu, C. and Fu, X., 2003a. A comparative analysis of productivity performance of the world's major airports: summary report of the ATRS global airport benchmarking research report - 2002. *Journal of Air Transport Management* **9**, 285–297.

Oum, T. H., Zhang, H. and Zhang, Y., 2003b. Concession profit and its efficiency implications on alternative forms of economic regulation of airports. *The 7ʰ ATRS World Conference,* Toulouse.

Oum, T. H., Adler, N. and Yu, C., 2006. Privatization, corporatization, ownership forms and their effects on the performance of the world's major airports. *Journal of Air Transport Management* **12**, 109–121.

Starkie, D., 2001. *A new deal for airports. In: Robinson,* Colin, ed. RegulatingUtilities -New Issues, 145-165. Edward Elgar Publishing, London.

Vasigh and Hamzaee, 1998. A comparative analysis of economic performance of US commercial airports. *Journal of Air Transport Management,* **4,** 209-216.

In: Airports: Performance, Risks, and Problems

Editors: P.B. Larauge et al, pp. 179-187

ISBN: 978-1-60692-393-1

© 2009 Nova Science Publishers, Inc.

# AVIATION METEOROLOGICAL FORECASTS AND WARNINGS: AN AIRPORT MANAGEMENT TOOL

## M.P. de Villiers

Weather Services International (Europe), Birmingham, United Kingdom

## Abstract

In times gone by the aviation meteorological forecaster was concerned with the issue weather forecasts for the departure airport, en-route and the destination airport. These days the airport aviation meteorologist is increasingly being required to be more knowledgeable about the airport environment and more intimately involved in, the day to day operational decision making and activities at airports so as to increase safety and productivity, lower costs and minimise environmental effects. The increased diversity of aviation meteorological forecasting for airports is commented on by briefly looking at the role the forecaster plays in the issue of forecasts and warnings to air traffic controllers, airside managers, ground operators and airlines as well as a comment on modern trends in the dissemination of the information and into the future.

## 1. Introduction

In the past the aviation meteorological forecaster was concerned with the issue of weather forecasts for the departure airport, en-route and the destination airport. This was accomplished by the issue of routine forecasts such as Terminal Area Forecasts (TAFs), Route Forecasts (ROFORs), Area Forecasts (ARFORs) and Significant Meteorological reports (SIGMETs) [21, 30]. These were either written forecasts to be collected by the pilot or airline dispatcher, or issued by telephone. For widespread regional and international use the coded forecasts were communicated to users via the Global Telecommunications System (GTS) [29] and the Aeronautical Fixed Telecommunication Network (AFTN) [20]. A secondary task was to provide local weather warning information to the airport air traffic controllers.

These days the airport aviation meteorologist is increasingly required to be much more intimately involved in the day to day operational decision making at airports so as to increase safety and productivity, lower costs and minimise environmental effects. This entails a closer working relationship with air traffic controllers, the airlines and airport ground operators. Dr. Olli Turpeinen, the Chief of Meteorology for the International Civil Aviation Organization (ICAO) "believes that coordination and cooperation between meteorological services and other aviation fields will intensify in the future. In fact, with the growing traffic volume, it is the only way forward" [27]. Communication methods have also become more diverse. These now include the Internet, telephone conferencing, mobile phone voice communication and txt messaging. Another growing form of communication is providing in-flight forecast weather information, including wind shear and microburst information to the aircraft cockpit [19].

The diversity of clients, although all may work on the same airport, means that the forecaster must be aware of a wide range of operational requirements and therefore different warning criteria and even a difference in the weather parameters required. This paper is a commentary on the diverse nature of aviation meteorological forecasting for airports.

# 2. Air Traffic Control

Air traffic controllers (ATC) are interested in getting aircraft safely and efficiently into the air and back onto the ground at an airport. Conditions on the ground at the airport are of much less interest to them, unless these have an effect on the runway, and departure and arrival rates. To complicate matters for forecasters, not all airports have the same operational limitations.

Thunderstorms pose a problem for all aircraft operations [11], but more specifically ATC are concerned about thunderstorms that will pass through the Terminal Manoeuvring Area (TMA) and across the approach and departure paths to and from an airport. Advance warning of thunder cloud activity from the forecaster means ATC can pre-plan and be ready for requests from pilots for deviations from approach routes to avoid thunderstorm cells. There may also be requests for a change of runway if there is a thunderstorm on the final approach path to the present designated runway and even notice of intention to divert to another airport. Aircraft ready to depart may request a delayed departure time due to a thunderstorm on the departure path, or the use of another runway. The size of TMAs, as well as the number of approach and departure routes, can vary from location to location. It is therefore important that the forecaster is familiar with the different airport approach and departure paths and TMAs.

Strong winds can be a problem at an airport, such as tail winds on preferred runways that can exceed the wind velocity at which aircraft can land, or take off, at an airport. This is particularly so if there is a strong crosswind component that exceeds the maximum velocity allowed for a particular aircraft [26]. The result can be diversions and delayed departures. While a forecaster cannot be expected to know the limitations of aircraft, there is usually a mean wind speed and/or gust speed above which a warning must be issued. There is an additional consideration and that is the wind velocity on the approach. Although approach airspeeds will remain the same, a stronger headwind on the approach means slower approach ground speeds and therefore, for safety, aircraft approach separation is increased. As a result the airport landing rate will decrease. At peak arrival times at an airport operating at, or near, traffic capacity, this will result in delayed approaches.

Wind shear is particularly important and it has been the "direct cause of accidents" [13]. An aircraft relies on air flow over the wings to remain airborne. If the air flow over the wing decreases to below a critical speed the aircraft will stall, that is begin to sink. Near the ground, at the approach and landing stage, this is dangerous. Wind speed at higher levels is usually stronger than nearer to the ground and this will result in a decrease in the speed of the air over the wings. Pilots allow for this. However, it is incumbent on the forecaster to issue a warning when wind shear conditions are expected. Under certain conditions, the wind may also decrease with height, which is equally dangerous for aircraft taking off. Conditions that become worthy of considering wind shear are when the surface wind exceeds 20 kn, the wind velocity difference between the surface and 2000 ft is ≥40 kn, thunderstorms are within 8 km and/or when already reported by pilots in the area [13, 25]. Criteria vary, at Abu Dhabi International Airport, for instance, the warning threshold is ≥5kn/100ft change in headwind component with ≥12kn/100ft for a severe wind shear warning. For similar reasons surface temperature inversions are also potentially dangerous. Higher temperatures above the surface lead to degradation of engine performance instead of improved performance in the normally lower temperatures higher in the atmosphere. Less dense air due to the higher temperature also results in less lift and aircraft sink [22, 26]. Air temperature ≥10°C than the surface up to 1000 ft above the ground is considered worthy of a warning [12].

Getting the wind direction correct is also important. It is not an easy matter changing the runways in use at a very busy airport, such as London Heathrow. An added problem is that London City Airport has its own traffic almost under the approaches to runways 27L and 27R [2]. Local terrain also plays a role. Due to the surrounding terrain it may not be a simple matter of making the change from one end of the runway to the other as higher ILS intercepts may be required on the new runway. Aircraft always land into the wind, but a preferred runway may to be used with a tailwind until the limit is reached before this velocity becomes unacceptable and a change has to be made. However, if it is known a surface tailwind of say 050 degrees 4 kn, is going to change to 230 degrees 10 kn in the next few hours it is worthwhile using runway 23 with a 4 kn tailwind, provided it is safe, until it changes to 230 degrees and a headwind.

Delayed approaches at peak capacity will result in arriving aircraft having to be held in the stack. Aircraft in the stack awaiting times to approach are held vertically over a navigation point and are separated by flight levels that are dictated by the air pressure. When the air pressure lowers these flight, or pressure, levels descend nearer to the ground. This means that the lowest level, or lower levels, may become unsafe to use due to ground proximity and/or interference with the controlled air space of airports in the vicinity. Once again the forecaster needs to know the critical pressure so as to trigger a timely alert. To complicate matters some locations also apply increased separation when the surface temperature falls to excessively low temperatures. Of course thunderstorms in the vicinity of a navigation holding point means that this particular holding point may not be used and this will put further strain on the other holding points. Delays of this nature and the reduced landing rate may cause instructions for the imposition of delayed departure times for aircraft from other airports to the affected airport. It is therefore important that the forecaster is familiar with the locations and names of holding points.

The forecaster needs to be aware of the applicable Low Visibility Procedure (LVP) criteria at airports. For example, most airports in the United Kingdom (UK) adopt LVP "when the cloud base lowers to 300 ft and is expected to lower further, or the Runway Visual Range

(RVR) falls to 1200 metres and is expected to deteriorate further. They should be fully in place by the time the cloud base reaches 200 ft or the RVR falls to 600 metres [3]. Cloud base and visibility below these limits means that certain precautions have to be taken by the ATC and ground operators [2]. Due to lessened visibility these can be restrictions on the movement of vehicles and exclusion from certain areas of the airport. When LVP is in force a reduced landing rate can be expected due to the need for increased spacing between arriving aircraft. At London Heathrow these are reduced to 34 per hour below 1000 metres Runway Visual Range (RVR) and down to less than 20 below 150 metres RVR [6]. London City Airport has a higher cloud base limit that depends on the airline operator and this varies between 400 and 500 ft. This is higher than the 200 ft for a certified CAT I ILS, but, although the airport ILS conforms to a CAT I, it cannot be fully certified due to signal disruption caused by its location amongst tall city buildings [2].

## 3. Ground Operators

"Besides snow and ice, other adverse weather conditions affect the safety of aircraft operations on aprons, principally strong surface winds and low visibility conditions" [8].

Ground operators are particularly concerned about snow and need an advance warning that includes when it will start and end, the intensity and amount of ground accumulation with a confidence level. At London City Airport no operations are permitted when there is more than 3 mm of standing water, ice or slush to a depth of 3 mm is exceeded and dry snow to a depth of 10 mm [2]. Although "take-off should not be attempted in depths of dry snow greater than 60 mm or depths of water, slush or wet snow greater than 15 mm. If the snow is very dry, the depth limit may be increased to 80 mm" [9]. It is important to be aware of preparation times for advance planning and the positioning of resources at different airports. Requirements with respect to the time length of advance warning can be up to 24 hours, while others may only require 6 hours. Obviously false alarms from the forecaster can be costly to the client and in the shorter term result in unnecessary use and deployment of de-icing and anti-icing equipment and material.

Ground frost and ice are other important weather parameters and, therefore, so are runway, taxiway and walkway surface temperatures. Frost and ice on walkways are a danger to passengers who may slip and injure themselves. This is of particular concern to airport management who need to take pre-emptive measures by passing the warning on to ground operators and treating these surfaces [8]. Airline operators, too, are greatly concerned about structural icing that occurs on standing aircraft, which is usually produced by snow, or frost [10, 17]. Although colder conditions after rain, freezing rain and freezing fog are other causes of ice on aircraft. These are all weather conditions that require warnings,which indicate the duration, intensity and risk of occurrence. The aircraft then needs to be de-iced and anti-iced before take off, because not only does the ice form on the wings and degrade their aerodynamic efficiency, but it can block important instrument probes, such as those of the indicated airspeed indicator and the altimeter as well as critical engine instruments. These were contributory causes for the after take off crash of an aircraft at Washington [1, 23].

Another source of concern is cold soak. Aircraft wings are also said to be cold-soaked when wing fuel tanks contain very cold fuel [17]. Cold fuel can cool the wings to the point where clear ice forms if the wings are damp, for example due to rain, drizzle and fog, even at air temperatures as high as 15°C [15]. The clear ice can be difficult to see and go unnoticed. Factors that contribute to cold soak are the length of time at very cold temperatures at high altitude prior to landing, or having been refuelled with very cold fuel and the time since refuelling, the quantity of fuel in the wings, the type and location of fuel cells.

Strong wind speed and gusts at an airport can hamper cargo operations. For example there are mean wind speed and gust limits above which aircraft cargo doors may not be opened, or remain open, if already open. A strong wind is also a source of concern for loading and unloading baggage from aircraft with the risk of baggage trolleys being blown over, or blown out of control on the apron, or flying debris causing human injury and damage to vehicles and equipment. Airside management needs to be warned of these conditions as they are usually required to "promptly relay" it to airlines and operators [8].

Mention of cargo operation and baggage trolleys brings to mind that in the desert climate at Abu Dhabi and Al Ain, in the United Arab Emirates, when necessary, a 24 hour advance rainfall warning is issued in the morning to apron control so that cargo and airfield equipment that are usually not under cover can be protected. Warnings are also issued for dust and sand storms and dust haze when the visibility deteriorates below 1000 metres.

A thunderstorm overhead an airport, or in the immediate vicinity of an airport is a particular danger to airport ground operations. When lightning is within 5 km all outdoor operations, such as aircraft refuelling, loading and unloading and passenger movement to and from aircraft should cease [18].

## 4. Airport Environment

It is important to know the local environment and weather peculiarities around individual airports. For example, Aberdeen Dyce airport in north-eastern Scotland is about 15 km inland from the North Sea with higher ground to the north-west and west. It is very well sheltered from the west where the Highlands and Grampian mountains rise to over 4000ft. It is very exposed to any wind direction veering from the north around to the south, and especially from an easterly direction. Moderate to severe turbulence and wind shear may be experienced on the approaches to all runways when the 1000 ft wind exceeds 15 kn from 200 degrees through to 320 degrees off the hills inland [4]. Heavy snow can occur with northerly to north-easterly Arctic maritime winds off the North Sea, and also cloud down to the ground in a moist south-easterly flow from the sea. Temperatures can plummet overnight with winds from the west, but are heavily modified by the sea temperatures when the wind is from an easterly direction. During early summer when the North Sea is at its coldest, Doncaster - Robin Hood airport inland from the east coast of England is subject to low Stratus cloud and fog, known as Haar. It is also prone to snow falls brought by Polar continental north-easterly to south-easterly winds. Annual incidence of snow falling is 15-20 days [25].

Cardiff airport, which is close to the sea, has a sharp drop in terrain to the sea at its southern end so that mechanical (terrain induced) turbulence will be experienced on short finals when landing on runway 30 in strong westerly to south-westerly winds. Mechanical turbulence is also likely at the threshold of runway 12 during strong north-westerly to north-easterly winds due to the hanger north-east of the runway 12 threshold [7]. Furthermore, sea fog can lap up against the edge of the southern end of the runway if it is deeper than 200 ft.

It is also useful to know the preferred runway that will be in use under differing conditions and operational limitations. For example runway 22 is the preferred landing runway and 04 is the preferred departure runway at Belfast City Airport. Wind shear on these runway directions is also a well known occurrence when the surface wind direction is between 100° and 160° and >15 kn [5]. Birmingham airport is also known for wind across its 15/33 runway, particularly from a south-westerly crosswind with a difficult approach to runway 15 when the centre of a deep low pressure cell passes to the north, or a marked trough approaches from the west. Due to Edinburgh's position alongside the Firth of Forth in a lowland valley extending to the west to Glasgow with the Scottish Highlands to the north and high ground to the south, is subject to a wind funnel effect that results in predominantly west-south-westerly and east-north-easterly winds that accelerate through the valley. A similar characteristic is evident at Geneva in the narrow north-east to south-west gap between the Alps to the south and the Jura Mountains to the north.

The forecaster also needs to be aware of operational hours and peak operating periods and be more alert to severe weather during these times. At London Heathrow peak landing traffic is between 0600Z to 1200Z with a peak departure time in the evening. Noise restrictions also limit the hours of operation [6]. Landings and departures are not permitted 2300Z to 0400Z at Geneva with runway restrictions until 0500Z [24]. Due to its position almost in the heart of London, the London City Airport is severely restricted with respect to hours of operation, noise control and types and number of aircraft permitted to fly in and out. The operational hours are restricted to 0630Z to 2200Z on weekdays, 0630Z to 1230Z on Saturday, 1230Z to 2200Z on Sunday and 0900Z to 2200Z on public holidays [2].

# 5. Modern Solutions

Weather forecasts in the form of TAFs at departure and arrival airports and en-route forecasts are still issued, but these days the en-route weather is in the form of numerical weather prediction model charts of wind and temperatures at specific levels, either in map or tabular form, as well as forecaster edited significant weather charts. Complete flight planning packages are available via the Internet to pilots and airline dispatchers where all the information necessary to file a flight plan can be obtained. Data transfer via facsimile machine is also available, but this form of communication is rapidly becoming outdated. Forecasts can be tailored to individual client requirements and contain hour by hour weather parameters such as visibility, cloud base, wind velocity and gusts, air and ground runway surface temperatures, pressure and weather type (such as snow, ice, fog and thunderstorms). The parameters can be colour coded according to configurable critical thresholds, as well as the provision of warning alerts. Specialised 24 hour forecast scripts and longer time period planning forecasts as well as weather graphics, such as satellite and high resolution radar imagery and forecast graphics are also available [28].

Commercial aircraft, such as the A340-500, already have flight endurance of 19 hours, while the A380 typically carries 525 passengers and up to 555. This implies that en-route and destination aviation forecasts, obtained at the departure airport, can become obsolete and inaccurate before the aircraft arrives at its destination. Therefore, for safety and economy of operation, aviation weather forecasts will need to be more accurate over longer forecast periods. Equally as important they have to be accessible to pilots in flight. Hence the development of in-flight systems that can provide information such as the latest destination and diversion airport METARs and TAFs, significant weather reports (SIGMETs) and pilot reports (PIREPs)[28]. At present this is in its infancy and mainly limited to North America and the Caribbean.

A future potentially controversial trend will be the production of TAFs by accredited private companies, or organisations, other than the National Meteorological and Hydrological Service (NMHS) of a country [14]. This is already possible in the United States of America where private companies produce TAFs for airline use that are written under the approved airline's Enhanced Weather Information System (EWINS) [16]. However, a requirement has arisen for these to be issued for airline use in some other parts of the world due to the non-availability of a state NMHS TAF, or due to unreliable communication. Without a TAF airline operators are forced to carry extra fuel, thereby increasing operating costs.

## 6. Conclusion

While forecast formats such as TAFs will still be used by ATC and ground operators and airlines at airports they do not provide enough detailed information for timely, safe and cost effective decision making. This has made it necessary for the aviation meteorologist to be increasingly knowledgeable about the airport weather environment, not only locally, but globally as well, and be more intimately involved in operational requirements in order to provide a better service. This, in turn, has given rise to private companies that can provide value added forecasts tailored to the clients specific and changing needs. These can take the form of detailed airport hour-by-hour forecasts to ATC, airport operators and airline dispatchers that are easily and quickly accessible via the Internet and other modern communication methods. These services are also increasingly being provided by private companies. The author expects that in future this demand will increase, particularly as airports near their peak capacity and there is better appreciation of weather forecasts as a management tool. The proliferation of bigger and longer range commercial aircraft will also increase the requirement for the provision of timelier destination airport forecasts via ground to in-flight communication systems.

## References

[1]    Beaty, D. *The Naked Pilot.* Airlife Publishing: Ramsbury, England, 1995, pp 33, 101-105, 243.
[2]    Civil Aviation Authority (United Kingdom). *AIP AD 2-EGLC-1* (13 Mar 08). 2008, pp 1, 5-7.
[3]    Civil Aviation Authority (United Kingdom). *Aerodrome/Heliport availability.* AD 1.1 (14 Feb 08), AD 1.1.2. 2008, pp 7.
[4]    Civil Aviation Authority (United Kingdom). *AIP AD 2-EGPD-1* (17 Jan 08). 2008, pp 9.
[5]    Civil Aviation Authority (United Kingdom). *AIP AD 2-EGAC-1* (13 Mar 08). 2008, pp7.
[6]    Civil Aviation Authority (United Kingdom). *AIP AD 2-EGLL-1* (12 Apr 07). 2007, pp12, 14-17.
[7]    Civil Aviation Authority (United Kingdom). *AIP AD 2-EGFF-1* (5 Jul 07). 2007, pp 8.

[8]   Civil Aviation Authority (United Kingdom). *Airside Safety Management.* CAP 642, 5 September 2006. 2005, chapter 2, section 15.3, pp 37-39.

[9]   Civil Aviation Authority (United Kingdom). *Risks and factors associated with operations on runways affected by snow, slush or water.* AIC 86/2007, 13 September, pp 3.

[10]  Civil Aviation Authority (United Kingdom). *Recommendations for de-icing/anti-icing of aircraft on the ground.* AIC 1/2005 6 January. 2005.

[11]  Civil Aviation Authority (United Kingdom). The effect of thunderstorms and associated turbulence on aircraft operations. AIC 81/2004, 19 August, pp 1-3.

[12]  Civil Aviation Authority (United Kingdom). *Manual of Flight Information Services. Part B. Aerodrome.* CAP 410, 7 March 2002. 2002, chapter 12, pp1.

[13]  Civil Aviation Authority (United Kingdom). Low Altitude Wind Shear. AIC 19/2002, 4 April, pp 1 & 5.

[14]  Civil Aviation Regulation Advisory Council (CARAC, Canada). *Air navigation Services (Part VIII).* Chapter 2, paragraph 2.2, 1998. [http://www.tc.gc.ca/civilaviation/ RegServ/Affairs/carac/NPAs/ANS/Archives/sep98/Chapter1.htm].

[15]  Civil Aviation Safety Authority (CASA) Australia. *Ground De-icing and Anti-icing Programme.* Air operator Certification Manual. Version 5.3, December 2007, chapter 6.22, pp 6-22-1.

[16]  Federal Aviation Administration (U.S.A.). *Principle Operations Inspector Handbook.* HBAT 8400.10 CHG 42. Vol 3, chapter 7, section 5, 2006, pp 3-687-3-691.

[17]  Federal Aviation Administration (FAA U.S.A.). *Pilot Guide. Flight in icing conditions.* AC 91-74, date 12/12/02. 2002, pp 51-53.

[18]  Federal Committee for Meteorological Services and Supporting Research. *Weather information for Surface Transportation.* FCM-R26-2006. . Office of the Federal Coordinator for Meteorological Services and Supporting Research: Silver Spring, MA, 2006, August, pp 4 and Appendix B-6 pp 2.

[19]  International Civil Aviation Organization. *Uplink and downlink of weather information – recent development in Hong Kong, China.* CNS/MET SG/11-IP/12 Agenda Item 12(4). Bangkok, Thailand, 16-20 July 2007. ICAO: Montreal, 2007.

[20]  International Civil Aviation Organization. *Standards and Recommended Practices. Aeronautical Telecommunications.* Annex 10, volume II (up to 24 November 2005). ICAO: Montreal 2005.

[21]  International Civil Aviation Organization. *International Standards and Recommended Practices. Meteorological Service for International Air Navigation.* Annex 3. ICAO: Montreal, 2004, chapter 6 pp 6-1 to 6-2, chapter 7, pp 7-1 to 7-2, appendix 5, pp 5-1 to 5-6, appendix 6, pp 6-1 to 6-4.

[22]  Kermode, A. C. *Mechanics of flight.* Eighth edition. Pitman Publishing: London, 1976, pp 234.

[23]  National Transportation Safety Board (USA). *Aircraft Accident Report.* NTSB-AAR-82-8, 9 September 1982.

[24]  Skyguide (Swiss Air Navigation Services Ltd, Switzerland). *AIP LSGG AD 2* (20 Dec 2007). 2007, pp13-17 and 21-23.

[25]  United Kingdom Meteorological Office. *Source Book to the Forecasters' Reference Book.* Met.O.1024. Meteorological Office College, 1997, chapter 5, pp 5-6 to 5-12 and 5-28-5-29, chapter 6 pp 6-5 and 6-6.

[26] United Kingdom Meteorological Office. *Handbook of Aviation Meteorology.* Third edition HMSO: London, 1994, pp 39, 44.

[27] Utela, P.; Metso, M (2006). Future trends in aeronautical Meteorology. Changes in ICAO regulations 2007. [http://www.vaisala.com/newsandmedia/vaisalanews/vaisalanews171/articles/future%20trends%20in%20aeronautical%20meteorology.pdf], Vaisala News, No 171/2006. Vaisala: Helsinki, pp 6-7. Accessed 2008-03-31.

[28] Weather Services International. WSI InFlight. The *weather you trust where you need it most* [http://www.wsi.com/aviation/products/inflight/] 2007. Accessed 2008-03-26.

[29] World Meteorological Organization. Manual on the Global Telecommunication System. Technical Regulations. WMO No 386, Volume 1 (annex III). WMO: Geneva, July 2007, pp A-I-1.

[30] World Meteorological Organization. *Manual on Codes. International Codes.* Technical Regulations. WMO No 306. Volume I.I, Part A – Alphanumeric Codes. WMO: Geneva, 1995, FM 51-XII, FM 53-X, FM 54-X, pp109-120.

In: Airports: Performance, Risks, and Problems  
Editors: P.B. Larauge et al, pp. 189-197

ISBN: 978-1-60692-393-1  
© 2009 Nova Science Publishers, Inc.

# CHALLENGES OF AIRPORTS IN MULTI-AIRPORT REGIONS (MARS)

## Becky P.Y. Loo

Department of Geography, The University of Hong Kong

## Abstract

In traditional single-airport regions, air traffic forecasting is often a simple case of nearest-centre assignment based on national forecasts and local market shares. However, the emergence of multi-airport regions (MARs) has challenged the "golden rule" that air passengers would naturally choose the nearest airports. Within MARs, air passengers may bypass the nearest airports but travel longer distances for cheaper air fares, more frequent flights, more convenient departure/arrival time or services of particular airlines. In this Chapter, the characteristics of MARs are first discussed. Then, the implications of MARs on the airports' relationships with air passengers, airlines and other airports operating within the same MARs are analyzed. This Chapter concludes by highlighting the need for more research on air passengers' travel behaviour, the benefits of fostering closer relationships between airlines and airports, and the opportunities for strengthening coordination among airports.

## Introduction

Multi-airport regions (MARs) are sometimes called "multi-airport systems" (de Neufville, 1995; Reynolds & Feighan, 1998) or "multiple-airport regions" (Ashford & Bencheman, 1987; Brooke, Caves, & Pitfield, 1994). In the mid-1990s, de Neufville (1995) identified 26 MARs in different parts of the world. As the international air traffic grew, MARs continued to become more significant not only in the developed but also developing economies. The better studied MARs include the San Francis Bay Area MAR (Harvey, 1987; Pels, Nijkamp and Rietveld, 2001, 2003) and the Baltimore-Washington MAR (Skinner, 1976) in North America, the Greater London MAR (Hess and Polak, 2006) in Europe and the Hong Kong-Pearl River Delta (HK-PRD) MAR in Asia (Loo, 2008; Loo, Wong and Ho, 2005).

Geographically, the significance of MARs in air transport lies in their three major distinct characteristics. First of all, MARs often occupies large territorial extent. Notably, an MAR needs not be confined to any single administrative jurisdiction, whether a city, a state/province or even a country. For instance, the Boston MAR spans three states including Boston Logan International Airport (BOS) and Worcester Regional Airport (ORH) in Massachusetts, Providence T.F. Green Airport (PVD) in Rhone Island and Manchester-Boston Regional Airport (MHT) in New Hampshire (de Neufville, 1995). Moreover, the cross-country Amsterdam-Eindhoven-Brussels MAR was formed in Europe even before the full liberalization of air transport among members of the European Union in 1997 (Bradley, 1998; Graham and Goetz, 2008). Conceptually, MARs are characterized by a unified air travel market whereby air passengers in the region consider a set of airports in their travel decisions. These alternative airports are typically separated by 15 km or above. However, the San Francisco Bay Area MAR, New York-Newark MAR and HK-PRD MAR are having alternative airports separated by over 100 km (Loo, Ho and Wong, 2005).

Apart from their territorial size, MARs are significant because they are major air traffic generating regions with at least 10 million originating air passengers. Thus, any economic or geographical analysis of the global air transport market would almost inevitably include MARs. Table 1 shows the top 15 world airports in 2007 in terms of passenger turnover. Due to the different geographical factors shaping air freight and their distribution, this paper is devoted mainly to the analysis of air passengers. Rows with airports being identified as operating within MARs are shaded in grey. These identified airports were all leading airports in their respective MARs. The total air passenger turnover of these airports reached over 487.4 millions in 2007, representing more than 55.2% of all the top 15 world airports.

**Table 1. Top 15 World Airports by Air Passenger Turnover (2007)**

| Rank | City | Country | Name of Airport | Total Air Passenger Turnover (millions) |
|------|------|---------|-----------------|-----------------------------------------|
| 1 | Atlanta | USA | Hartsfield-Jackson Atlanta International Airport (ATL) | 89.4 |
| 2 | Chicago | USA | O'Hare International Airport (ORD) | 76.2 |
| 3 | London | Great Britain | London Heathrow Airport (LHR) | 68.1 |
| 4 | Tokyo | Japan | Haneda Airport (HND), formally Tokyo International Airport | 66.7 |
| 5 | Los Angeles | USA | Los Angeles Airport (LAX) | 61.9 |
| 6 | Paris | France | Paris Charles de Gaulle Airport (CDG) | 59.9 |
| 7 | Dallas/FT Worth | USA | Dallas Fort Worth International Airport (DFW) | 59.8 |
| 8 | Frankfurt | Germany | Frankfurt am Main International Airport (FRA) | 54.2 |

**Table 1. Continued.**

| Rank | City | Country | Name of Airport | Total Air Passenger Turnover (millions) |
|------|------|---------|-----------------|-----------------------------------------|
| 9 | Beijing | China | Beijing Capital International Airport (PEK) | 53.7 |
| 10 | Madrid | Spain | Madrid Barajas International Airport (MAD) | 52.1 |
| 11 | Denver | USA | Denver International Airport (DEN) | 50.0 |
| 12 | New York | USA | John F Kennedy International Airport (JFK) | 47.8 |
| 13 | Amsterdam | Netherlands | Amsterdam Schiphol Airport (AMS) | 47.8 |
| 14 | Las Vegas | USA | Las Vegas McCarran International Airport (LAS) | 47.6 |
| 15 | Hong Kong | China | Hong Kong International Airport (HKG) | 47.0 |

**Source**: ACI (2007).

Last but not least, there is a strong functional integration among jurisdictions operating within the same MARs. Hence, they are often associated with the geographic concept of extended metropolitan regions (Loo, 1999). In other words, an MAR is not simply identified by the existence of more than one airport in the vicinity (e.g. within 3-hour travel time) of a primary airport. The formation of MARs is often associated with close intra-regional cooperation and strong flows of people, goods and information within the region. Moreover, a *de facto* division of labour among the airports can be detected in many MARs, with the secondary airports capturing niche markets which do not directly overlap with the primary airports. Though there is no hard and fast rule, secondary airports within MARs are typically operating at a scale about one-third of the primary airports (de Neufville, 1995).

Thus, it is not surprising to find that MARs represent a key focus in air transport research (Vowels, 2001; Windle and Dresner, 2002). The emergence of MARs has fundamentally affected the geography of air passenger flows (Loo, Ho and Wong, 2005). In particular, MARs are affecting the air passengers' choice, airline strategies, and airport cooperation and competition. These aspects will be discussed in the following sections.

## Relationship with Air Passengers

When airports are viewed as service points (rather than just intermediate stops), air passenger turnovers are best conceptualised as the results of aggregate personal decisions to use airport facilities. Within MARs, air passengers do not necessarily choose the nearest airports but may travel longer distances for cheaper air fares, more frequent flights, more convenient boarding/arrival time or services of particular airlines. Airport choice is affected by facility attributes including a set of primary level-of-service (LOS) factors, which relate to the price and frequency of flights, and a set of secondary LOS factors about the quality of airports and airlines. In particular, secondary LOS factors tend to dominate within MARs where differences in primary LOS factors and distances between airports are not great (Bradley, 1998; Rubin and Fagan, 1976). Within MARs, services offered at different airports are not homogenous but differentiated.

In the pioneer study of Skinner (1976) on airport choice in the Baltimore-Washington MAR, ground accessibility was found to be as important as the air carriers' LOS, such as frequency of flights. Similarly, Harvey (1987)'s study in the San Francisco Bay Area MAR found that ground access time and the frequency of direct flights were the most important in affecting air passengers' choice of departure airports in 1980. In Europe, Ndoh, Pitfield and Caves (1990) used revealed preference data to examine air passengers' choice of departure airports among the Central England airports, that is, East Midlands (EMA), Birmingham (BHX), Manchester (MAN), and Liverpool (LPL) Airports. The results showed that airport access time was the most significant LOS attribute. Nonetheless, the study of Thompson and Caves (1993) suggested that flight frequency was the most important in the airport choice among the air passengers in Northern England.

More recently, Bradley (1998) found that the air passengers' choice among competitive departure airports in Europe was affected by at least twelve LOS factors. They are air fare, access modes, travel time to the airport, timing of flights, airport congestion, extra journey time for transfer, airlines services, parking facilities, check-in facilities, ancillary airport facilities (like shops), transfer facilities, and baggage (and immigration and customs) facilities. Among these twelve LOS variables, air ticket price was found to be the primary consideration. His findings were based on a stated preference survey reflecting air passengers' choice among alternative airports with different attributes. Using a hypothetical example and later the San Francisco Bay Area MAR case study, Pels, Nijkamp and Rietveld (2000, 2001, 2003) used the nested multinomial logit model to show that ground accessibility (especially time, as opposed to cost) was the most important factor in affecting airport choice within MARs. In the Asia-Pacific region, Loo (2008) used stated preference data to analyze airport choice within the HK-PRD MAR. Her findings also indicated that airport access time, flight frequency and air fare were the most important LOS attributes affecting passengers' airport choice. In addition, research studies also show that there is significant heterogeneity in preferences among different market segments, notably air passengers making business and non-business trips (Windle and Dresner, 1995; Hess and Polak, 2006; Loo, 2008). In other words, there is a better understanding of the relative importance of different airport LOS factors. Nonetheless, the exact trade-offs varied greatly for air passengers in different MARs and the use of these findings on air traffic forecasting and airport planning is still rare (Loo, Ho and Wong, 2005).

## Relationship with Airlines

While the distribution of traffic among airports may be the concerns of policy-makers and transport researchers, airport operators consider airlines as their primary customers. Airlines entered into legally binding contracts with airports to use airport capacity and airport operators receive aeronautical revenues from airlines. In Europe, aeronautical revenues typically accounted for about 56% of airport income (Graham, 2001). In smaller airports, aeronautical revenues would have accounted for a higher share (around 75%) of the total airport revenues (Francis, Humphrey and Ison, 2004). Table 1 lists the major sources of airport revenues worldwide.

**Table 2. Major Sources of Revenues for Airports**

| Type of Airport Revenues | Detailed Breakdowns |
|---|---|
| Aeronautical revenues | Aircraft landing, departure and parking fees |
| | Passenger charges (on a per passenger basis) |
| | Freight charges (on a per tonne of freight handled basis) |
| | Security charges |
| | Apron services and aircraft handling |
| Non-aeronautical revenues | Royalties |
| | Concessions/rentals |
| | Advertising |
| | Car park |
| | Others (including consultancy, property development, etc.) |

Under airline regulation, all details of the air routes, including fares, frequency, capacity, number of carriers and routes, were strictly regulated bilaterally. Airfares were negotiated through the Traffic Conferences of the International Air Transport Association (IATA) to ensure that there is no cut-throat competition. Under this system, the relationship between the airports and the airlines is almost predetermined and is stable. Basically, all airlines offering air service between two cities must use the "designated" airports of the cities and pay the aeronautical revenues to them.

Since the deregulation of the United States' domestic airline market, new airlines began to emerge. In particular, price competition among airlines was allowed. Full-service (legacy) carriers began to face fierce competition from low-cost carriers (LCCs), and the air travel market became more volatile. Airline bankruptcy and the emergence of new airlines, particularly LCCs, make the airport-airline relationship more complicated. With increasing liberalization of the air travel market, airports are under increasing pressure to raise non-aeronautical revenues. Furthermore, the greater ease to offer new air routes and cancel existing air routes gives airlines much higher bargaining power in negotiating with airport operators about the aeronautical revenues. In particular, the hub-and-spoke structure means that air traffic is typically very concentrated. Airports would stand to lose much should the airlines opt to shift their hubbing operations elsewhere. According to Graham and Goetz (2008), most hub airports were dominated by single carriers which controlled more than 70% of the airport traffic.

While the above challenges brought about by airline deregulation are applicable to all airports, airports operating within MARs are particularly affected. While primary airports within MARs may be facing congestion, secondary and other airports within MARs are typically facing spare capacity. Given that airports are large-scale infrastructure, the marginal cost of accommodating extra traffic at these secondary airports is low. Table 3 shows the average unit costs for airports at different scales measured in work load unit (WLU), which is a passenger or 100 kilogram of freight.

**Table 3. Average Unit Costs of Airports at Different Capacities**

| WLU | Average unit costs per WLU (US dollars) |
|---|---|
| <300,000 | $15 |
| 300,000-2.5 millions | $9.4 |
| 2.5-25 millions | $8 |

Source: Graham (2001).

Typically, a critical mass of 1 million WLU is required to make airport operation financially viable and efficient. Many non-aeronautical revenues also critically depend on passenger turnovers. Attractive and diversified retail and catering activities, for instance, are only viable in airports with large passenger turnovers. Hence, smaller airports tend to depend heavily on aeronautical revenues. For airports with less than 300,000 WLUs, it is not surprising that more than 75% of the airport revenue would come from aeronautical revenues (Graham, 2001). Against this background, many LCCs managed to negotiate contracts which significantly reduce aeronautical charges at secondary airports within MARs (Francis, Humphrey and Ison, 2004). Also, LCCs sometimes require dedicated LCC terminals closest to the terminal, no air-bridge charge, and no sophisticated baggage transfer services, to ensure fast turnaround time and efficient use of apron. In some situations, these conscientious efforts to attract LCCs have enabled smaller peripheral airports to cut into the catchment areas of large hub airports (Gillen and Lall, 2004; Mason, 2000). Nonetheless, the high volatility of the airline market, with bankruptcy and merger, is also posing risks on airports entering into long-term contractual relationships with airlines, particularly LCCs, that required investment on airport facilities.

## Relationship among Airports

In a sense, airports operating within MARs share with each other the air passengers in the same extended metropolitan region. Nonetheless, there is also a trend that airports within MARs are increasingly differentiated not only by size but also function. In particular, many secondary airports are serving niche market within the lucrative air transport market of the MARs. Apart from specializing in serving LCCs, a division of labour for international and domestic flights (like the case in the Greater Tokyo MAR) would differentiate airport functions. Within MARs, airports compete with each other for air passengers. At a boarder spatial scale, they compete as a group with airports in nearby regions.

Thus, there is much room for airport coordination within MARs. The advantages are particularly obvious in two situations. First, airport coordination is desirable when airport (or even runway) expansion is difficult at the primary airport but congestion is already very serious. A notable example is the London Heathrow Airport (LHR) in the Greater London MAR. The increasing air traffic not only puts further stress on airport facilities like gates, air bridges and terminal capacities but also their associated air-traffic control systems and the ground transport network. However, considerations of noise and air pollution have made further expansion difficult and controversial. Second, airport coordination is desirable when there is huge excess capacity at the secondary airports. Examples include the Shenzhen (SZX) and Macau (MFM) International Airport in the HK-PRD MAR, Stansted (STN) in the Greater London MAR, Newark (EWR) in the New York MAR, Mirabel (YMX) in the Montreal MAR and Dulles (IAD) in the Baltimore-Washington MAR (de Neufville, 1995; Loo, Wong and Ho, 2003; Loo, Ho and Wong, 2005). These secondary airports are operating below the critical mass. Hence, the marginal cost of utilizing the excess capacity at these secondary airports is very low. They are criticized to be white elephants which fail to generate the expected economic benefits to the local economies.

In practice, airport coordination may be fostered under the same ownership, through airport alliance, or directed by the government or a regulatory authority. In the Tokyo, Baltimore-Washington, Osaka and Montreal MARs, the governments actually mandated international flights to use the more distant airports. In addition, the French government directed Air France, the national carrier, to use Charles de Gaulle (CDG) in the Paris MAR (de Neufville, 1995). Furthermore, technical restrictions have prevented flights from using the most accessible primary airports in the Baltimore-Washington, Taipei, Houston-Galveston and Buenos Aires MARs (de Neufville, 1995). In Australia, the coordination between the primary airport of Kingsford Smith (SYD) and Sydney West (SWZ) has been very successful. Nonetheless, the form and scope of airport coordination needs to be carefully considered by taking into account the special geographical characteristics of the MARs under consideration.

# Conclusion

All in all, the emergence and growing importance of MARs have posed significant challenges to air transport researchers. In particular, the airport-air passenger relationship, airport-airline relationship and airport-airport relationship have been changed. There is a need to further strengthen research on airport choice among air passengers. These studies would inform airport operators not only about their relationships with air passengers (this would directly affect airport revenues through the generation of non-aeronautical revenues) but also their potential bargaining power with airlines. Within MARs, there is much more uncertainty about the airline-airport relationships. In relation, there is room for better airport coordination (orchestrated by an outside authority, like a government or a regulatory authority) and/or cooperation (fostered by voluntary or commercial interests, like the formation of alliance) within MARs.

# References

Airports Council International (ACI) (2008) Passenger traffic 2007 preliminary (last update: March 12, 2008). Available at http://www.aci.aero/cda/aci_common/ display/main/ aci_content07_c.jsp?zn=aci&cp=1-5-54-55_666_2__ (last accessed on June 17, 2008).

Ashford, N., & Bencheman, M. (1987). Passengers' choice of airport: an application of the multinomial logit model. In Transportation Research Board, National Research Council (Ed.), *Air transportation issues* (pp. 1-5). Washington, DC: Transportation Research Board.

Bradley, M.A. (1998). Behavioural models or airport choice and air route choice. In J. de D. Ortuzar, D. Hensher, and S. Jara-Diaz (Eds.), *Travel behaviour research: updating the state of play* (pp. 141-159). Amsterdam: Elsevier.

Brooke, A.S., Caves R.E., & Pitfield, D.E. (1994). Methodology for predicting European short-haul air transport demand from regional airports. *Journal of Air Transport Management*, **1**(1), 37-46.

de Neufville, R. (1995). Management of multi-airport systems. *Journal of Air Transport Management*, **2**(2), 99-110.

Francis, G., Humphreys, I., & Ison, S. (2004). Airports' perspectives on the growth of low-cost airlines and the remodeling of the airport-airline relationship. *Tourism Management*, **25**, 507-514.

Gillen, D. & Lall, A. (2004). Competitive advantage of low-cost carriers: some implications for airports. *Journal of Air Transport Management*, **10**, 41-50.

Graham, A. (2001) *Managing airports: an international perspective*. Oxford: Butterworth Heinemann.

Graham, B., & Goetz, A.R. (2008) Global air transport. In R. Knowles, J. Shaw & I. Docherty (Eds.), *Transport Geographies: Mobilities, Flows and Spaces* (pp. 137-155). Malden: Blackwell.

Harvey, G. (1987). Airport choice in a multiple airport region. *Transportation Research A* **21** (6), 439-449.

Hess, S., & Polak, J.W. (2006). Exploring the potential for cross-nesting structures in airport-choice analysis: a case study of the Greater London area. *Transportation Research Part E*, **42**, 63-81.

Loo, B.P.Y. (1999). Formation of a regional transport network: some lessons from the Zhujiang Delta. *Journal of Transport Geography*, **7**, 43-63.

Loo, B.P.Y. (2008) Passengers' airport choice within multi-airport regions (MARs): Some insights from a stated preference survey at Hong Kong International Airport. *Journal of Transport Geography*, **16**, 117-125.

Loo, B.P.Y., Ho, H.W., & Wong, S.C. (2005) An application of the continuous equilibrium modelling approach in understanding the geography of air passenger flows in a multi-airport region. *Applied Geography*, **25**, 169-199.

Loo, B.P.Y., Wong, S.C., & Ho, H.W. (2003) Competition among airports in the Hong Kong-Zhujiang Delta region. In G. Chen, Y. Zhou, A.G.O. Yeh and V.F.S. Sit (Eds), *Enhancing the Competitiveness of the Greater Zhujiang Delta* (pp. 293-323). Guangzhou: Zhongshan University Press.

Mason, K.J. (2000). The propensity of business travellers to use low cost airlines. *Journal of Transport Geography*, **8**, 107-119.

Ndoh, N.N., Pitfield, D.E. & Caves, R.E. (1990). Air transportation passenger route choice: a nested multinomial logit analysis. In M.M. Fischer, P. Nijkamp & Y.Y. Papageorgiou (Eds.), *Spatial choices and process* (pp. 349-365). Amsterdam: North-Holland.

Pels, E., Nijkamp, P., & Rietveld, P. (2000). Airport and airline competition for passengers departing from a large metropolitan area. *Journal of Urban Economics*, **48**, 29-45.

Pels, E., Nijkamp, P., & Rietveld, P. (2001). Airport and airline choice in a multiple airport region: an empirical analysis for the San Francisco Bay area. *Regional Studies*, **35** (1), 1-9.

Pels, E., Nijkamp, P., & Rietveld, P. (2003). Access to a competition between airports: a case study for the San Francisco Bay Area. *Transportation Research A*, **37**(1), 71-83.

Reynolds-Feighan, A.J. (1998). The impact of U.S. airline deregulation on airport traffic patterns. *Geographical Analysis*, **30**(3), 234-253.

Rubin, D. & Fagan, L.N. (1976). Forecasting air passengers in a multiairport region. In Transportation Research Board, National Research Council (Ed.), *Airport and air transport planning* (pp. 1-5). Washington, DC: Transportation Research Board.

Skinner, R.E. (1976). Airport choice: an empirical study. *Journal of Transportation Engineering* **102** (4), 871-882.

Thompson, A., & Caves, R. (1993). The projected market share for a new small airport in the North of England. *Regional Studies*, **27** (2), 137-47.

Vowles, T.M. (2001). The "Southwest Effect" in multi-airport regions. *Journal of Air Transport Management*, **7**, 251-258.

Windle, R., & Dresner, M. (2002). Airport choice in multiple-airport regions. *Journal of Transportation Engineering*, **121**(4), 332-337.

In: Airports: Performance, Risks, and Problems
Editors: P.B. Larauge et al, pp. 199-205

ISBN 978-1-60692-393-1
© 2009 Nova Science Publishers, Inc.

# COMPLEX NETWORK VIEW OF PERFORMANCE AND RISKS ON AIRPORT NETWORKS

*Ganesh Bagler*
National Centre for Biological Sciences,
Tata Institute of Fundamental Research,
Bangalore, India 560065

### Abstract

Air transportation has been becoming a major part of transportation infrastructure worldwide. Hence the study of the Airports Networks, the backbone of air transportation, is becoming increasingly important. In complex systems domain, airport networks are modeled as graphs (networks) comprising of airports (vertices or nodes) that are linked by flight connectivities among the airports. A complex network analysis of such a model offers holistic insight about the performance and risks in such a network. We review the performance and risks of networks with the help of studies that have been done on some of the airport networks. We present various network parameters those could be potentially used as a measure of performance and risks on airport networks. We will also see how various risks, such as break down of airports, spread of diseases across the airport network could be assessed based on the network parameters. Further we review how these insights could possibly be used to shape more efficient and safer airport networks.

## 1. Introduction

Air transportation has become an important component of transportation across the world for long-distance as well as short-distance travel. Air transportation has enormous impact on the national and international economies. Airport networks form the crucial backbone of the air transportation infrastructure. Hence study of airport networks for their performance and the risks posing them, is quite imperative. Airport networks could be classified as complex systems by virtue of their topological as well as their dynamical complexity. Lately there has been growing interest in studying a variety of systems from complex systems viewpoint [1,2]. Airports networks too are one of the interesting complex systems which are studied at various scales for various reasons [3–11]. According to network dogma, airport network is represented as a graph comprised of 'n' nodes (vertices; airports) and 'e' links (edges; air-connectivities). Thus represented, airport network looks like a graph (network) whose properties could be computed using graph theoretical formalism. Airport network could further be represented as weighted network by considering the (say) number of flights plying on a route as the 'weight' of that particular link. Various network parameters give an idea of the performance of the network as well as risks involved in the functioning of the network. In this paper, we will discuss various parameters that could be used as a measure of performance and risks on airport networks and discuss how possibly we could construct future airport networks.

## 2.  Performance of Airport Network

Airport network is a complex entity by virtue of its topology and traffic dynamics over it. It is a task to define what one means by the performance of the airport network. One way to define performance would be to consider efficient functioning of the network as a whole, while the other could be to consider the ease with which the passengers can travel across the network. Many of the network parameters express efficiency and performance of the network. Following is a list of parameters and features that could serve as a measure of performance of airport network.

**Characteristic Path Length ($L$)**

Characteristic path length ($L$) is defined as,

$$L = \frac{1}{N(N-1)} \sum_{\substack{i,j=1 \\ i \neq j}}^{N} L_{ij}, \tag{1}$$

where, $N$ is total number of nodes in the network, and $L_{ij}$ is the shortest path length between nodes $i$ and $j$. Clearly characteristic path length is an average of the shortest path lengths between all possible pairs of nodes. The smaller the $L$, the more compact and reachable the network is. Thus $L$ could be used as an indicator of the performance of the airport network, the performance of the network being inversely proportional to the $L$.

Among the Airport Network of India (ANI) ($L = 2.2593$), Airport Network of China (ANC) ($L = 2.067$), World-wide Airport Network (WAN) ($L = 4.37$), and Italian Airport Network (IAN) ($L = 1.98$) the IAN turns out to be most efficient. But it should also be kept in mind that WAN is a much larger network with 3880 airports whereas IAN has only 42 airports in it.

**Clustering Coefficient ($C$)**

Clustering coefficient ($C$) is defined as,

$$C = \frac{1}{N} \sum_{i=1}^{N} C_i, \tag{2}$$

where $N$ is total number of nodes in the network, and $C_i$ is clustering coefficient of node $i$. The clustering coefficient of a node is defined as the ratio of number of links amongst its neighboring nodes to the maximum number of links they could have had. It essentially enumerates the probability that two nodes are connected to each other given that they are already (independently) both connected to a common node.

Clustering coefficient could be used as a measure of performance of airport network. It will represent, on an average, what is the fraction of closed triangles in the airport network. The higher the clustering coefficient the better accessible is the network and hence better is its performance. In an ideal condition the clustering coefficient would be 1 and hence every airport would be connected to every other airport by a direct air-link. Note that the clustering coefficient in a random network (random connectivities) of the same size and average degree would be significantly smaller, than found in the real-world networks [4, 5].

By this criterion, among ANI ($C = 0.6574$), ANC ($C = 0.733$), and IAN ($C = 0.10$), the ANC turns out to be the best in terms of reachability as defined by clustering coefficient. Interestingly, IAN has clustering that is comparable to a random model.

**Small-World Nature**

High Clustering Coefficient ($C$) along with small Characteristic Path Length ($L$) are two indicators of the small-world nature of the network. But, incidentally all airport networks studied so far have been observed to be small-world networks [3–6], indicating that this network feature is not good enough to adjudge the performance of the network. Perhaps $C$ and $L$ independently are better measures of performance of the network as discussed above.

**Closeness ($L_i$)**

Closeness ($L_i$) is defined as the average of $(N - 1)$ shortest paths between node '$i$' and the rest of the nodes. While 'Characteristic path length' gives a gross average of shortest paths over the whole network, 'Closeness' specifically gives the average of shortest paths that are connected to node '$i$'. Hence 'Closeness' is a better measure of connectivity of 'a node' to the rest of the network. A plot of '$L_i$ x $i$' gives a complete picture of local connectivity across the whole network. The lower the Closeness of a node, the better is the network connectivity to and from that node, and hence better is the node's performance.

**"Shortest Path Length" Plot**

Another way of visualizing the performance of the airport network is to plot Frequency of the Flight-routes versus the Shortest Path Length. So this plot will indicate how many flight-routes exist in the network for a given shortest path length. Ideally, in a well-performing network such a plot should be populated on the low shortest path length side and it should have a nonexistent or a thin tail.

As shown in the Figure 1, the ANI has a peak at shortest path length 2 and has a thin tail between 4 and 5.

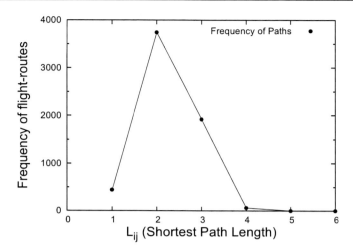

Figure 1. Shortest path distribution in Airport Network of India (ANI). The ANI comprises of 79 airports and 449 one-way flight routes. The network is put together by 11 airlines, largely domestic and a few international.

## 3.   Risks on Airport Network

An airport network could be subjected to variety of risks, varying from traffic congestion, airport shutdown to terrorist attack. In this paper, we will consider risks that involves connectivity, connectivity pattern, breakdown of airports due to natural or human causes, and spread of information (diseases) over the airport network. Earlier, forecast and control of epidemics has been attempted in a world connected by global airport network [8, 10].

**Betweenness ($B_k$)**

Betweenness ($B_k$) [12] of a node 'k' is defined as the ratio of number of shortest paths passing through 'k' to the total number shortest paths in the network. Essentially Betweenness is a parameter that enumerates the importance of a node in terms of it being central to the traffic in the network. Given that it also represents the importance of the airport (node) to the entire traffic dynamics and hence the risk posed by possible malfunctioning of the airport. This indicates at the list of possible airports that need to be taken special care of, to keep the traffic flow in regulation. It has been shown for the Italian Airport Network that the betweenness follows a Double Pareto Law [6].

**Coefficient of Assortatvity ($r$)**

A network is said to show assortative mixing or assortative, if the high-degree nodes in the network tend to be connected with other high-degree nodes, and 'disassortative' when the high-degree nodes tend to connect to low-degree nodes [13]. Clearly this parameter enumerates degree-degree connectivity. It is defined such that it is between -1 and +1. It lies between 0 and +1, if the high degree, high degree connections dominate. In case high degree, poor degree connections are dominant, the coefficient of assortativity lies between 0 and -1.

From computational simulations, it is observed that assortative networks percolate easily [13]. At the same time the subset of the network to which the percolation is restricted to is 'smaller' in the case of assortative network, as opposed to that of disassortative network. This has implication to the spread of diseases over the network. A disease would spread faster on an assortative network, while the set of airports that would form reservoir of the disease would be smaller. Note that WAN (especially weighted WAN) has been shown to be having assortative nature while a regional airport network such as ANI has been shown to be having disassortative nature.

Assortativity also has bearing on resilience. It has been found that assortative networks are resilient to simple targeted attacks [13]. In assortatvive networks, removing high-degree nodes is a relatively inefficient strategy for destroying network connectivity. This implies that to avoid destruction of network connectivity due to node (airport) malfunctioning as a result of natural disaster or because of human cause, it is better to have the network with assortative degree mixing.

## 4.   Design of Future Airports

Understanding of network parameters that relate to performance and risk on the airport may not be simply be an academic issue, restricted to theoretical studies. The implications coming out of theoretical and computational studies could well be used for implementing into real-life airport networks.

Section 2. offers us $L$, $C$ and $L_i$ as possible measures of network performance. Incidentally, in the real-life airport networks all networks have a low $L$ and significantly high $C$ (except for IAN) compared to the random network model. It is not clear whether decreasing $L$ further or stretching $C$ to it's maximum possible value would improve the performance of the network in terms of making it easy to travel across the network. To improve the connectivity of an airport ,'i', with rest of network, simulations could be done to figure out the network topology for best possible value of $L_i$. At any point of time one may have possible alterations to the topology of the network of which only a few may be better in terms of having improved network performance.

The degree, number of flight links that a airport has, of an airport is not necessarily linked to its traffic centrality as defined by betweenness ($B_k$). One could use betweenness as a parameter to decide traffic dynamics-wise important airports and provide some appropriate facilities there.

Keeping in view the above points mentioned in Section 3. regarding the risks, if one engineers the network to be disassortative to avoid the fast spread of diseases on the airport network, one is risking disruption of the network in case of airport(s) malfunctioning. And vice versa. This puts us in a dilemma as to how to engineer the degree correlations of future airport networks. Perhaps the unweighted network could be engineered as an assortative network, so that any possible natural or man-made disaster could not easily disrupt it. While at the same time, the weighted network could be designed as a disassortative network, so that diseases could not spread (percolate) fast on this network.

# 5.  Conclusion

Air transportation, and thereby, airport networks are increasingly becoming important for transportation across the world. Hence study of airport networks for their performance and risks is of crucial for maintenance and engineering of the airport networks.

By virtue of its nature airport network is amenable for modeling using complex network paradigm. It has discrete elements (airports) that are connected by links (air connectivity). Various network parameters and features could be used as a measure of performance and risks in the airport network. Not every parameter could be useful for this purpose as not every parameter may enumerate the performance or risk on the network.

Characteristic Path Length ($L$) and Clustering Coefficient ($C$) very well enumerate the performance of the airport network. $L$ is inversely while $C$ is directly proportional to the performance of the network. Incidentally, small-world nature is not necessarily a good indicator of an efficient network. While $L$ and $C$ offer a global view of performance of network, Closeness gives a local view of performance of the network.

The results on spread (percolation) and resilience of the networks suggests that design of future airports is not a straightforward task. While tweaking a parameter might improve a certain feature, it might as well impair some other network feature. One may have to deal with tweaking network parameters of weighted and unweighted airport network simultaneously to achieve the desired result. Importantly tweaking a parameter may be easy or difficult job depending on the task. For example, as an engineer it may be relatively easier to create an assortative unweighted network by introducing some flight routes and rerouting a few. But creating a disassortative weighted network may be a tough task as it involves changing the number of flights which are solely governed by passengers' demand.

# References

[1] Réka Albert and Albert-László Barabási. Statistical mechanics of complex networks. *Rev. Mod. Phys.*, **74**:47–97, 2002.

[2] S. N. Dorogovtsev and J. F. F. Mendes. *Evolution of Networks: From Biological Nets to Internet and WWW*. Oxford Univ. Press, Oxford, 2003.

[3] Alain Barrat, Marc Barthélémy, Romualdo Pastor-Satorras, and Alessandro Vespignani. The architecture of complex weighted networks. *Proc. Natl. Acad. Sci. (USA)*, **101**:3747–3752, 2004.

[4] Ganesh Bagler. Analysis of Airport Network of India as a complex weighted network. *Physica A*, **387**:2972–2980, 2008.

[5] W. Li and X. Cai. Statistical analysis of Airport Network of China. *Phys. Rev. E*, **69**:046106, 2003.

[6] M Guida and F. Maria. Topology of the Italian airport network: A scale-free small-world network with a fractal structure? *Chaos: Solitons and Fractals*, **31**:527–536, 2007.

[7]  Carlos Pestana Barrosa and Peter U.C. Dieke. Performance evaluation of italian air-
     ports: A data envelopment analysis. *J. of Air Transport Management*, **13**:184–191,
     2007.

[8]  L. Hufnagel, D. Brockmann, and T. Geisel. Forecast and control of epidemics in
     aglobalized world. *Proc. Natl. Acad. Sci. (USA)*, **101**:15124–15129, 2004.

[9]  R. Guimerà, S. Mossa, A. Turtschi, and L. A. N. Amaral. The worldwide air trans-
     portation network: Anomalous centrality, community structure, and cities' global
     roles. *Proc. Natl. Acad. Sci. (USA)*, **102**:7794–7799, 2005.

[10] Vittoria Colizza, Alain Barrat, Marc Barthelemy, and Alessandro Vespignani. The
     role of the airline transportation network in the prediction and predictability of global
     epidemics. *Proc. Natl. Acad. Sci. (USA)*, **103**:2015–2020, 2006.

[11] R. Guimerà and L. A. N. Amaral. Modeling the world-wide airport network. *Eur.
     Phys. J. B*, **38**:381–385, 2004.

[12] L.C. Freeman. A set of measures of centrality based on betweenness. *Sociometry*,
     **40**:35–41, 1977.

[13] M. E. J. Newman. Assortative mixing in networks. *Phys. Rev. Lett.*, **89**:208701, 2002.

# INDEX

**F**

**G**

**Q**

**R**

**S**

## T

## U

## V

## W

## Y